SECOND EDITION

COMMUNICATION RESEARCH

by
Kathryn Lancioni

Chapters 2, 4, 5, 6, and 7 are borrowed from Straight Talk About Communication Research Methods, Third Edition, by Christine S. Davis, Heather Powell, and Kenneth A. Lachlan.

Cover image © Shutterstock.com

Kendall Hunt
publishing company

www.kendallhunt.com
Send all inquiries to:
4050 Westmark Drive
Dubuque, IA 52004-1840

Copyright © 2018, 2020 by Kendall Hunt Publishing Company

PAK ISBN 978-1-7924-0102-2
Text Alone ISBN 978-1-7924-0100-8

All rights reserved. No part of this publication may be reproduced, stored in a retrieval system, or transmitted, in any form or by any means, electronic, mechanical, photocopying, recording, or otherwise, without the prior written permission of the copyright owner.

Published in the United States of America

CONTENTS

About the Author   xi

Chapter 1: Communication Research Defined   1

What Is Research?   1
     Communication Research versus Traditional Research   2
     Research Characteristics   3
     Types of Research   4
Why Is Research Conducted?   5
     Research Methods   6
     Types of Research Methods and Research Example   6
     Quantitative Research Methods   9
     So What?   9
Glossary   10
References   10

Chapter 2: Research Questions, Objectives, and Hypotheses   11

Chapter Outline   11
Key Terms   11
Chapter Objectives   11
How Do You Design Good Quality Research through Appropriate Questions and Hypotheses?   12
What Are the Functions of Theory, Research Objectives, Research Questions, and Hypotheses?   12
What Are Research Objectives?   13
How Do You Ask Research Questions?   16
     Types of Research Questions about Communication   17
        Questions of Definition   17
        Questions of Fact   18
What Are Research Hypotheses?   19
     Null Hypotheses   21
     Forms of Relationships in Hypotheses   22
     Directional and Nondirectional Hypotheses   23

How Do You Set Up Good Research Questions? 24
    Conceptual Definitions 24
    Operational Definitions 25
What Are the Boundaries of Research Questions and Hypotheses? 26
How Is Metatheory Related to Research Questions and Hypotheses? 26
So What? 27
Glossary 27
References 28

Chapter 3: Understanding Communication Research Ethics 29
Chapter Outline 29
Key Terms 29
Chapter Objectives 29
Why Are Ethics Important? 30
How Do Ethics Influence Research? 31
Why Are Ethics Important in Research? 31
The Connection Between Communication Research and Ethics 33
The Tenets of the Belmont Report 33
    Principal #1: Respect for Persons 34
    Principal #2: Nonmaleficence and Beneficence 35
    Principal #3: Justice 37
Conducting Communication Research 38
Promoting Ethical Conduct in Science 39
So What? 40
Glossary 41
References 41

Chapter 4: Understanding Variables 43
Chapter Outline 43
Key Terms 44
Chapter Objectives 44
What Is the Function of Variables in Communication Research? 44
What Is a Variable? 45
Revisiting Conceptual and Operational Definitions 45
    Conceptual Definitions 45
    Operational Definitions 45
        Measured Operational Definitions 46
        Experimental Operational Definitions 46
Operationalizing: Matching Your Variables to Your Study 47
    Conceptual Fit 47
    Measuring Variables 47
        Self-Report 48
            Social Desirability Bias in Self-Report Data 48
        Other Report 48

        Limitations in Other Reports   48
    Observing Behavior   49
        Hawthorne Effect Bias in Observing Behaviors   49
Triangulation   49
Measurement   50
    Nominal Level Measurement   50
    Ordinal Level Measurement   51
    Interval Level Measurement   51
        Likert Scale   53
        Semantic Differential Scale   54
    Ratio Level Measurement   55
Types of Variables   56
    Independent Variables   56
    Dependent Variables   57
        Examples of Independent and Dependent Variables   57
    Extraneous Variables   58
        Confounding Variables   58
        Mediating Variables   60
        Moderating Variables   60
The Different Types of Relationships between Variables   61
    Reversible and Irreversible Relationships   61
    Deterministic and Stochastic Relationships   61
    Sequential and Coextensive Relationships   62
    Sufficient and Contingent Relationships   62
    Necessary and Substitutable Relationships   62
The Dimensions of Variables   63
    Unidimensional Concepts   63
    Multidimensional Concepts   63
So What?   64
Glossary   64
References   65

Chapter 5: Understanding Sampling   67

Chapter Outline   67
Key Terms   67
Chapter Objectives   68
How Important Is Sampling?   68
Sampling Theory   68
    Generalizability and Representation   68
    Sampling Frame   70
    Unit of Analysis or Sampling Units   71
Sampling in Quantitative Research   71
    Sampling Methods   71
        Random Sampling   71

Simple Random Sample 71
   Systematic Random Sample 72
Stratified Sample 72
Proportional Stratified Sample 73
Cluster Sampling 73
Nonrandom Sampling 74
Convenience Sample 74
Volunteer Sample 75
Snowball Sampling 75
   Network Sampling 75
      Advantages And Disadvantages 76
Response Rate and Refusal Rate 76
Sample Size and Power 77
Sampling in Qualitative Research 81
   Sampling Methods 81
      Purposive Sampling 81
      Quota Sampling 82
      Maximum Variation Sampling 83
      Theoretical Construct Sampling 83
      Typical and Extreme Instance Sampling 83
   Sample Size and Data Saturation 84
So What? 84
Glossary 85
References 86

Chapter 6: Survey Research 89

Chapter Outline 89
Key Terms 89
Chapter Objectives 90
Why Surveys? 90
Survey Research 90
   Applications of Survey Research 91
      Survey Research Measuring Attitudes 91
      Survey Research Measuring Retrospective Behaviors 92
      Political Polls 94
      Evaluation Research 94
      Market Research 95
   Design Concerns 95
      Sampling 95
      Cross-Sectional Design 96
      Longitudinal Design 98
         Trend Study 98
         Cohort Study 98

        Panel Study   99
    Measurement Techniques   100
Constructing a Survey Questionnaire   101
    Writing Survey Questions   101
        Strategies for Questions   101
    Types of Questions   104
    Structure and Arrangement of Questions   105
        How to Choose the Right Format   106
    Survey Administration   106
        Researcher-Administered   107
        Self-Administered   107
        Interviews   108
So What?   111
Glossary   112
References   112

Chapter 7: Experiments   115

Chapter Outline   115
Key Terms   115
Chapter Objectives   116
What Is an Experiment?   116
    Independent and Dependent Variables   116
        What Are Independent Variables?   117
        What Are Dependent Variables?   117
    Good Questions for Experiments   117
Understanding Experimental Notation and Language   118
    Observation   119
    Induction   119
    Random Assignment   119
    Terminology   120
Designs and Validity   120
Preexperimental Designs   121
    One Shot Case Study Design   121
    One Group Pretest Posttest Design   121
    Static Group Comparison Design   122
Quasi-Experimental Designs   122
    Time-Series Design   122
    Nonequivalent Control Group Design   123
    Multiple Time-Series Design   123
True Experimental Designs   123
    Pretest Posttest Control Group Design   124
    Posttest-Only Control Group Design   124
    Solomon Four-Group Design   125

Factorial Design   126
Field and Natural Experiments   128
So What?   130
Glossary   130
References   131

Chapter 8: Qualitative Research and Case Studies   133

Chapter Outline   133
Key Terms   133
Chapter Objectives   133
When Should You Use a Case Study Approach?   135
What Is a Case?   135
Limiting Your Case Study   136
Determining the Type of Case Study   137
    Yin's Case Study Ideas   137
    Stake's Case Study Ideas   138
Single or Multiple Case Study Designs: 139
    A Single Case Study   139
    Multiple Case Studies   140
    Propositions   140
    Propositions versus Issues   141
Types of Decisions   142
Data Management   143
Analysis   143
Reporting a Case Study   144
Strategies for Achieving Trustworthiness
   in Case Study Research   145
So What?   146
Glossary   146
References   147

Chapter 9: Putting It All Together   149

Chapter Outline   149
Key Terms   149
Chapter Objectives   150
Developing the Basics of Your Communication Research Toolkit   150
Research Theory and Logic   151
Research Objectives and the Research Question   151
Research Hypothesis   152
Determining Your Variables   152
Relationships Between Variables   153

Research Techniques: Sampling   154
    Establishing a Sampling Framework   155
Research Techniques: Surveys   156
    Benefits of Survey Research   156
    Designing Your Survey   157
        Specifics of Longitudinal Design   158
        Building a Survey Questionnaire   159
        Arranging the Survey Questions   159
        Administering a Research Survey   160
Research Technique: Experiments   161
    Building Blocks of an Experiment   161
    Important Terms in Experiment Design   161
    Designing Your Experiment   162
Research Techniques: Field Work   162
Research Techniques: Focus Groups   163
Candidate Selection   163
Budgets   164
Timelines   165
Research Study Checklist   165
So What?   166
Glossary   166

Chapter 10: Applying Your Survey Research   169

Chapter Outline   169
Key Terms   169
Chapter Objectives   170
Importance of Communicating Your Research Findings   170
Application of Research Findings   172
    What Effective Research Communication Involves   173
    Understanding your audience   173
Defining the Target Audience   174
    Consider the Breadth of Your Target Research Audience   175
Types of Research Users   175
Understanding Your Research Audience's Wants and Needs   176
Learning More About Your Target Research Audience   176
Developing Your Research Messages   177
Clarifying Your Research Findings   177
Identifying the Implications of Your Study   178
Imagining the "What If" of Your Research   178
Out-of-the-Box Applications of Your Work   179
Writing Your Key Messages   180
Broadcasting Your Content   181
Which Medium? Think About the Consumption Habits of Your Target Market   182

So What?   186
Glossary   186
References   186

Chapter 11: Case Studies in Communication Research   189

Chapter Outline   189
Chapter Objectives   189
University of Minnesota: "The Other Hangover"   190
Domino's Social Media Crisis Communication   191
A Whale of a Problem: A Strategic Communication Analysis of SeaWorld Entertainment's Multiyear *Blackfish* Crisis   193
    Connecticut Light & Power's (CL&P) Crisis Communication Response   196
    The Jersey Shore and Superstorm Sandy   199
    Deflated: The Strategic Impact of the "Deflategate" Scandal on the NFL and Its Golden Boy   202
References   204

Chapter 12: Outline   205

ABOUT THE AUTHOR

With more than twenty-five years of experience in the communication industry, Kathryn Lancioni has a deep understanding of the world global communication. She is a nationally recognized expert in the fields of public relations and corporate communications. She has worked as a journalist, a public relations executive, a college professor and an executive coach.

Over the past two decades Ms. Lancioni, has helped dozens of domestic and multi-national companies conquer their market research, branding, public relations and investor relations challenges. She has worked with media of the highest levels, taken companies public on the New York Stock Exchange, directed global communications program, counseled clients through monumental crises and relaunched lagging brands.

In recent years, Ms. Lancioni has developed a fascination for the world of communication research. Her book, *Communication Research*, is designed to provide students with a wholistic view of the communication research process. The book walks students through the concept of communication research, explaining the nuances and prevalent techniques currently dominating the field. It also explores the challenges and opportunities that come with the publication of research findings and identifying viable publication channels. It covers everything from qualitative and quantitative research techniques to case study methodology. It is the ideal resource for any student looking for an overview of this rapidly changing field.

Currently, Ms. Lancioni is a Professor of Communication in the College of Communication and the Arts at Seton Hall University. She has served on the faculty of Rutgers University, Farleigh Dickinson University, Montclair State University, St. John Fisher College and William Paterson University. She has guest lectured at Columbia Business School, Cornell University, Rutgers University and Seton Hall University. Her articles about the communications field have been published in several national and regional magazines and she is a featured guest speaker throughout the New York tri-state area.

Ms. Lancioni earned a Bachelor's of Science in Communications from Cornell University and a Master's of Science in Journalism from the Graduate School of Journalism of Columbia University. For more information, please visit: www.kathrynlancioni.com.

Research Process

- Conduct a Study
- Analyze Data
- Draft Article
- Submit for Publication
- Peer Review
- Article Published
- New Research Inspired
- Design Study

COMMUNICATION RESEARCH DEFINED

Welcome to the word of communication research! Before we explore the many theories, paradigms, and approaches, as well as techniques and tools, it is important to first define the concept of research and then specifically focus on communication research.

What Is Research?

Research is a careful study of a specific problem or concern using scientific methods, tools, and instruments. It can be about anything that the researcher finds interesting or peculiar. The many types of research conducted in the marketplace include scientific research, basic research, applied research, market research, qualitative market research, quantitative market research, problem-oriented research, and problem-solving research. If it seems kind of daunting, it is. The truth of the matter is that anyone can conduct research on anything. To begin researching something, you just need to have a question you would like answered, a problem you would like solved or a concern that needs a solution.

Every research study begins with asking the right research questions. The next step is to select the appropriate research method to support the study. Then, you carry out the research study using research tools to gather the necessary data. Finally, you pull together your statistics and observation, do an analysis, and, hopefully, reach a conclusion.

research
A careful study of a specific problem or concern using scientific methods, tools, and instruments.

© davooda/Shutterstock.com

Communication Research versus Traditional Research

Now that we have explained the basic concept of research, let's go a bit deeper and get into the difference between communication research and traditional research. Market researchers define **communication research** as "the qualitative and quantitative research methodology followed to understand about the communication phenomena. Communication Research helps in confirming and discovering patterns in communication behavior of people, and helps the scholars to develop useful Communication theories." (Source: mbaskool.com). Communication researchers tend to examine different contexts for communication, such as interpersonal communication, group communication, organizational communication, and mass communication. (Source: Thompsen)

In general, individuals conducting a communication research study use one of two methodologies—quantitative or qualitative. We will explore these concepts throughout the book, but, in general, it can be said that quantitative research relies primarily on numbers and statistics, while qualitative focuses on behaviors and observations.

communication researcher
The study of a specific communications phenomena using a blend of qualitative and quantitative techniques.

The following is an explanation of the Communication Research Cycle:

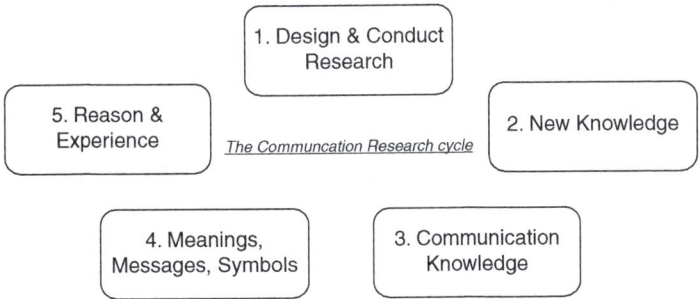

At its base level, regardless of whether it is traditional research or communication research, the idea of research and a research study stays the same. According to the American sociologist, Earl Robert Babbie, "Research is a systematic inquiry to describe, explain, predict and control the observed phenomenon. Research involves inductive and deductive methods" (Source: Bhat).

Inductive research methods help researchers *analyze* observed phenomenon, while **deductive methods** are used to *verify* the observed phenomenon. Inductive approaches are associated with qualitative research, and deductive methods are more commonly associated with quantitative research. Typically, research studies are carried out to explore a concept or investigate an issue. One of the most important things to come out of a research study is the statistics associated with it and the conclusions resulting from the work (Source: Bhat).

inductive research
Research methods employed to help researchers analyze observed behavior.

deductive research
Research techniques used to help researchers very observed behavior.

Research Characteristics

In general, most research studies share a set of common characteristics (Source: Bhat):

1. All research studies are conducted using a systematic approach. Rules and processes are critical as they help define and determine the objective of a research process.
2. Research is based on logical reasoning and involves a combination of inductive and deductive methods.
3. Regardless of the way the data is captured, it is done in real time with actual observations and in a natural environment.
4. All of the data captured is part of the analysis, unless something within the experiment goes wrong.
5. Research creates an opportunity for generating new questions and ultimately generating additional research opportunities.

6. Control and accuracy are two of the most essential elements in conducting a research study. All of the information collected during a research study should be accurate and true to its nature as much as possible.
7. All studies start off with Research Question and Hypothesis. Sometimes, the results confirm the hypothesis and other times they refute it. It is impossible to predict the outcome prior to executing the study. It is okay to wind up with a null hypothesis.

Types of Research

Despite the fact that all research studies share a series of common traits, there is huge variance in the types of research that is conducted. Here is a brief synopsis of the types of research methods you can choose from:

- **Basic research:** Basic research is usually conducted to enhance overall knowledge about a particular subject or industry. The objective of this research is knowledge expansion. It is a not commercial research and doesn't lead to the creation or invention of anything. An experiment is a good example of basic research.
- **Applied research:** Applied research focuses on analyzing and solving real-world problems. This type of research refers to a study that helps solve practical problems using scientific methods. This research plays an important role in solving issues that impact society. For example, finding a cure for a life-threatening disease.

- **Problem-oriented research:** Problem-oriented research is done to understand the exact nature of a problem with the hope of discovering possible solutions.
- **Problem-solving research**: Problem-solving research is conducted by companies to understand and fix their own problems.
- **Qualitative research:** Qualitative research is a process of inquiry that provides an in-depth understanding of problems or issues in their natural settings. It relies heavily on the experience of researchers and the structure of questions to generate results. The sample size is usually restricted to 6 to 10 people and open-ended questions. The hope is that one response leads to another. The purpose of asking open-ended questions is to gather as much information as possible from the population being tested.
- **Quantitative research:** Quantitative research is a structured way of collecting data and analyzing it to develop conclusions. Unlike qualitative research, this research method is mathematically focused and uses a computational, statistical methodology to collect and analyze data. It involves a bigger sample size as a larger number of people result in more data. Owing to the manner in which the data is collected, it can be analyzed more quickly than in a qualitative study. This type of research method uses closed-ended questions because researchers are typically looking at measuring the extent and gathering foolproof statistical data. (Source: Bhat)

Why Is Research Conducted?

Now that we have talked about the types of research possibilities and the commonalities across research studies, let's look at why research is conducted. Typically, it comes down to three simple reasons: exploration, description, and explanation:

1. **Exploratory research:** Exploratory research is done (as the name implies) to *explore* research questions. It may or may not provide a final conclusion to the research carried out. Usually, it is done to handle new problems that haven't been examined before. Exploratory research sets the foundation for more precise research and data collection. For example, an exploratory research study could be done to discover the level of customer satisfaction at a restaurant.

2. **Descriptive research:** Descriptive research provides greater insight into issues through a process of focused, precise data collection. These studies describe the behavior of a sample population. With this type of research, only one variable is required to conduct the study. The three primary reasons for conducting descriptive research are to describe, explain, and validate findings.
3. **Explanatory/causal research:** Explanatory research is done to understand the impact of changes on an environment. Experiments are the most popular form of casual research.

	Exploratory Research	Descriptive Research	Explanatory Research
Approach	Unstructured	Structured	Highly structured
Conducted	Asking research questions	Asking research questions	By using research hypotheses.
Timing	Early stages of decision making	Later stages of decision making	Later stages of decision making

The following is a comparative analysis of these three rationales (Source: Bhat):

Research Methods

Now that we have defined the concept of research, explored why research studies are conducted, and investigated the types of research approaches that are used, it is important to talk about methods of research.

A **research method** is defined as the tool used to fulfill the goals and objectives of a research process. Simply put, it is the process by which the tools or instruments will be used to carry out the study.

research method
Any type of research technique used to support a specific research study.

Types of Research Methods and Research Example

In general, research techniques can be put into one of two categories: Quantitative or Qualitative. These techniques support the type of approach being taken, as discussed earlier in this chapter.

As noted earlier, Qualitative research is an approach that gathers data using conversational methods, where participants involved in the research are asked open-ended questions. The responses collected aren't numerical. This method helps a researcher understand not only "what" participants think but also "why" they think it (Source: Bhat).

Some examples of **qualitative research methods** include:

- **One-to-one Interview:** This interview technique is conducted with one participant at a given point in time. One-to-one

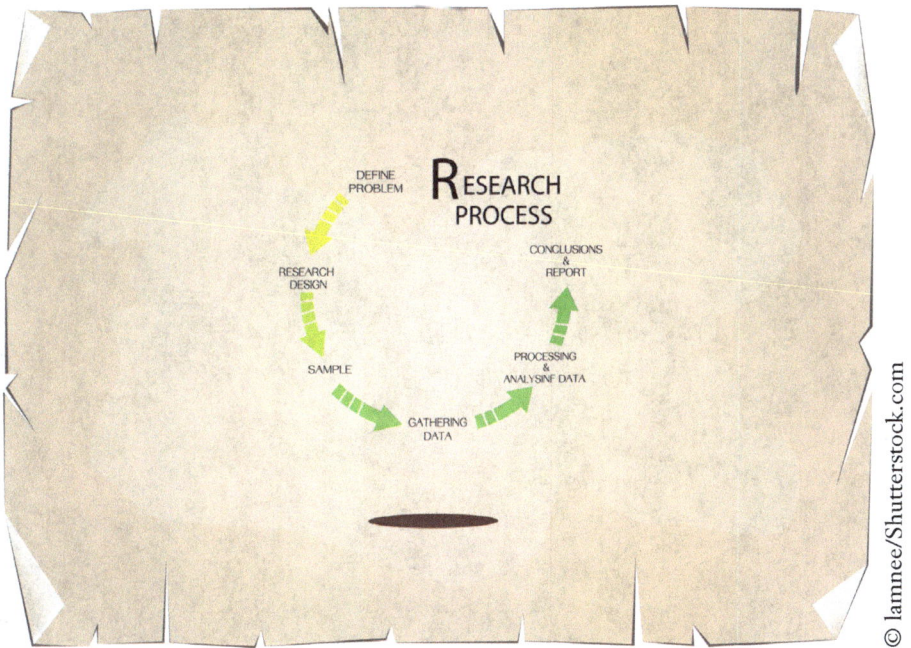

interviews require the researcher to prepare questions in advance and to make sure the researcher asks only the most important questions to the participant. This type of interview usually lasts between 20 and 30 minutes.

- **Focus groups:** Focus groups are small groups consisting of 6 to 10 participants who are asked to provide their opinion about a product, service, or concept. Participants can be representatives of a potential target market or be experts in the field or industry. A moderator is assigned to run the focus group. Their role is to facilitate discussion among group members. A moderator's experience in running focus groups plays an important role. With the proper techniques, an experienced moderator can probe the participants to yield the collection of sizable amounts of data related to the research (Source: Bhat).
- **Ethnographic research:** Ethnographic research is an in-depth form of research where people are observed in their natural environment. This method can be very demanding as it requires the researcher to adapt to the natural environment of the target audience. Geographic locations can pose an immense challenge in this type of research method. Rather than conducting interviews, a researcher needs to experience the settings in person to collect information (Source: Bhat).

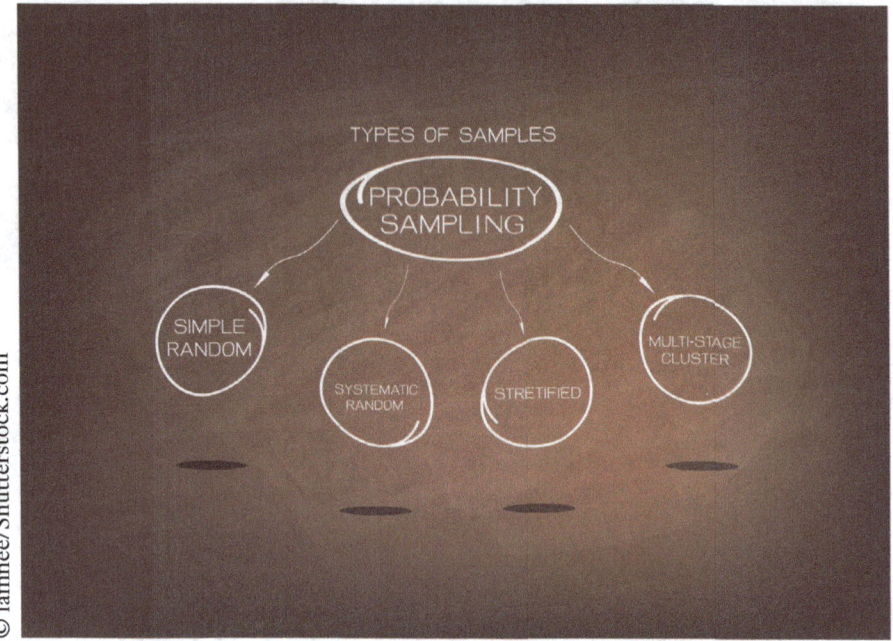

- **Sampling:** Sampling is the process of selecting units (e.g., people, organizations) from a population of interest and studying the sample for feedback in a research study. Use of this technique allows researchers to generalize results back to the population from which they were chosen. Typically, sampling is used with the research of consumer products and other items that require direct, personal feedback.
- **Text analysis:** Text analysis varies greatly from other qualitative research methods. It is used to analyze society through the decoding of words, texts, and so forth through any available form of documentation. The analysis itself involves "digging deeper into the meaning of the text." The researcher studies and understands the context in which the documents are furnished with the information and then tries to draw meaningful inferences from it. In modern times, researchers follow activities on a social media platform and try and understand the pattern of thoughts (Source: Hutchinson).
- **Case study research:** Case study research, as the name suggests, is used to study an organization or an entity. It is used in fields such as the education sector and philosophical and psychological studies (Source: Bhat).

Quantitative Research Methods

Quantitative research methods focus on numbers and anything that can be dealt with in a measurable form. They are used to answer questions for justifying relationships with measurable variables to either explain, predict, or control a phenomenon. The most popular methods of quantitative research are the following:

- **Survey research:** The ultimate goal of survey research is to learn about a large population through the deployment of a survey. Most surveys are conducted online as it is the fastest, least expensive, and most efficient way of carrying it out. A researcher designs a survey with most relevant questions and distributes it. Once the researcher receives the responses, the results are tabulated, and an analysis is performed.
- **Descriptive research**: Descriptive research focuses on identifying the characteristics of an observed phenomenon and collecting additional information about it. This research method is designed to depict the participants in a very systematic and accurate way.
- **Correlational research:** Correlational research is a nonexperimental method of research in which a researcher measures two variables and understands and assesses the statistical relationship between them with no influence from any external factors (Source: Bhat).

So What?

After reading this chapter, you should now have a very general sense of what the world of communication research involves. We've defined the overall idea of research, compared it with communication research, talked about various research characteristics, looked at the possible types of research that you could conduct, and finally looked at specific research tools. Now that all of that is behind us, let's dive into the World of Communication Research!

Glossary

Communication researcher
The study of a specific communications phenomena using a blend of qualitative and quantitative techniques.

Deductive research
Research techniques used to help researchers very observed behavior.

Inductive research
Research methods employed to help researchers analyze observed behavior.

Research
A careful study of a specific problem or concern using scientific methods, tools, and instruments.

Research method
Any type of research technique used to support a specific research study.

References

Dr. Thompsen. February 4, 2014. *"On Defining Communication Research," Dr. Phillip A. Thompsen*. Accessed November 11, 2019. http://drthompsen.com.

Hutchinson, Patti. n.d. "Different Ways of Analyzing the Text," edhelper.com.

MBASkool. n.d. Accessed November 11, 2019. https://www.mbaskool.com/business-concepts/marketing-and-strategy-terms/6777-communication-research.html.

QuestionPro. n.d. Accessed November 11, 2019. https://www.questionpro.com/blog/what-is-research/.

RESEARCH QUESTIONS, OBJECTIVES, AND HYPOTHESES

Chapter Outline

1. How Do You Design Good Quality Research through Appropriate Questions and Hypotheses?
2. What Are the Functions of Theory, Research Objectives, Research Questions, and Hypotheses?
3. What Are Research Objectives?
4. How Do You Ask Research Questions?
   a. Types of Research Questions about Communication
      i. Questions of Definition
      ii. Questions of Fact
5. What Are Research Hypotheses?
   a. Null Hypotheses
   b. Forms of Relationships in Hypotheses
   c. Directional and Nondirectional Hypotheses
6. How Do You Set Up Good Research Questions?
   a. Conceptual Definitions
   b. Operational Definitions
7. What Are the Boundaries of Research Questions and Hypotheses?
8. How Is Metatheory Related to Research Questions and Hypotheses?
9. So What?

Key Terms

Conceptual definition
Fact pattern
Hypothesis

Null hypothesis
Operational definition
Research objectives

Research question

Chapter Objectives

1. To understand the purpose of research questions
2. To explain the different types of research questions
3. To understand research hypotheses
4. To learn how to evaluate research questions
5. To consider the boundaries of research questions and hypotheses

How Do You Design Good Quality Research through Appropriate Questions and Hypotheses?

If we do our job as instructors and mentors, by the time you graduate, you will know maybe the answers to some questions, but most importantly—how to ask good questions (Miller & Nicholson, 1976). In this chapter, you will consider the role of objectives, questions, and hypotheses construction in good research design. Your study objectives, the questions you ask, and the hypotheses you write are grounded in metatheory, and collectively they contribute to your understanding of communication theory. This chapter will focus on research objectives, questions, and hypotheses, how they are driven by our metatheoretical consideration, and subsequently, how these research objectives, questions, and hypotheses drive the methodological choices we make in research design.

What Are the Functions of Theory, Research Objectives, Research Questions, and Hypotheses?

In communication research, theories, research questions and hypotheses allow us to organize and summarize information, while simultaneously focusing our attention on important questions or ideas. They also give us a framework for developing and contributing to knowledge, and they function to explain, predict, and/or control. Specifically, theory, research questions, and hypotheses help to explain or make sense of reality, linking interrelated constructs and processes and essentially answering the question of "Why?" (see Barnlund, 1968; Bross, 1953; Dance, 1982; Hall & Lidzey, 1970; Hawes, 1975; Kaplan, 1964; Kuhn, 1970; Littlejohn, 1996; and Poole, 1990). Questions and hypotheses also allow us to predict or forecast what will happen in the future, essentially telling us what we can expect to observe when certain conditions are satisfied. In terms of control, once we understand how a process works, to some extent this understanding allows us to control it. Ultimately, the primary function of research questions, hypotheses, and theory is heuristic, allowing us to generate new knowledge, learning, and understanding. Notice that under this paradigm, research questions and hypotheses are built on existing theory—either extending, testing, or explicating a theory. This type of research falls under the positivist paradigm, using deductive reasoning, and researchers who conduct research in this paradigm believe that reality is fixed, measurable, controllable, orderly, and objective.

Also recall that research can be conducted under the inductive model, in which researchers seek to answer more open-ended questions and end up with, perhaps, a theory, or a deeper understanding of an extant phenomenon. This model of research falls under the interpretive paradigm, and researchers who subscribe to this metatheory tend to believe that reality is subjective, constructed, and chaotic. Note that theory—in terms of providing an organization or framework for knowledge, or understanding of reality—has its place in both paradigms and philosophies of research.

Theories begin with either a **fact pattern** or a question. A fact pattern is a factual relationship occurring repeatedly. A good example of a fact pattern in Communication is what we call *divergence* or *convergence*. Have you ever noticed how when you are in a conversation with someone you like, or perhaps someone you need to impress, you adjust your style of speaking to match hers? This is an example of convergence. What about when you are in a conversation with someone you feel dissimilar to or dislike in some way? Do you tend to match him? Research suggests you will maintain your own style of communicating. This is an example of divergence. Convergence and divergence provide the basis for Communication Accommodation Theory (CAT). Giles and his colleagues have studied CAT in a variety of contexts; for example, one study examined how we adjust our communication behaviors when interacting with the elderly (McCann & Giles, 2006). A researcher working out of the positivist philosophy might design a study to see if CAT affects the therapeutic value of medical communication. A researcher working with interpretivist assumptions might instead look at medical communication in a more open-ended sense, and might in the end use CAT to help explain what they found in their study.

Theories might also begin with a question—a search for an answer to why something happens. As Miller and Nicholson (1976) suggest, "People incessantly ask questions" (p. 10). This search for answers, via questions posed, is really at the heart of the process of inquiry, the search for understanding. In our case, we will focus on the process of communication inquiry, but that does not mean the process of writing and examining research questions we will discuss is inappropriate for other forums of inquiry. However, what is unique to our approach is our substantive vantage point; we are interested in human interaction via communication.

fact pattern
A factual relationship occurring repeatedly.

What Are Research Objectives?

Research objectives represent the reasons you give for undertaking your own research project. They are the step between your research topic, your "I wonder if . . ." musing, and your research questions or hypothesis. When

research objectives
are the reasons or primary rationale for the execution of a research project.

you are given an assignment to conduct a research study, the first thing you will do is determine your general area of inquiry. Several of the previous chapters mentioned areas of inquiry in our field of study: organizational communication, health communication, interpersonal communication, mass media, or public relations. From your general area of inquiry, you would need to narrow your focus to a slightly more specific topic for your research. We would suggest you start with something that interests you most—keeping it related to communication, of course. You should work on narrowing your topic until you have something specific enough to build a research study on it.

Next, narrow it by adding modifying words and phrases to each of your topic ideas. For example, if you are interested in the general field of health communication, you might decide you are very interested in patient-provider communication. That's good, but not specific enough. Let's add some modifiers: What types of patients? How about terminally ill patients? What types of healthcare providers? How about physicians? What types of communication? How about giving the bad news about their terminal diagnosis? Ahh, so *now* we see it . . . you're interested in studying how physicians give terminal diagnoses to people with terminal illness. Now, *that's* a research topic! Always think in terms of narrowing down to very specific questions addressing very specific variables. The need for this specificity will become even more apparent in later chapters when we discuss measurement and research procedures. Beginner social scientists often try to answer questions that are too broad to be definitively addressed in a single study. If you find yourself asking, "is this too specific?" the answer is, "probably not."

Now, let's turn your topic into a research objective. Research objectives are your statements of what you ultimately want to accomplish through this research. For many studies, your research objective can be determined by filling in the blanks of this statement: "I am studying _____, because I want to find out [who/what/when/where/whether/how] _____ is, in order to understand _____" (see Booth, Colomb, & Williams, 1995). For the example above, your research objective may be stated as, "I am studying patient-provider communication, because I want to find out how physicians give terminal diagnoses to patients, in order to understand the different ways to break bad medical news." Notice that we added a new part: "in order to understand the different ways to break bad medical news." This last section answers a significance or "so what" element. All research studies should connect to a bigger picture in some way. In the example above, you might be developing a theory about terminal diagnosis communication, or you might be testing an existing theory within this specific context. You might be understanding something that's important to society, or you might be describing something that will have public policy implications, or you might be measuring something that will have financial ramifications. There are lots of ways your study should answer the "so what" question, but you should know—up front—the significance of your own research. Given our arguments above considering specificity, this means that you are likely addressing or informing one small part of a much larger question or phenomenon. That's okay, and it is the nature of scientific inquiry. We take on small questions and problems one at a time, and try to replicate them in different contexts and settings, in an attempt to contribute to the answers to these larger questions. Researchers from the interpretive paradigm might tackle broader questions or issues, but even these must have defined boundaries.

Research objectives are frequently turned into research questions or hypotheses, but qualitative researchers also frequently stop at the research objective stage when designing their qualitative study. Countless qualitative studies simply have one of these two objectives: to understand _____ or to describe _____. In some types of qualitative research, such research objectives are actually unstated. For example, in an autoethnographic narrative (we'll explain more about this in Chapter 11), Davis (2005) wrote a story about her experience with the last week of her mother's life. The unstated objective of that research was to describe that experience. Green's 2002 study of having a child with a disability is another good example of qualitative research that had the (unstated) objective to understand or describe an experience. In her paper, she says that:

> *This work offers a glimpse into the emotional and social experience of disability through the lens of my own experience of mothering a child with severe cerebral palsy. (p. 21)*

Johnson's 2002 essay (textual analysis) on the performance of black American gospel music by white Australian gospel choirs states his objectives in the abstract, as the objectives of his essay are to prove two points—his conclusions, in fact:

> *This essay examines how the medium of gospel music facilitates a dialogic performance of "blackness." This essay also addresses the politics of appropriation, highlighting the ways in which Australians explain their interest in and performance of gospel music and the ironies that underlie these explanations. (p. 99)*

What metatheoretical perspectives do you think these researchers tend toward? Researchers "seeking to understand or describe" reality tend to lean toward the interpretivist tradition. They are using the open-ended study objective (rather than the more specific research question and even more precise hypothesis, to be explained in the next section) to study a reality they believe to be chaotic and subjective.

How Do You Ask Research Questions?

research question
Questions scholars ask about the way things work.

What is a **research question**? Research questions are questions scholars ask about the way things work. Just as research can be basic or applied research questions can be either basic or applied. In our field, most research questions are about the nature of communication or about the relationship between two or more variables later in the book. We'll talk more about variables later in the book but for now you should know that when you are stating a communication research question that relates two variables, at least one of the two variables must be a communication variable, because we are scholars of the process of communication.

While research *objectives* are used by communication researchers to design open-ended research about a topic, other communication researchers pose research questions when they want to find out certain information about a topic without making a prediction ahead of time. Research questions are good starting points for new areas of inquiry, as opposed to formal hypotheses (which we will discuss shortly).

Fundamentally, a communication research question must be concerned with communication, must be empirical (which means it can be experienced and is practical and/or pragmatic), and must have some level of specificity. Typically, research questions ask about the *who*, *what*, *when*, *where*, and *how* of communication. They ask about: *Who* is impacted by, or involved in, this communication act; *what* does this communication act look like; *what* are the parts of the communication act; *what* are the categories of the communication act; *what* is the outcome of the communication act; *when* do the parts of the communication act occur; *where* does the communication act occur—what is the environment and context of the communication; *how* does this communication act relate to other things (society, community, power, culture, outcomes, etc.); and/or *how* does this communication act happen?

Consider some examples of research questions about the nature of communication. How much violence is depicted during Saturday morning cartoons? What persuasive techniques are used on late night infomercials? How do couples use touch to signal relationship status in public? All of these questions are concerned with some basic question about communication behavior.

Now consider some examples of research questions exploring the relationship between two variables (remember one must be a communication variable). Do children who watch a lot of cartoons behave more aggressively on the playground? Are couples who touch less in public as happy as couples who touch more in public? How have persuasive techniques in late night infomercials changed over time? Remember, research questions are simply questions that scholars are seeking answers to; there is not a statement or assertion of what will happen, just a question the research attempts to answer.

The research question is symbolized as the capital letters RQ, followed with a numeric subscript (RQ_1). The numeric subscript refers to the number of the research question in a particular study. In a complicated study, you may have several research questions and numbering allows us to keep track of what research question is being analyzed and discussed. Here's an example of a research question from a quantitative study conducted by Segrin, Powell, Givertz, and Brackin (2003):

RQ_1: Do members of dating couples exhibit symptoms of depression that are indicative of emotional contagion?

And, here's an example of research questions from a qualitative study conducted by Davis (2009):

RQ_1: What reality does hospice construct for patients and families through communication?

RQ_2: How does hospice use communication to construct this reality?

Notice that the first stated RQ, for the Segrin et al. 2003 study, reflects positivist tendencies, toward a reality that is observable and measurable, while the RQs for the Davis 2009 research reflect interpretivist tendencies, toward a reality that is constructed and subjective.

Types of Research Questions about Communication

Questions of Definition. One common type of research question is a question of definition. There is some debate as to whether questions of definition are in fact research questions, because they are not empirical questions with definitive answers. However, these types of questions are important to the process of communication inquiry, so we will discuss them here. In fact, there is a very common question of definition that you have probably already wrestled with in prior coursework: how exactly do you define communication? Often in introductory communication courses, we debate all the possible forms and definitions of communication and what constitutes communication and what does not. Most students of communication are familiar with Watzlawick, Beavin Bavelas, and Jackson (1967), whose statement, "one cannot not communicate" (p. 51) provides ongoing debate and ardor. In fact, because the boundaries of our field are so difficult to agree upon, most textbooks as a matter of course (including ours) stipulate their own definition for the term *communication*, so as to alleviate some of the likelihood of misunderstanding. This is true for other types of questions that concern communication. Consider the question, "What communication patterns cause conflict in marriage?" Before you even address this question, you must agree upon the definition of *conflict*. Many scholars have attempted to define conflict in organizations and relationships (e.g., Gottman & Notarius, 2004; Pondy, 1967; Schmidt & Kochan, 1972).

We should note that questions of definition are an important part of the process of communication inquiry (Miller & Nicholson, 1976). We are always concerned with the way in which we define the concepts we desire to study, and definitions have a huge impact on the ways in which we choose to measure our variables. However, it is necessary to understand that if you are unclear about your definition, your research questions will suffer, and as a result your research design will encounter problems. It all begins with asking a good question—your measurement and design decisions can only be as good as the place from which you begin. Writing a good research question is more difficult and arduous than it seems at first glance. If you don't believe us, trying writing one!

Questions of Fact. Another common type of research question is the question of fact. Much communication scholarship focuses on questions of fact, wherein you ask questions regarding what has happened or will happen in the future. These questions concern what is going on in the world. For example, "Will your instructor give you a pop quiz next class period over your reading?" As you know, there is, in fact, an answer to that question that has yet to be determined. Interestingly, these types of questions can only be answered in the known external world. These questions can be confirmed or disconfirmed, essentially locating an affirmative or negative answer, a simple yes or no. For example, "Do men interrupt in conversations more than women?" This is a question of fact, with a simple yes or no answer. As we pointed out earlier, the question itself drives from the decisions scholars make about how to design and conduct research. If you return to your pop quiz example, how can you determine the answer to your question, in other words, how do you research the answer? Well, the easiest way is to attend the next research methods class period and observe whether your teacher administers a pop quiz. How could you find the answer to your question about who interrupts in conversations more, women or men? Well, again, observation would be a likely candidate. It is unlikely that you could ascertain the correct answer utilizing surveys, for instance.

So far, the questions of fact we posed are quite simple. However, we don't want to suggest all questions of fact are so simple, because they can be much more complicated. Take for instance the following question: "Are fear appeals effective instruments of persuasion?" If you have already taken a persuasion course, you know this question is much more involved than it initially appears. Other message components must be considered as potential caveats to this question: the message source, for example, and the receiver's previous knowledge, beliefs, and attitudes, as well as personality. Further, it may be the case that a particular degree of fear may be ideal—enough to motivate a response, but not so much as to lead to hopelessness—and that this degree of fear may vary from one persuasive campaign to another. So, while this question is a question of fact, a simple yes or no answer is essentially impossible.

Here are two other examples of research questions—these are ones posed in a qualitative study. This research (Kramer, 2004) uses ethnography to look at the dialectical tensions in group communication in a community theater group. Kramer asks:

RQ_1: What dialectical tensions are experienced by community theater group members as they communicate to produce a group performance?

RQ_2: How do members of a community theater group manage the dialectical tensions through their communication?

Note that both of these questions are questions of fact, even though they are very much open-ended questions based in the interpretivist tradition.

Here is another way to look at research questions. How many observations are necessary to make a valid conclusion about the answer? In the pop quiz example, you need only attend class on the next occasion to answer the question. With the questions about who interrupts more, whether fear appeals work in health messages, or how members of a theater group manage dialectical tensions, the number of observations necessary increase exponentially. So, again, you begin to see that the question you ask drives the research design process, including what methodology is an appropriate choice.

Research questions can ask about a relationship of association ("Do families with a child with a disability experience closed communication?"), or about a relationship of causation ("Does depression in a relational partner affect the number of conversational turns in a communication act?"). We'll talk more about those relationships in the next section and in future chapters.

What Are Research Hypotheses?

A research hypothesis is used when the researcher knows enough about the topic under study to make a prediction. A **hypothesis** is a statement the researcher makes about the relationship between at least two variables (a dependent and independent variable). It is often predictive, specifying how two concepts are believed to be related. Most of you are already familiar with the common definition of a hypothesis—an educated guess. And that's exactly what a hypothesis is: an educated guess about what will

hypothesis
A statement a researcher makes about the relationship between a dependent and an independent variable.

happen in a relationship between variables, based on what is known from existing theory.

This educated guess is based upon some previous knowledge and/or scholarship into related ideas. Frequently (since hypotheses fall under the deductive model), your hypothesis is based on a theory you found in your library research. Perhaps, for example, you want to study communication between hospice physicians and their patients. Your library research may have found Spiers' 2002 study on the interpersonal contexts within which care is negotiated between home care nurses and their patients. Spiers identified six communication contexts (territoriality, shared perceptions of the situation, an amicable working relationship, role synchronization, knowledge, and taboo topics) that affect the therapeutic value of the communication, and perhaps you think some of these contexts might be relevant to hospice communication as well. You might write a hypothesis based on this previous research: "When hospice physicians and patients share the same perceptions of the situation, communication is perceived by the patients as being more therapeutic."

The research hypothesis is symbolized by a capital letter H, followed with a numeric subscript (H_1). This numeric subscript refers to the number of the hypothesis in a particular study. In a complicated study, you may have several hypotheses and numbering helps you to keep track of what hypothesis is being analyzed and discussed. Some scholars add letters to denote related hypotheses (H_{1a}, H_{1b}, etc.), though we would discourage you from doing do; simply numbering the hypotheses in order is the easiest approach for most readers to follow. The symbol and numeric subscript is then followed with a statement concerning how you think the two variables will be related.

Here are some examples from Segrin et al. (2003):

H_1: There will be a negative association between depression and relational quality in dating relationships.

H_2: The poor relational quality associated with depression will be associated with increased loneliness.

Notice that both of these hypotheses have at least two variables: depression and relational quality, and depression and loneliness, respectively. Notice, also, that these Hs reflect positivist tendencies, studying a reality that is believed to be orderly, fixed, objective, observed, and measurable.

Consider these examples:

H_1: The more people watch soap operas, the more extramarital affairs they will have.

H_1: Adolescent males report greater enjoyment of slasher films than do adolescent females.

What are the two variables in each of these hypotheses? For the first hypothesis, the two variables are soap opera viewing and extramarital affairs; in the second hypothesis, the variables are gender and slasher film enjoyment. Can you identify the independent and dependent variables?

Null Hypotheses

Technically, although statistically testing your research hypothesis to see if it's true, you are actually testing whether your hypothesis is *not* true. In other words, the research hypothesis is always contrasted with a **null hypothesis**, which simply says the research hypothesis is wrong. In other words, there is no (null) relationship between the variables that the research predicted. The null hypothesis, when written, is symbolized by a capital letter H, followed with a numeric subscript of zero (H_0). Consider the null hypotheses for the original hypothesis from Segrin, Powell, Givertz, and Brackin (2003):

> H_1: There will be a negative association between depression and relational quality in dating relationships.
>
> H_0: There will be *no association* between depression and relational quality in dating relationships.

And,

> H_2: The poor relational quality associated with depression will be associated with increased loneliness.
>
> H_0: The poor relational quality associated with depression will *not be associated* with increased loneliness.

Are you getting the idea? Simply substitute in the phrase "no relationship" or "no association" to turn a research hypothesis into a null hypothesis.

What are the null hypotheses for these research hypotheses?

> H_1: The more people watch soap operas, the more extramarital affairs they will have.
>
> H_1: Adolescent males report greater enjoyment of slasher films than do adolescent females.

The correct answers are as follows:

> H_0: There is no relationship between exposure to soap viewing and extramarital affairs.
>
> H_0: Males and females do not report different enjoyment of slasher films.

Although you should be familiar with the concept of the null hypothesis, it is implied from the research hypothesis and is almost never written out in

null hypothesis
A statement that the research hypothesis is wrong. In other words, there is no (null) relationship between the variables that the research predicted.

actual research studies. However, as we move toward analysis and statistics, it is imperative that you understand the concept.

Forms of Relationships in Hypotheses

There are two key types of relationship specified in a hypothesis: relationship of association ("associational relationship") and relationship of causation ("causal relationship"). A relationship of association implies that where one variable is found, the other also will be found. For example, the format for a relationship of association in a hypothesis would be: If A, then B (A and B are different variables). An example of a relationship of association would be "interpersonal conversation and friends go together." We're not implying that having friends causes conversation, or that conversation causes a person to have friends, or even that the *more* conversation you have the *more* friends you have. We're just hypothesizing that the two occur together. It's entirely possible that a third variable (high intelligence, perhaps) causes both of these two variables to occur. Or that they co-occur for another reason. We don't know enough to make a causal statement about the two. We're simply predicting association—that if one happens, the other also tends to happen. If we word our earlier hypothesis as "H_1: People who watch soap operas have extramarital affairs," it is an example of an associational relationship.

A causal relationship implies that one variable causes a change in the direction of the other variable. The format for a relationship of causation in a hypothesis would be: An increase in "A" causes an increase in "B." It could also be: A decrease in "A" causes a decrease in "B"; an increase in "A" causes a decrease in "B"; or a decrease in "A" causes an increase in "B." Or, simply, it could be "A" causes "B." Note that many words can be used in our hypothesis to mean "cause": results in, affects, creates, induces, and so on. If we word our earlier hypothesis as "H_1: Watching soap operas causes people to have extramarital affairs," this is an example of a causal relationship.

Possible forms of relationships include positive and linear relationship (as A increases, B increases), negative and linear relationship (as A increases, B decreases), and curvilinear relationships (U shape, inverted U shape, and other more complicated curves). A U curvilinear relationship implies that as A increases, B decreases for awhile, then B increases. (Perhaps the more you drink, the less inhibited you are up to a point; then if you drink enough, you will become more inhibited.) One of your authors (Christine Davis) once conducted research on children's mental health treatment team meetings and found that meeting communication was less dialogic (called "wraparound fidelity score" in the graph) as team leader experience rose—up to six to ten years of experience. Then, meeting communication became more dialogic as team leader experience rose past eleven years of experience.

An inverted U shape implies that as "A" increases, "B" increases for a while then decreases. Davis once conducted research that found that the more people in attendance at children's mental health treatment team meetings, the more dialogic the meeting communication was up to a point 7 to 10 attendees, in fact. After 10 attendees, the dialogic nature of the meeting communication decreased.

If you consider the previous work cited in this chapter by Segrin and colleagues (2003):

H_1: There will be a negative association between depression and relational quality in dating relationships,

this is predicting a negative and linear associational relationship, such that as depression increases, the quality of dating relationships will decrease; and

H_2: The poor relational quality associated with depression will be associated with increased loneliness,

indicates a positive and linear associational relationship. In other words, they predicted that more depression is related to more loneliness.

What about the form of the relationship in the following hypotheses?

H_1: The more people watch soap operas, the more extramarital affairs they will have.

H_1: Adolescent males report greater enjoyment of slasher films than do adolescent females.

In the first hypothesis, we have a positive and linear associational relationship, as we do in the second (males like slasher films more than females).

Now, what about those curvilinear relationships? An example of a communication study that considers a curvilinear relationship is the use of touch across relational stage. Guerrero and Andersen (1991) found that touch in public spaces follows a curvilinear relationship, such that couples that are either in the early stages or later stages of relationship development exhibit less touch than couples between these two stages. This is a curvilinear relationship—actually an inverted U.

Directional and Nondirectional Hypotheses

Another component of hypotheses that becomes increasingly important to you is whether the hypothesis is directional. Some hypotheses are written specifying the direction of the relationship. Consider stating, "People from the South speak more slowly than people from the North." This is an example of a directional hypothesis because of the specific nature of the relationship between the variables. If, however, you had said, "People from the North and South speak at different rates," you have not specified who you expect speaks faster or slower; thus you have not identified a direction. This is a nondirectional hypothesis. Again, both hypotheses are acceptable, but they should be based upon previous research and theory. Being able to identify a hypothesis as directional or not becomes important when we approach statistical analysis in subsequent chapters. Directional hypotheses are called *one-tailed*, because you know where you expect to find your result. This identifies which tail end of the distribution your result will be associated with—based upon what your hypothesis identifies. A nondirectional hypothesis tells you that you must consider a result that could occur on either end of your distribution—thus it is *two-tailed*. This is because you are unsure about where the result will occur. We will return to the notion of one and two-tailed inferences in later chapters.

▼ How Do You Set Up Good Research Questions?

While there are many possible ways to critique a research question, you need to keep in mind that the best way to define what makes a good research question is based on utility, not a sense of correctness or incorrectness. In fact, we try to avoid thinking in terms of correctness and incorrectness when formulating these research questions. In other words, is the research question helpful to use in advancing your understanding of a particular communication problem or issue? Does it allow you to get at an important, narrowly defined, unanswered question in the field? If it does, then you have a successful research question.

When we ask our students to write questions, they often struggle to write a solid research question. The most common mistake they make is writing a question that has already been answered. We suggest that they dig a little deeper, perhaps there's a new and interesting way to expand that area that they and other scholars have not considered; this is often accomplished through the narrowing down process we discussed earlier in this chapter. Another important tool for evaluating research questions is the concept of quality. In other words, that you have quality variables and the relationship among your variables. While we will talk later about types of validity (or accuracy), the question of validity begins to be answered when you write your research question and/or hypothesis.

Conceptual Definitions

conceptual definition
How the concept or variable that is being studied is defined.

A quality research question and/or hypothesis begins with a solid **conceptual definition**. A conceptual definition is how you define the concept or variable that you are going to study. This is not as easy as it sounds.

Think of the concept as the pieces of the research question or the hypothesis. They are the nouns in the question or statement. For example, we like to ask our classes to define the word *violence*, something many of our mass media scholars are interested in pursuing as a variable. Remarkably, the definitions of this word vary a great deal from student to student. Some people see violence as an act or behavioral situation, while others more broadly define violence to include verbal attacks. We could likely debate the merits of each type of definition for a long time; however, that is not the point. Your conceptual definition must be clear and explain to other scholars what you consider violence to be. Most successful communication scholars will explore their variable's conceptual definitions somewhere within their literature review. Consider another example. Imagine that you believe people engage in matching behavior when they desire intimacy with another person. Your first consideration is to define, conceptually, what you mean by intimacy. What if you mean "romantic and sexual interest" when you talk about intimacy, and we mean "caring and giving concern" when we talk about intimacy? There are potentially as many conceptual definitions as there are people to define them. It is essential that you make sure you know what you mean when you talk about your concepts.

Operational Definitions

The second consideration you must make in determining whether you have a quality research question and/or hypothesis is how you define your variables operationally. An **operational definition** is how you plan to measure and/or observe the concept or variable of interest. In the violence example, you must specify how you plan to determine whether behavior in the television programs you watch is to be coded as violent. What do you count as violence? What are the categories you'll use? Do you code physical violence, the different types of physical violence, the outcome of the violence? Do you code the verbal violence? How will you do that exactly? Will it be just the verbal content that determines verbal violence, or will you also take into account nonverbal components of the message such as tone of voice, volume, and paralanguage?

operational definition
How the concept or variable of interest is measured and/or observed.

Operational definitions are important as they minimize confusion within our scholarly field, provide an opportunity for others to replicate your work, and provide some *control* over the variable you study. What about the intimacy example? Obviously, it depends upon what conceptual definition you agree upon. Then, based upon that definition, you need to create an operational definition that will determine what types of questions you ask or what you measure as you observe relational couples.

Both a solid conceptual definition and operational definition are necessary for a quality research question and/or hypothesis. Yet, the key is that conceptual and operational definitions need to match. A quality research question and/or hypothesis will be certain that they do. You can't write a conceptual definition about violence that includes verbal aggression and then not include it in your operational definition.

What Are the Boundaries of Research Questions and Hypotheses?

Another important consideration for both research questions and hypotheses is whether you wish to impose any boundaries upon them. In other words, under which conditions do you suspect your research question and/or hypotheses may be true? If you expect there to be boundaries, you need to specify this information in the question and/or hypothesis. If you don't expect there to be boundaries, there is no need to include this type of information in the question and/or hypothesis. Time, place, people, and situations could all be boundaries you place upon your questions and hypotheses. For example, do you suspect that the age of the individual matters? We generally assume that most research is based in current time, but is there a reason to consider that history or time might have some effect? Place, which could be culture and/or location, may matter a lot, depending on the question and/or hypothesis. What about the situation? Is it possible that this communication behavior you are interested in only occurs in certain situations? We have a graduate student currently interested in the communication scripts that occur in a speed-dating situation. This type of event—speed dating—is very different than any other type of dating situation. This must be included in the question.

Essentially, here you are considering, what are the limits on your research question? The key is to consider boundaries that might influence the process of inquiry. This can even be an opportunity to generate new research questions. Is there something specific about communication students at UNCC or UCONN that will influence the outcome of your study? If so, this may be a limitation to generalization and an example of how boundaries can influence your process of inquiry. It does not mean that you shouldn't ask the question; rather it means that you need to be aware of the level of specificity you offer. As you will see later, when we discuss each methodology, no one methodology is perfect; rather they are types of inquiry rife with tradeoffs. What one method offers as its strength, another has as its weakness. That is why we insist our students be exposed to a variety of methodologies because no one method is right for every study. In fact, we want you to consider how the question and/or hypotheses you write actually influence the methodology you should use, and the type of analysis you will conduct.

How Is Metatheory Related to Research Questions and Hypotheses?

It is important to consider the relationship between metatheory and the overall research process. This is because what we find most interesting about reading a variety of communication research questions and/or hypotheses is how much metatheory seeps out from beneath the question or hypothesis. What we mean is that even when students are still grappling with the abstract concepts of metatheory, once they begin writing research questions, these concepts become a little clearer to them. Both your epistemological and ontological entailments drive how you write a particular question. In other words, you approach any question or hypothesis you write with certain assumptions about the world.

So What?

In summary, your research objectives, questions, and hypotheses are driven by the way you see the world and the assumptions you make about reality; but they are also driven by your curiosities and interests, as well as the research other people have conducted, and the theories, concepts, and conclusions they have come to in your area of interest. In previous chapters, we have shown you how to begin your research search in the library—among the mounds and mounds of research that has come before you. In this chapter, we've shown you how to pull your unique research idea out of that history, find the important questions left to be explored, and formulate good, solid objectives, questions, and/or hypotheses that will result in good quality research. The next several chapters will help you further design your research study as we show you how every decision you make in the research process—from choosing your method to designing your study to analyzing your results—depends on the objectives, research questions, and/or hypotheses you set out to address.

Glossary

Conceptual definition
 How the concept or variable that is being studied is defined.

Fact pattern
 A factual relationship occurring repeatedly.

Hypothesis
 A statement a researcher makes about the relationship between a dependent and an independent variable.

Null hypothesis
 A statement that the research hypothesis is wrong. In other words, there is no (null) relationship between the variables that the research predicted.

Operational definition
 How the concept or variable of interest is measured and/or observed.

Research objectives
 Are the reasons or primary rationale for the execution of a research project.

Research question
 Questions scholars ask about the way things work.

References

Barnlund, D. C. (1968). *Interpersonal communication: Survey and studies*. Boston: Houghton Mifflin.

Booth, W. C., Colomb, G. G., & Williams, J. M. (1995). *The craft of research*. Chicago: University of Chicago Press.

Bross, I. B. J. (1953). *Design for decisions*. New York: Macmillan.

Dance, F. E. X. (1982). Essays in human communication theory: A comparative overview. In F. E. X. Dance (Ed.), *Human communication theory: Comparative essays* (pp. 286–299). New York: Harper & Row.

Davis, C. S. (2005). Home. *Qualitative Inquiry 11*(2), 392–409.

Davis, C. S. (2009). *Death: The beginning of a relationship*. Cresskill, NJ: Hampton Press.

Davis, C. S., & Dollard, N. (2005). *Team process and adherence to wraparound principles in a children's community mental health care system of care*. Tampa, FL: Louis de la Parte Florida Mental Health Institute, University of South Florida.

Gottman, J. M., & Notarius, C. I. (2004). Decade review: Observing marital interaction. *Journal of Marriage and Family, 62*, 927–947.

Green, S. (2002). Mothering Amanda: Musings on the experience of raising a child with cerebral palsy. *Journal of Loss and Trauma, 7*, 21–34.

Guerrero, L. K., & Andersen, P. A. (1991). The waxing and waning of relational intimacy: Touch as a function of relational stage, gender and touch avoidance. *Journal of Social and Personal Relationships, 8*(2), 147–165.

Hall, C. S., & Lidzey, G. (1970). *Theories of personality* (2nd ed.). New York: Wiley.

Hawes, L. C. (1975). *Pragmatics of analoguing: Theory and model construction in communication*. Reading, MA: Addison-Wesley.

Johnson, E. P. (2002). Performing blackness down under: The café of the gate of salvation. *Text and Performance Quarterly, 22*(2), 99–119.

Kaplan, A. (1964). *The conduct of inquiry*. New York: Harper & Row.

Kramer, M. W. (2004). Toward a communication theory of group dialectics: An ethnographic study of a community theater group. *Communication Monographs, 71*(3), 311–332.

Kuhn, T. S. (1970). *The structure of scientific revolutions*. Chicago: University of Chicago Press.

Littlejohn, S. W. (1996). *Theories of human communication* (5th ed.). Belmont, CA: Wadsworth.

McCann, R., & Giles, H. (2006). Communication with people of different ages in the workplace: Thai and American data. *Human Communication Research, 32*(1), 74–108.

Miller, G. R., & Nicholson, H. E. (1976). *Communication inquiry: A perspective on a process*. Reading, MA: Addison-Wesley.

Pondy, L. R. (1967). Organizational conflict: Concepts and models. *Administrative Science Quarterly, 12*, 296–320.

Poole, M. S. (1990). Do we have any theories of group communication? *Communication Studies, 41*, 237–247.

Schmidt, S. M., & Kochan, T. A. (1972). Conflict: Towards conceptual clarity. *Administrative Science Quarterly, 17*, 359–370.

Segrin, C., Powell, H. L., Givertz, M., & Brackin, A. (2003). Symptoms of depression, relational quality, and loneliness in dating relationships. *Personal Relationships, 10*, 25–36.

Spiers, J. A. (2002). The interpersonal contexts of negotiating care in home care nurse-patient interactions. *Qualitative Health Research, 12*(8), 1033–1057.

Watzlawick, P., Beavin Bavelas, J., & Jackson, D. D. (1967). *Pragmatics of human communication. A study of interactional patterns, pathologies and paradoxes*. New York: W. W. Norton & Company.fact pattern

A factual relationship occurring repeatedly.

UNDERSTANDING COMMUNICATION RESEARCH ETHICS

CHAPTER OUTLINE

1. What are Ethics Important?
2. How do Ethics Influence Research?
3. Why do Ethics Matter in Research?
4. What is the Belmont Report? Why Is It Important?
5. The Role of Ethics in Communication Research
6. Ethical Conduct in the Social Sciences
7. So What?

KEY TERMS

Anonymity
Authoethnographic Research
Belmont Report
Beneficence
Confidentiality
Ethical Norms
Ethical Research
Informed Consent
IRB
Justice
Nonmaleficence
Norms of Conduct
Research Ethics
Respect for Persons

CHAPTER OBJECTIVES

1. Realize the ethical and proper way of conducting a communication research study
2. Understand the important role that ethics play in both the execution of a research study and the protection of its participants
3. Appreciate how to conduct a research study that has appropriate representation and legitimation of its findings

norms of conduct
These guidelines explain the difference between acceptable and unacceptable behavior.

When most people think of ethics, they think of rules for distinguishing between right and wrong. This is the most common way of defining "ethics": **norms for conduct** that explain the difference between acceptable and unacceptable behavior (Source: Resnik). Most of us learn these norms very early in life, typically in early to midchildhood. We begin to develop our ethical foundation through lessons learned at home, school, or in other community settings. By the time most people hit adolescence, they have a keen sense of what's right and what's wrong.

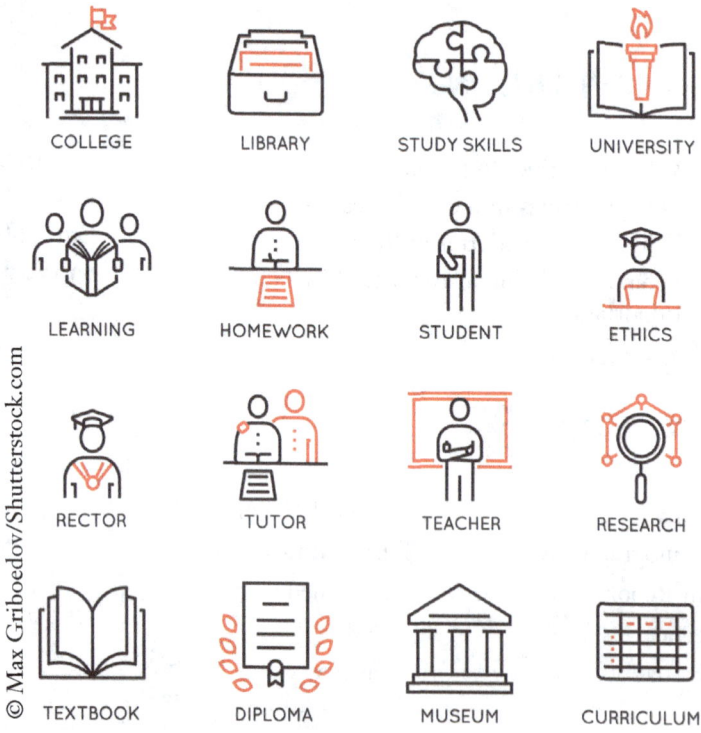

Why Are Ethics Important?

As explained by George L. Head, Director Emeritus of the American Institute, "Each individual's set of ethics provides the fundamental principles or beliefs by which that person distinguishes, consciously after some thought or unconsciously and seemingly by instinct, between morally acceptable and morally unacceptable behavior in that person's eyes." In terms of the world of research, an individual's ethics and beliefs guide the way they will conduct their research. A person's moral code provides the foundation on which they will decide what to study, how to study it, and, ultimately, the way they interpret the results (IRMI, 2006).

How Do Ethics Influence Research?

Simply put, ethics have a huge influence on the world of research. Because each person "draws portions, sometimes bits and pieces, of their personal and business ethics from an almost random variety of sources, such as their childhood upbringing, a dramatic or otherwise pivotal life experience, religious beliefs, discussions with family, colleagues, and friends" (Source: Head), it is virtually impossible to determine the perspective they may have on a subject or issue. This comes into play with both researchers and individuals being studied. As a result, before a study begins, researchers are often forced to generalize how respondents will react to a situation or feel about a product. What's ironic is that the judgment for this generalization comes from the researcher's own bias.

The other huge challenge with research and ethics is that an individual's moral code changes over time. Despite the fact an individual's moral foundation is formed by the time he or she reaches adolescence, moral development occurs throughout life. Regardless of the type of research being conducted, this poses continual challenges for researchers. Ultimately, it is impossible to know how someone feels about an issue or idea until you ask them. In addition, **ethical norms**—what is considered right and wrong—varies between societies. For research, this means that what is right and wrong can vary between cultures. Researchers must be keenly aware of this variance when they are sampling subjects from a diverse population (National Institute of Environment Health Sciences, 2015)

ethical norms
The societal codes of conduct.

Why Are Ethics Important in Research?

Ethical norms support the aims or goals of researchers and apply to people who conduct scientific research or other creative activities. There are many reasons it is important to stick to ethical norms in research. First, norms promote the aims of research, such as knowledge, truth, and objectivity. For example, rules against making up, falsifying, or misrepresenting research data promote the truth and minimize error (Source: Resnick).

Second, as research usually involves cooperation and coordination among many people in different disciplines and institutions, ethical standards promote the values that are vital to collaborative work, such as trust, accountability, mutual respect, and fairness. With a view to guiding the process of research, ethical norms such as guidelines for authorship, copyright, patents, data sharing, and confidentiality have been established to protect intellectual property interests while facilitating collaboration. Most researchers enjoy receiving credit for their ideas and contributions. They do not want to have their ideas stolen, copied, or attributed to someone else (Source: Resnick).

Third, many ethical norms help ensure researchers are held accountable to the public. For instance, federal policies on research misconduct, conflicts of interest, the protection of human subjects, and animal care are necessary in order to make sure that researchers who are funded by public money can be held accountable to the public (Source: Resnick).

Fourth, ethical norms help garner public support for research. People are more likely to fund a research project if they trust the quality and integrity of research. Finally, many of the norms of research promote a variety of other important moral and social values, such as social responsibility, human rights, and compliance with the law. Without ethics in research, serious problems could arise that could ultimately cause harm to the general population. For example, a researcher who alters data in a clinical trial may harm or even kill patients, or a researcher who fails to follow regulations and guidelines relating to radiation or biological safety may compromise his or her health and safety or the health and safety of those involved in the study (Source: Resnick). As you can see, even the slightest deviation from guidelines or safety precautions could have a significant impact on the safety of a study.

The Connection Between Communication Research and Ethics

It is clear that ethics are critical in the field of research. But what is ethical research? Two important terms need to be explained: **research ethics** and **ethical research**. **Research ethics** are the principles, rules, guidelines, and norms of research behavior that a research community has decided are fair and appropriate. **Ethical research** is research designed and carried out in a valid, reliable, and legitimate way that protects a participant's rights (Davis, Powell and Lachlan, 2017). Ethical research not only protects a participant's rights, but also ensures the research being conducted is reliable, valid, and truly representative of the sample set. So, as you can see, the concept of research applies not only to the design of the study but also to the execution and interpretation of the findings. The most important thing it protects is a participant's rights.

In 1979, the U.S. government issued a document called "Ethical Principles and Guidelines for the Protection of Human Subjects," commonly referred to as the **Belmont Report** (The National Commission for the Protection of Human Subjects of Biomedical and Behavioral Research, 1979). This document provides the basis for all of the federal regulations for the protection of human research participants. The three major tenets of the Belmont Report are respect for persons, beneficence/nonmaleficence and justice (Murphy & Dingwall, 2001).

research ethics
The principles, rules and norms of research behavior considered acceptable by a research community.

ethical research
Research designed and executed in a way that protects a particpant's rights.

Belmont Report
The first Federal report to specify the rights of participants in a research study.

The Tenets of the Belmont Report

The big question: How do researchers adhere to ethics? Let's explain this in conjunction with exploring the basic principles of the Belmont Report.

Principal #1: Respect for Persons

respect for persons
A principal that covers two major concepts: the autonomy and protection of research participants.

The first one—**respect for persons**—covers two things: autonomy and protection of participants. Under the terms of this first tenet, participants should have autonomy while participating in a research study. This means they are independent and capable of making decisions on their own as long as they have been properly informed. According to the principle of respect for persons, "researchers must acknowledge the considered opinions and choices of research subjects. In other words, individuals must be given the choice whether to participate in research, and they must be provided sufficient information and possess the mental competence to make that choice" (Bailey, 2004, p. 5).

Respect for persons also recognizes that some people are incapable of making decisions or choices that are in their best interest. "Individuals with diminished decision-making capacity may lack the ability to comprehend study procedures or how participating in a study might adversely affect them" (Bailey, 2004, p. 6). As a result, it specifies that special care should be used to protect those with "diminished capacity to the point of excluding individuals who are not able to give meaningful consent to participate in research" (Bailey, 2004, p. 6).

Minors also fall into a special category with research. Usually, a parent or legal guardian must give permission for a child to participate in a research project or study. Researchers must also ask a minor for his or her consent by explaining the study in language and terms that are age appropriate (Bailey, 2004, p. 7).

informed consent
The idea of providing participants with full information about a research study and letting them make their own decision about it.

The principle of participant autonomy led to the development of **informed consent**, where participants are provided with full information about the research study and are left to independently decide whether they would like to participate in it or not.

The process of informed consent involves three main facets:

1. Disclosing information needed to make an informed decision
2. Ensuring an understanding of what has been disclosed
3. Promoting the true volunteering of information and overall participation in the study (Bailey, 2004, p. 8)

Participants must receive full information about the focus of the study and research techniques being used and be provided with statements about confidentiality. In addition, they must be provided with information about withdrawing from the study without penalty, if they choose to do so (Creswell, 2007).

SEARCH AND ANALYSIS

Principal #2: Nonmaleficence and Beneficence

The second principle—**nonmaleficence and beneficence**—supports the underlying tenet that research is ethical if the benefits outweigh the risk of harm to participants. The term **nonmaleficence** means no avoidable harm should come to participants, and **beneficence** suggests that the outcome of research should be positive and beneficial (Davis, Powell & Lachlan, 2017). Together, these two ideas help to safeguard the participants in a research study.

Two rules have been created to ensure the application of beneficence in research: (1) do not harm and (2) maximize possible benefits and minimize possible harms. The reality is that most communication research does not directly benefit participants, and the potential for harm is minimal. The most common risks of harm are psychological distress and unintentional disclosure of private information. For example, studies involving issues of sexuality or mental health may create feelings of duress or embarrassment or cause harm to a participant's reputation if personal information that would ordinarily not be disclosed is released (Bailey, 2004, p. 9).

To safeguard against such issues, researchers often use codes or pseudonyms to protect the privacy of participants. Such techniques usually work; but when pieces of information are pieced together, it may be enough to determine the identity of a participant. Although rare, it does occasionally happen. As a result, when conducting a communication research study, it is incredibly important to do everything possible to protect a participant's rights by ensuring privacy of their identity and confidentiality of their responses. The concept of **anonymity** safeguards a participant's rights to

nonmaleficence
The concept that no avoidable harm should be done to participants.

beneficence
The idea that the outcome of research should be positive and beneficial.

anonymity
Protects a research participant's rights to privacy.

confidentiality
Prohibits a research participant's name from being revealed in a study.

privacy. Under the terms, no one is allowed to link a participant's responses to their identity. The concept of **confidentiality** takes privacy one step further by ensuring that researchers do not disclose a participant's name when writing or reporting their summary (Davis, Powell and Lachlan, 2017).

Periodically, there are times when it is simply impossible or not in the best interest of participants to maintain confidentiality. Typically, this comes into play when a researcher is conducting certain types of qualitative research studies such as a narrative or autoethnographic research. As explained by researchers Carolyn Ellis, Tony E. Adams, and Arthur P. Bochner, **Autoethnographic research** is an approach "to research and writing that seeks to describe and systematically analyze personal experience in order to understand cultural experience" (Ellis, Adams, & Bochner, 2011). When using this form of qualitative research, the researcher must disclose that he or she is using this technique as well as attempt to ensure the greatest care when publishing the results.

autoethnographic research
A Research approach that attempts to describe and analyze personal experience as a means of understanding culture.

Although most researchers go out of their way to ensure adherence to ethical policies, occasionally there are some studies that are strategically designed to deceive participants. According to researchers at Oregon State University, deception occurs when researchers provide "false or incomplete information to participants for the purpose of misleading research subjects." Deception is considered an acceptable practice in research according to the Institutional Review Board (IRB) as long as it is justified by the researchers (Deception in Research, 2019).

When employing deception, according to the IRB, researchers must

- Confirm the design of the study meets all of the criteria for a waiver of consent
- Provide a justification for the use of deception
- Rationalize why deception was chosen and ultimately selected as a technique over other possible methods
- Include a description of the type of deception and how it will take place
- Offer an explanation as to why the use of deception is necessary and whether it poses an increased risk to participants
- Give an indication whether the use of deception may hamper an individual's desire to participate in the study
- Show a description of the poststudy memo that gives individuals the right to have their data removed from the study
- Provide a description of any prior uses of deception in comparable research studies and a summary of participants' reaction to its use (Deception in Research, 2019).

Principal #3: Justice

The third principle of the Belmont Report is **justice**. In the world of communication research, the concept of justice focuses on the way participants are selected, as opposed to how the actual research is conducted. The principle of justice suggests participants should be selected from all factions of society, regardless of race, ethnicity, gender, age, and so on, and

justice
The idea that all classifications of people should be equally exposed to the risks and benefits of research.

receive equal rights if selected. When applying the concept of justice to research participants, researchers need to consider the selection process so that individuals are chosen objectively, on the basis of the focus of the study (Davis, Powell & Lachlan, 2017).

It also mandates "the benefits and burdens of research are equitably distributed - that is, no individual or population is exposed to risks of harm while other individuals or populations receive the benefits" (Bailey, 2004, p. 12). Simply put, it is incredibly important that all participants are cautiously and fairly exposed to the same techniques and elements in a study. In addition, in regard to the design of the study itself, the concept of justice requires that researchers are "dissuaded from prioritizing the perspective of the entire or privileged while downplaying the views of the less fortunate" (Davis, Powell & Lachlan, 2017, p. 68).

Psychologist Joan E. Sieber suggests the research question itself and the interpretation of the findings may contain bias that singles out a particular group of individuals and leads to unfair treatment of that group: "One historically sensitive area of the application of research findings is examining racial differences. Another example relates to the use of psychological test results in order to promote a policy of sterilization for the mentally retarded population" (Sieber and Stanley, 1988, pp. 49–55).

On the concept of justice, Sieber summarizes: Justice and equitable treatment refer to issues of procedural and distributive justice that may arise at any stage of the research process. An idea that creates prejudices against some sector of society is unfair. An experimental treatment is also unfair if resources known to be vital to subjects' well-being are withheld from subjects in one group and given to those in another (Sieber & Stanley 1988, pp. 49–55).

Now that we have explored the concepts of the Belmont Report, let's examine its influence on the world of Communication Research.

▼ Conducting Communication Research

With the adherence to ethics and the implementation of an ethical code being one of the fundamental parts of a research study, it should come as no surprise that most universities, associations, institutions, and government agencies have very specific rules and policies that guide their research studies. This ranges from government agencies such as the National Institutes of Health (NIH) and the Environmental Protection Agency (EPA) to associations such as the American Psychological Association and the American Heart Association. Across these various organizations, there are some common ethical principles that are found—(*Adapted from Shamoo*

A and D. Resnik. 2015. Responsible Conduct of Research. 3rd ed. New York: Oxford University Press).

- **Maintain honesty:** Strive for honesty across all facets of a study—reporting of data, results, methods and procedures, and publication of findings. Do not fabricate, falsify any aspect of the study, or deliberately deceive colleagues, or the public.
- **Ensure objectivity:** Avoid bias in the design of the experiment, analysis of the data, interpretation of the findings, and other aspects of the project where objectivity is expected or required. Be sure to disclose personal or financial relationships that may affect research objectivity.
- **Strive for integrity:** Adhere to promises and agreements and aim for consistency throughout the study.
- **Be careful:** Avoid silly errors, and carefully examine your own work and those of others involved in the project. Maintain detailed records of research activities, especially during the data collection process.
- **Respect intellectual property:** Adhere to patents, copyrights, and other forms of intellectual property. Do not use unpublished materials without proper permission, and give credit for all contributions to research. Don't copy other people's work.
- **Maintain confidentiality:** Honor the right to anonymity of participants and safeguard any data, records, or private materials solicited as part of a study.
- **Avoid discrimination:** Stay objective and avoid rendering judgment against participants or colleagues on the basis of sex, race, ethnicity, religion, or other factors.
- **Don't lie or engage in legal actions:** Obey the law across all facets of the research study, and respect any related corporate or institutional policies.
- **Protect participants:** When working with people in a study, be aware of any risk or harm that could come to them. Be sure to respect their rights to privacy, autonomy, and dignity. Take extra care of vulnerable populations (minors, physically/mentally challenged), and try to allocate the burdens and benefits of a research study fairly.

Promoting Ethical Conduct in Science

Most academic research institutions in the United States require students to have some education in the responsible conduct of research (RCR).

Very often, students who are taking courses in research ethics wonder why they are required to take such a class. Most of us perceive that we know the difference between right and wrong and understand the serious ramifications of plagiarizing. So what is the point in taking such a class? It is simply a precaution. The reality is that research studies have proven that deliberate misconduct in research is very rare (Bailey, 2004, p. 14). In fact, researchers estimate the rate of misconduct in research to range between 0.01% and 1% per year (Shamoo and Resnick, 2015.)

In the rare instances when misconduct does deliberately occur in research, it is usually for a few simple reasons. One possible reason is the pressure and constraints put on researchers by universities and other institutions. The pressure to publish, secure research grants, or reveal the findings of landmark study can cause individuals to purposely commit fraud or violate basic ethical rules (Shamoo and Resnik 2015). Sadly, incorrect or deliberately concocted research often goes overlooked or isn't discovered for years.

Many of the ethical violations that occur in research happen out of pure ignorance. Very often, researchers just overlook or fail to consider the ethical ramifications of their actions. Periodically, some unethical authorship practices simply reflect traditions and practices that have not been questioned until recently. For example, if the lead scientist at a lab is named as an author on every paper, even if he or she does not make a large contribution, is that wrong? Or a researcher may perceive that having a financial relationship with a drug company that sponsors a research study is perfectly acceptable (Bailey, 2004, p.17). There are countless examples of situations that might be considered ethical by some individuals or professions yet unacceptable to others.

The reality is that at the end of the day, we each have an ethical code that we live by that affects not only how we live our life but also the way we interact with others. How we elect to follow that ethical code is up to each of us. When it comes to conducting communication research studies, it is important to consider not only the objectives and goals of the work but also the ramifications of the study on the participants.

So What?

In conclusion, as researchers it is our responsibility to do our very best to ensure that our research studies are responsibly designed, scientifically sound and produce credible results. In doing so, it is important to keep in mind the principals of the Belmont Report and that all aspects of the study adhere to the guidelines set forth by the IRB. We must do our best to ensure the rights and protection of participants across all phases of the research process. In the end, our research is only as good as the moral foundation and ethical code it is built upon.

Glossary

Anonymity
Protects a research participant's rights to privacy.

Autoethnographic research
A research approach that attempts to describe and analyze personal experience as a means of understanding culture.

Belmont Report
The first Federal report to specify the rights of participants in a research study.

Beneficence
The idea that the outcome of research should be positive and beneficial.

Confidentiality
Prohibits a research participant's name from being revealed in a study.

Ethical norms
The societal codes of conduct.

Ethical research
Research designed and executed in a way that protects a particpant's rights.

Informed consent
The idea of providing participants with full information about a research study and letting them make their own decision about it.

Justice
The idea that all classifications of people should be equally exposed to the risks and benefits of research.

Nonmaleficence
The concept that no avoidable harm should be done to participants.

Norms of conduct
These guidelines explain the difference between acceptable and unacceptable behavior.

Research ethics
The principles, rules and norms of research behavior considered acceptable by a research community.

Respect for persons
A principal that covers two major concepts: the autonomy and protection of research participants.

References

Bailey, Lisa Robinson. January 2004. Duke University, "Historical and Ethical Principles—SBE." CITI Program. Original Publication Date: January 2004. Updated: January 2014.

Carolyn Ellis, Tony E. Adams and Arthur P. Bochner. January 2011. "Autoethnography: An Overview" *12* (1), 10. Accessed November 11, 2019. http://qualitiaitve-research.net.

Creswell, John. 2009. Research Design: Qualitative, Quantitative and Mixed Methods Approaches, 3rd edition. Sage Publications.

Davis, Christine S., Heather Powell and Kenneth A. Lachlan. 2017. *Chapter 4: Straight Talk About Communication Research Methods.* 3rd edition. Kendall Hunt Publishing Company.

"Deception in Research." 2019. Accessed November 11, 2019. http://research.oregonstate.edu.

IRMI. March 2006. Where Our Ethics Come From By George L. Head. Accessed November 11, 2019. https://www.irmi.com/articles/expert-commentary/where-our-ethics-come-from.

Elizabeth Murphy and Robert Dingwell. 2001. *The Ethics of Ethnography.* In Handbook of Ethnography, edited by Paul Atkinson, Amanda Coffey, Sara Delamont, John Lofland & Lyn Lofland (pp. 339-351). Sage Publications.

National Institute of Environment Health Sciences. 2015. *What is Ethics in Research & Why is it Important?* Accessed November 11, 2019. https://www.niehs.nih.gov/research/resources/bioethics/whatis/index.cfm.

Sieber, Joan E., and Barbara Stanley. 1988. "Ethical and professional dimensions of socially sensitive research." *American Psychologist, 43*(1):49-55.

Shamoo A and D. Resnik. 2015. *Responsible Conduct of Research*, 3rd ed. New York: Oxford University Press.

"The Belmont Report: Ethical Principles and Guidelines for the Protection of Human Subjects of Research," published by The National Commission for the Protection of Human Subjects of Biomedical and Behavioral Research, Dept. of Health, Education and Welfare, 18 April 1979.

4

UNDERSTANDING VARIABLES

Chapter Outline

1. What Is the Function of Variables in Communication Research?
2. What Is a Variable?
3. Revisiting Conceptual and Operational Definitions
   a. Conceptual Definitions
   b. Operational Definitions
      i. Measured Operational Definitions
      ii. Experimental Operational Definitions
4. Operationalizing: Matching Your Variables to Your Study
   a. Conceptual Fit
   b. Measuring Variables
      i. Self-Report
         A. Social Desirability Bias in Self-Report Data
      ii. Other Report
         A. Limitations in Other Reports
      iii. Observing Behavior
         A. Hawthorne Effect Bias in Observing Behaviors
   c. Triangulation
   d. Measurement
      i. Nominal Level Measurement
      ii. Ordinal Level Measurement
      iii. Interval Level Measurement
         A. Likert Scale
         B. Semantic Differential Scale
      iv. Ratio Level Measurement
5. Types of Variables
   a. Independent Variables
   b. Dependent Variables
      i. Examples of Independent and Dependent Variables
   c. Extraneous Variables
      i. Confounding Variables
      ii. Mediating Variables
      iii. Moderating Variables
6. The Different Types of Relationships between Variables
   a. Reversible and Irreversible Relationships
   b. Deterministic and Stochastic Relationships
   c. Sequential and Coextensive Relationships
   d. Sufficient and Contingent Relationships
   e. Necessary and Substitutable Relationships
7. The Dimensions of Variables
   a. Unidimensional Concepts
   b. Multidimensional Concepts
8. So What?

KEY TERMS

Coextensive relationships
Conceptual fit
Confounding variable
Contingent relationships
Dependent variable
Deterministic relationships
Hawthorne effect
Independent variable
Interval level measurement
Irreversible relationships
Measurement
Multidimensional concepts
Necessary relationships
Nominal level measurement
Ordinal level measurement
Ratio level measurement
Reversible relationships
Self-report
Sequential relationships
Social desirability
Stochastic relationships
Substitutable relationships
Sufficient relationships
Unidimensional concepts

CHAPTER OBJECTIVES

1. To understand the function of variables
2. To explore the relationships that occur between variables
3. To understand confounding variables
4. To become familiar with the process of variable measurement

▼ What Is the Function of Variables in Communication Research?

measurement
A process of determining the characteristics and/ or quantity of a variable through systematic recording and organization of observations.

In this chapter, we will examine what variables are, how we think about variables, and how variables are used in communication research. We will consider the types of variables, both independent and dependent, while revisiting the importance of how we operationally define variables at the outset of our research. We will also explore, in depth, the types of relationships between variables. Additionally, we discuss problematic variables, called extraneous variables, that we should be mindful of as we design our research studies. Finally, we consider **measurement** theory, levels of measurement, and whether variables are unidimensional or multidimensional. Our focus will remain on how all of the decisions we make along the way inform the subsequent methodological choices we make.

Chapter 4 Understanding Variables ▼ 45

What Is a Variable?

Variables can be any concepts that have the ability to take on more than one value. In other words, a single object cannot be a variable because it is incapable of taking on more than one value. In communication, we are interested in concepts that can vary. They can vary from person to person, vary in time, and vary in intensity. Remember that we have suggested that the variables of the study are the nouns in our research question or hypothesis.

Revisiting Conceptual and Operational Definitions

Although we discussed the concepts of conceptual definitions and operational definitions in Chapter 5 when we discussed research questions and hypotheses, we need to revisit our discussion on that topic, as that is an important consideration you make when choosing what variables to study in your research. Without a strong understanding of our conceptual and operational definitions we cannot establish variables that adequately answer our research questions and hypotheses.

Conceptual Definitions

Remember that a conceptual definition is simply how you define the variable you plan to study. In Chapter 4, we used the example of defining the word *violence*, illustrating that we might all have a slightly unique definition of what counts as violence. The goal of a conceptual definition is to delineate clearly what you mean, when you are identifying your variables of interest. It allows the reader of the research and others who wish to study the same construct to know without a doubt what you mean when you study a particular variable. The conceptual definition is really the written definition of the variables of the study. It allows you to define an often broad, obscure concept in terms of related, similar (often more concrete) concepts, and in some instances to establish the boundaries of what phenomena meet the definition you are using.

Operational Definitions

Operational definitions describe the observable characteristics of a concept, so that the characteristics can be measured or otherwise identified or represented. These definitions identify how the communication scholars plan to measure and/or observe the variable of interest. Having clear operational definitions allows researchers to replicate their studies and/or extend them into other domains, knowing that they are using the same procedures in terms of measurement. There are two types of operational definitions: measured operational definitions and experimental operational definitions. Both explore how you can measure a variable of interest, but they differ based on the methodological choices a scholar makes.

Measured Operational Definitions. A measured operational definition describes how a researcher can measure the existence or quantity of a variable—for example, intelligence measured with an IQ test, class performance with a letter grade, risk perception with Lachlan and Spence's (2010) hazard scale, dialogic communication with discourse analysis, communicating power with a close textual analysis.

Measured operational definitions are important in descriptive research too. For example, if you wanted to examine the frequency and context of violence in slashers films, like Weaver (1991) did, you must identify what you will count and how. In Weaver's study, "Each scene was coded for (a) duration (in seconds); (b) the number, gender, and dramatic role (i.e., protagonist vs. antagonist) of all characters; (c) the general type of action depicted; (d) the specific nature of each action; (e) the resolution, if any, of each action; and (f) the involvement of nudity" (p. 387). Here he identifies exactly what will be coded. He then becomes even more specific, "Acts of aggression, for example, were coded as involving verbal abuse, an attempted attack, or an attack on a person or persons" (1991, p. 387).

Experimental Operational Definitions. Experimental operational definitions specify how the researcher can manipulate a variable in an experiment, in order to produce at least two values or levels of an independent variable. For example, a variable with an experimental operational definition would describe how we manipulate exposure to differing levels of media violence: *The Dark Knight* vs. *Mama Mia!*, or persuasive message presented by an attractive vs. unattractive speaker—Randy Johnson vs. Michael Jordan.

In both measured and experimental operational definitions, the goal is to create a kind of a guidebook for other scholars in your field. Good operational definitions allow others to replicate previous work, while at the same time providing some control over what you study. Operational definitions steer how you observe and measure your variable, thus functioning as guidelines for some of your methodological choice making. However, ultimately, the key of both conceptual and operational definitions is that they need to match. They define the variables of interest in any communication research study, and in order to have valid research we must actually measure what it is that we claim we are measuring.

Operationalizing: Matching Your Variables to Your Study

Conceptual Fit

One of the primary goals of this textbook and of communication research methods courses across the country is to teach you to be a critical consumer of research. As such, we are not only interested in teaching you to be critical of the results of empirical work, but also of the methodological choices the researcher makes in building their work. While there is clearly no such thing as a perfect study, we expect you to learn how to evaluate the components of all communication research. It is important that you give consideration to how to evaluate operational definitions. The biggest concern in defining a variable, operationally, is in the **conceptual fit** between what is measured and what you set out to measure. This conceptual fit is really designed to be certain that the meaning of both your conceptual and operational definitions is preserved throughout the research process. One important question you can ask is as follows: Is the operational definition adequate or complete; does it include all of the essential aspects of a variable? For example, we might ask our students if they are comfortable with us determining whether they are a good student from their G.P.A. Not surprisingly, not all students are comfortable with this one measure having tapped into all of the aspects that should be considered when evaluating the relative success of a college student. Please recognize that while you strive to be as thorough as possible, most operationalizations are incomplete. It is nearly impossible to capture the complete meaning of some constructs with a single variable. The second question you should ask is: Is it accurate? In other words, do you agree with how the research measured the variable? Does it make sense? For example, you might ask whether hitting a Bobo doll (an inflatable child-size doll filled with sand and designed to be punched) is an accurate measure of aggression (see Bandura, Ross, & Ross, 1961; and Bandura, Ross, & Ross, 1963). Last, in evaluating both measured and manipulated operational definitions, the question you should ask is whether the researcher has made clear to us how the variable is measured or manipulated.

conceptual fit
How closely your operational definition matches your conceptual definition.

Measuring Variables

The last component of operational definitions we want to discuss has to do with the choices you make about the operational procedures for measured variables. There are three primary procedures you follow for measuring variables: self-report, other report, and observing behavior.

self-report
This procedure is good at measuring individual's beliefs, attitudes, and values, or in finding out about behaviors we might not be able to observe directly.

Self-Report.   **Self-report** procedures are familiar to most students. Think about the evaluation you make of professors and instructors at the end of each semester. Or perhaps, you find yourself consulting ratemyprofessor.com prior to enrolling in a class with a particular professor. These are good examples of self-report procedures (though despite students' beliefs to the contrary, one of these two methods is more accurate than the other; we will discuss sampling bias in Chapter 6). Self-report procedures are good at measuring an individual's beliefs, attitudes, and values, or in finding out about behaviors (after the fact) we might not be able to observe directly.

SOCIAL DESIRABILITY BIAS IN SELF-REPORT DATA.   Remember, research methods are about making the best choices with the tools at your disposal and none of the operational procedures for measured variables is without limitations. A well-documented limitation of self-report data collection is that it depends upon the participant's willingness to provide the information, as well as the ability to recall accurately something that has already happened. The most significant weakness of self-report is an issue we call **social desirability**. Social desirability is the idea that if you are asking participants to answer questions that are sensitive in nature, people might feel swayed to present themselves in a particular light, regardless of whether it is indeed true. An example of this can be seen in Oliver and Hyde's (1993) meta-analysis of sexual behavior by gender. This study found significant gender differences for sexual behavior, with eight of the nine measures reflecting greater experience for males. While this seems reasonable, the authors themselves note in the discussion that because all the studies they reviewed used self-report data, what they had found evidence of was "gender differences in reporting tendencies" (p. 45).

social desirability
The idea that if participants are asked to answer questions that are sensitive in nature, people will undoubtedly feel swayed to present themselves in a particular light, regardless of whether it is indeed true.

Other Report.   Another operational procedure for measured variables is an *other report*. In this method you ask others to report on the individual in question's behavior. The hope is that they may be more objective than an individual's self-report, eliminating your concern about social desirability.

LIMITATIONS IN OTHER REPORTS.   However, problems in asking people to rate others' behavior can include limited experience with the individual or limited prior exposure to her behavior. It is also possible that any kind of pre-existing relationship between subject and observer may bias the reporting of their behavior. Take for example the famous Bandura, Ross, and Ross's (1963) Bobo doll experiments. If you wanted to replicate these studies, you may want to measure children's aggression after viewing violent or nonviolent films by asking the classroom teachers to report on children's behavior. At the same time, it would be wise to pre-test the teachers making the observations to see if they have any existing biases toward identifying students who may be more or less inclined to exhibit violent behavior.

Observing Behavior. The third operational procedure you can use for measuring variables is observing behavior. For example, your author Christine Davis observes children's mental health treatment team meetings to assess communication in the meetings. Students often like to observe communication behaviors in research settings such as bars, shopping malls, or restaurants. Other communication researchers prefer to do their observations in laboratory settings. They might use an observation lab, which is a room set up like a living room (or conference room) with video cameras and/or one-way mirrors. Researchers give participants communication tasks (such as, "talk to each other on this subject") and observe them while they are carrying out the behavior.

The major strength of observing behavior is that it can sometimes be more accurate than self-report or other report, especially if the observations are conducted in a naturalistic setting. Imagine that we ask you to rate your communication competence in a communication task you complete with your significant other. Are you likely to be an objective judge of either your own skills in communication or even of your relational partner's skills? Perhaps. However, to guard against inaccuracies, we often have trained researchers assess communication competence in strangers. They tend to be much more objective. However, observation is not without its own inherent limitations. You can only assess what people do—not why they may behave in a particular way, what they believe, or what they feel. Therefore, scholars must observe the behavior they believe most accurately represents the concept of interest. This can pose potential problems; it can sometimes be challenging to be certain that the behavior indicates what you think it does.

HAWTHORNE EFFECT BIAS IN OBSERVING BEHAVIORS. Another potential limitation that occurs is the **Hawthorne Effect**. When you know others are observing you, do you change your behavior? Sure, most of us do alter our behavior slightly when we know that we are being observed. This is known as the Hawthorne effect. While the Hawthorne effect is most commonly associated with conscious observation, it should be noted that it can also occur in self-report and other-report studies too. Simply the awareness that someone will read your answers to a survey, or the suspicion that someone is looking at you from behind a one-way mirror in a laboratory setting, can be enough to induce Hawthorne.

Hawthorne Effect
An effect where people alter their behavior because they know they're being observed.

Triangulation

As you can see, each type of operational procedure for measured variables has both strengths and limitations associated with it. As is often the case, there is no solution to the limitations presented. As such, one solution is to combine a variety of different methods for measuring the variable in question. Triangulation is defined as "the comparison of two or more forms of evidence with respect to an object of research interest" (Lindlof & Taylor, 2002, pp. 240–241). There are actually several different types of triangulation: you can triangulate *sources*—multiple interviewees, multiple field sites, multiple cases, multiple observations; *methods*—qualitative methods plus quantitative methods, observation plus self-report plus other report; or *researchers*—multiple interviewers or observers (Lindlof & Taylor, 2002). However, not nearly enough scholars employ this technique in their research studies, and it is often the case that triangulation has to take place across multiple studies and entire programs of research. Triangulation moves you closer to understanding the variable in question and enhances the validity of the findings. For example, you might study communication competence and triangulate the methods by measuring the variable in three different ways: self-report, other report (rating their conversational partner), and trained coders' observational ratings.

Measurement

Regardless of what method you use to gather the information to measure your variables (self-report, other report, or observing behavior), you might need to use a scale as a questioning device to obtain a fairly precise and consistent measurement. Measurement is the process of determining the characteristics and/or quantity of a variable through systematic recording and organization of observations. Often, when conducting research, you use a scale to assign numbers and/or symbols to the characteristics of variables. There are four levels of measurement, which you consider from least specific to most specific: nominal, ordinal, interval, and ratio.

Nominal Level Measurement.

nominal level measurement
This type of measurement makes use of unordered categories, classifying the variable into qualitatively different and unique categories. These categories do not indicate any type of order or intensity of the degree to which a characteristic exists but represent the potential categories of some variable of interest.

Nominal level measurement makes use of unordered categories, classifying the variable into qualitatively different and unique categories. Nominal data does not have any true numerical value; the categories do not indicate any type of order or intensity of the degree to which a characteristic exists. Rather, they represent the potential categories of some variable of interest. For example, political party affiliation, religious affiliation, biological sex, and race are all variables measured at the nominal level. If you are unclear as to whether a scale is nominal, ask yourself whether there is some inherent order to the categories. If there is no order, the scale is nominal. There are two requirements for categorical representation: each category must be mutually exclusive and the list of categories must be exhaustive. Mutually exclusive categories have no overlap. You should be able to place an observation into one and only one category. One of the places you have likely encountered a categorical system that lacked mutually exclusive categories is when you have purchased music. Ever try to figure out what genre your favorite artist fits into? Is a CD by the Red Hot Chili Peppers likely to be found in Pop or Rock? Where do you look for a Taylor Swift CD, Country or Pop? In fact, Baccigalupo, Plaza, and Donaldson (2008) argue that genre is a fuzzy classification system for music, supporting our notion that genre is an example of a nominal categorical system violating the necessary mutually exclusive requirement of a categorical system. Second, the category system must be exhaustive. In other words, each category must represent the variable fully; each observation must be able to be classified by the measurement scheme. One of the ways scholars ensure that their category system is exhaustive is to identify the last category as *other*, thus ensuring that each observation will fit somewhere. For example, political party affiliation: Democrat, Republican, Independent, other.

Qualitative research frequently uses nominal measurements. Stephanie Houston Grey (2002), for example, analyzed the discourse of Japanese survivors of the Hiroshima and Nagasaki bombings in World War II as narratives of Christian transformation and meaning, redemptive knowing, and cultural authenticity. In another example, Warren and Kilgard (2001) studied a performance of Nathaniel Hawthorne's "The Birthmark" to understand the concepts (variables) of *whiteness*, *power*, and *privilege*—all nominal variables.

In quantitative research, nominal measurement is often used as a strategy to describe the sample of the study. For example, in their study on employee satisfaction with meetings, Rogelberg, Allen, Shanock, Scott, and Shuffler (2010) used nominal variables to describe participants' gender and organization type (publicly traded, privately held, private not for profit).

Ordinal Level Measurement. **Ordinal level measurement** is an ordered category or rank. Here we can determine whether an observation is greater than, less than, or equal to other observations, which cannot be determined from nominal level measurement. However, ordinal level measurement does not indicate the magnitude of that difference. Further, the intervals between the numbers on the scale are not necessarily equal. Ordinal level measurement examples include television programs classified as high, medium, or low in violence; the top five college football teams; and the top ten finishers in a NASCAR race. Any measure that uses ranking is ordinal level measurement.

Ordinal level measurement is often seen in the corporate world in terms of performance evaluation. For example, sales organizations often rank order their employees based on sales production. A life insurance company may hold a competition for life applications and rank a group of agents by number of applications in a month.

Interval Level Measurement. **Interval level measurement** specifies relative position and also establishes standard, equal distances between points on the scale. Most rating scales used in research are interval level

ordinal level measurement
This type of measurement has ordered categories or rank, and it can be determined whether an observation is greater than, less than, or equal to other observations. However, this type of measurement does not indicate how much the difference is; the amount separating levels is not known.

interval level measurement
This type of measurement specifies relative position and also establishes standard, equal distances between points on the scale.

measurement scales. Teacher evaluations are a good example of interval level measurements. When researchers ask participants to use a 5 or 7-point scale Likert scale (see below), most researchers assume that people recognize that the distances between points on the scale are equal. A benefit of interval level measurement is that if the differences between the numbers are meaningful, calculations (such as addition and subtraction) can be done. However, remember that the zero point is meaningless, and as a result it is impossible to make proportional statements. In other words, take the IQ (intelligence quotient) test, which is considered an interval level measurement; while the points between numbers are thought to be equal, there is no such thing as an IQ of zero. As such, someone with an IQ of 150 is not twice as smart as someone with an IQ of 75. Other examples of interval level measurement scales are both the Fahrenheit and the Celsius scales of temperature. The difference between 80 and 90 degrees is the same as the difference between 50 and 60; but 80 degrees isn't twice as hot as 40 degrees, because zero degrees does not indicate a total lack of temperature.

Interval measurement is pervasive throughout quantitative research methods, allowing us to study communication in marriage, patient satisfaction, employee dissent, and even communication strategies in a deceptive encounter. In fact, most any consumer survey you receive from the local grocery store, telephone company, voter attitude phone survey, or even the Nielsen television ratings use interval level measurement.

Table 4.1. Top Grossing Films in the USA (2015)

An Example of an Ordinal Level of Measurement	
1. *Star Wars: Episode 7*	$742,208,902
2. *Jurassic World*	$652,198,010
3. *The Avengers: Age of Ultron*	$459,005,868
4. *Inside Out*	$356,461,711
5. *Furious 7*	$351,032,910

Retrieved July 18, 2016, from http://www.the-numbers.com/market/2015/top-grossing-movies

Because interval level scales are so prominent in research, we should consider three types of interval level scales: Likert's method of summated ratings, Osgood's semantic differential, and the Thurstone scale. All three of these scales measure participants' feelings or attitudes. The key difference between them is the way they get at obtaining this information. We should take a second to note that not all researchers consider these three scales to be interval—some consider them to be ordinal scales. The determining factor is whether you believe that everyone sees the difference between 1 and 2 on a semantic differential, or *agree strongly* and *agree somewhat* on a Likert scale as the same. Most researchers in our field are willing to make that assumption and treat these scales as interval data.

LIKERT SCALE. The Likert scale is most common. You are probably already familiar with this interval scale, which measures participants' feelings or attitudes toward another person, issue, and event. The Likert scale is named after Rensis Likert (1932), an organizational psychologist who published a report detailing the use of this scale. Participants receive statements representing clear positions and are asked to indicate the extent to which they agree with each statement, usually on a 5- or 7-point scale (e.g., strongly agree, agree, neither agree nor disagree, disagree, strongly disagree). Often both positive and negative statements appear on the measure to be sure that participants are reading the questions, rather than responding without thought. Most human beings are quite patterned in their responses, so to avoid a response set, wherein they answer the same answer for each question, alternating the direction of a statement can alleviate this issue. Negative items are then reverse scored and scores are summed across the measure.

In their study on electronic multitasking in organization meetings, Stephens and Davis (2009, p. 71) utilized a Likert scale to measure the experience with technology variable. Participants were asked to rate their comfort with and skill with technology from "complete novice (1) to expert (7)."

Table 4.2. Example of a Likert Scale

Listening Measure
Please indicate the degree to which each statement applies to you by indicating whether you:
Strongly Disagree = 1; Disagree = 2; are Neutral = 3; Agree = 4; Strongly Agree = 5
_____ 1. I dislike speeches that don't interest me.
_____ 2. Usually I can listen to a speech that doesn't interest me.
_____ 3. I get restless and daydream when I listen to someone who doesn't interest me.
_____ 4. I listen even when the information in a speech doesn't interest me.
_____ 5. Listening to dull presenters about dull information makes me restless and causes me to daydream.
_____ 6. I do listen to dull presenters about dull information.
_____ 7. I don't usually listen to a presenter if there are distractions in the room.
_____ 8. I do listen when there are distractions during a presentation.

Table 4.2. Example of a Likert Scale (*Continued*)

_____ 9. I listen to presentations that are not directed at me.
_____ 10. I do not listen to presentations if they do not apply to me.
_____ 11. If I have other things on my mind, I don't pay attention to a presenter.
_____ 12. I listen to a presenter even if I have other things I'm thinking about.
_____ 13. I usually will not listen to a presentation that does not have a clear agenda.
_____ 14. I usually will listen even if a presentation has no clear agenda.
_____ 15. I am accepting of a presenter who does not give continuous feedback.
_____ 16. I am not accepting of a presenter who does not give continuous feedback.
_____ 17. I listen to presenters who do not give continuous feedback.
_____ 18. I will not listen to presenters who do not give continuous feedback.
_____ 19. I will listen to a presenter who has different opinions than mine.
_____ 20. I will not listen to a presenter who has different opinions than mine.
_____ 21. I will listen to a presenter who does not explain his/her subject matter.
_____ 22. I will not listen to a presenter if his/her subject matter is not defined.

SEMANTIC DIFFERENTIAL SCALE. Osgood's semantic differential scale is another interval level measurement technique, which measures the meanings participants assign to some stimulus (e.g., groups, types of music, a person, an idea). This scale, named after Charles Osgood (Osgood, Suci, & Tannenbaum, 1957), was initially used to measure the connotative meaning of concepts. This scale presents a stimulus at the top of a list of scales, wherein the scales are anchored at either end by pairs of polar-opposite adjectives (active-passive; warm-cold). Participants check a single point on the scale expressing their perception of the stimulus. A graduate school friend of one of your authors was interested in the music used during public service announcements. To pretest different types of music, we listened to five clips of music and rated them using a semantic differential scale (happy-sad; calm-anxious; relaxed-fearful, etc.). In a study by Uhlmann and Swanson (2004), they used a semantic differential scale to have participants measure their own and others' association of aggression. In other words, they reported where they fell on a scale from -3 to $+3$. The scale anchors were aggressive-peaceful, fighter-quiet, and combative-gentle.

Table 4.3. Example of a Semantic Differential Scale

Group Behavior Inventory, Friedlander (1966)
In this section, you are asked to judge the meaning of the concept Group Meeting (as it relates to _____ Department) in terms of each of the seven scales beneath it. Check one blank for each of the seven scales that best describes the meaning of the concept: _____ DEPARTMENT GROUP MEETINGS

good								bad
weak								strong
active								passive
pleasant								unpleasant
deep								shallow
relaxed								tense
valuable								worthless

Ratio Level Measurement. The most specific level of measure is the **ratio level measurement**, which not only has all of the characteristics of an interval scale, but also a true, meaningful zero point. Ratio scales also are assumed to be measured in equal intervals, and they can be mathematically measured, even to a decimal point or fraction of a point. Many variables have a true and meaningful measure of zero (e.g., age, heart rate, years at current address, the number of times you attended church in the last year, driving speed, income). The major advantage to ratio level measurement is that since there is a true, meaningful zero point, you can make proportional statements: Someone who is 50 is twice as old as someone who is 25 years of age. It is important to be able to identify whether a variable has been measured with a nominal, ordinal, interval, or ratio level of measurement, as the type of measurement level will determine the statistical techniques you can use to test your hypotheses and research questions.

Most often used in quantitative research studies, communication scholars use ratio measurement to examine relationships with a participant's age or measure a type of behavior of the participant. For example, Powell and Segrin (2004) used a ratio level to measure sexual behaviors, asking such questions as, "How many times in the last month did you engage in vaginal intercourse?" They also gathered the number of sexual partners over specific timeframes; this too, would constitute ratio level measurement.

> **ratio level measurement**
> As the most specific type of measurement, it has all of the characteristics of an interval scale, but also a true, meaningful zero point.

Table 4.4. Practice with Levels of Variable Measurement

Is the variable measured or manipulated? If the variable is measured: is it nominal, ordinal, interval, or ratio?
1. Preferred news source (self-report): newspaper, TV, magazine, other, none.
2. Length of acquaintance: Ask married people to report number of months they knew spouse prior to marriage.
3. Personal relevance of issue: Freshmen hear message advocating comprehensive exams for seniors; some told to begin next year, some told it will begin after they graduate.
4. Personal relevance of issue: Ask people to rate how personally important an issue is to them on a 7-point scale ranging from not at all important to very important.
5. Compliance-gaining strategies: Ask people to describe how they tried to gain compliance on one occasion, classify strategies.
6. Ask how successful the strategy was: not at all, somewhat, very.
7. Instruct people to use one of four different strategies to gain compliance from others in the context of collecting door-to-door for a charity.
8. Record amount of money donated to the charity.
Answer key: (1) measured, nominal; (2) measured, ratio; (3) manipulated; (4) measured, interval; (5) measured, nominal; (6) measured, ordinal; (7) manipulated; (8) measured, ratio.

Types of Variables

Now that we've discussed levels of measurement, let's review certain types of variables. There are two basic types of variables in communication research projects that follow an experimental design: independent and dependent variables. It is necessary that we know the differences between the two.

Independent Variables

independent variable
The variable that causes or determines the value in another variable.

An **independent variable** is the variable that is thought to predict or determine the value in another variable. For example, consider two variables: the number of cigarettes a person smokes and the probability of getting lung cancer. Both are variables because they can take on different values. One might have smoked zero cigarettes or might have smoked 3,000 in his or her lifetime. Even lung cancer is a variable because it can vary—you can have lung cancer, or not. Thus, the concept has more than one value, making it a variable. In this example, which one is your independent variable? If you guessed the number of cigarettes smoked, then you are correct. Consider another example. If we assume that your ratio of fat to lean is a function of how much you exercise, what is your independent variable? This seems a little trickier; reread and think it through. The amount of exercise is your independent variable, because it is thought to predict the value of your fat/lean ratio.

Dependent Variables

While we have been discussing these examples, there are other variables present—lung cancer and our ratio of fat/lean. In both of these cases, they are the **dependent variable**. The dependent variable is assumed to depend on or be predicted by another variable. In the examples above, cancer is presumed to be predicted by or dependent on the number of cigarettes smoked, while the ratio of fat/lean depends upon the amount of exercise one engages in. An easy way to remember it: outcomes are called dependent variables, because they depend on what happens with the independent variable.

dependent variable
The variable that is assumed to depend on or be caused by another variable.

Examples of Independent and Dependent Variables.

Another way to think about the independent variable is that this variable is likely to be what the researcher manipulates or what the research manipulates, while the dependent variable is what the researcher measures. So, for the first example, you will measure whether the participant has cancer, while you select a variety of people (who undoubtedly smoke a variety of number of cigarettes). And in the second example, you select a variety of people who exercise to varying degrees, and measure their fat/lean ratio.

An unusual, yet effective way to think about independent and dependent variables comes from ballroom dancing. When two dancers are dancing, they are in a partnership. As Tony Prado, Owner of Queen City Ballroom in Charlotte, explained it: Both partners have a job to do—one, the male (think independent variable), is in charge of where the couple moves to on the floor; he is in the lead. However, his task depends upon the woman's ability (think dependent variable) to follow his lead. In this example, the independent variable (the male lead dancer) predicts—or determines—which direction the dependent variable (the woman) goes.

As one last example, let's imagine that you do a survey of current college students measuring both marijuana smoking and grades. Imagine that you find that the more pot an individual smoked, the lower his or her grades. What is the independent variable, and what is the dependent variable? In other words, what caused what? How many of you think that the amount an individual smokes is the independent variable, causing the student to have lower grades (dependent variable)? Is it possible that it works the other way around? Is it possible that an individual might have poor grades (independent variable) and as a result begin smoking more marijuana (dependent variable)? Here, there is no clear answer; it is up to the researcher to identify the answer with his or her research question and/or hypotheses. The research questions and/or hypotheses identify what variable is the independent variable and what variable is the dependent variable. In other words, you as the researcher determine which is the independent variable or the dependent variable when you set up your experiment.

Table 4.5. Practice with Independent and Dependent Variables

Identify the independent and dependent variables for each of the following hypotheses:

1. People with high levels of exposure to television news will report greater satisfaction with life than people with low levels of exposure to television news.
2. Communicators with formal debate training will report higher levels of assertiveness than communicators without formal debate training.
3. When people are exposed to fear-arousing messages, as opposed to non-fear-arousing messages, they will report increased levels of anxiety.
4. The older one is, the greater will be the levels of stress perceived in one's life.
5. Children who stutter will have higher self-esteem than children who do not stutter.
6. Subjects reading persuasive messages by attractive sources will experience greater attitude change than subjects reading persuasive messages by unattractive sources.
7. Individuals with low communication apprehension will report significantly more positive parental behaviors and attitudes toward communication than individuals with high communication apprehension. [HINT: There are two dependent variables.]
8. Alcohol use and misuse would increase across adolescence.

Extraneous Variables

Sometimes a third (or more) variable will make finding the *true* relationship between the independent and dependent variables difficult to determine, because this additional variable is another possible cause (other than the independent variable) of the effect on the dependent variable. This is called an extraneous variable. An extraneous variable is one that is typically thought of as being unpredictable and uncontrolled by the researcher, or as being a variable that is not part of the research design. When searching for extraneous variables, researchers sometimes talk about the *third variable problem*—an unseen or unmeasured variable that is accounting for the changes seen in both the independent and dependent variables.

confounding variable
An extraneous variable that muddies the relationship between the independent and dependent variable.

Confounding Variables. A **confounding variable** is an extraneous variable that, because of its relationship to both the independent and dependent variables, cannot be distinguished from the independent variable in the analysis. Another way to define a confounding variable is when the effects of two variables cannot be separated from each other. For example, let's say a public speaking instructor not only asked students to practice their speeches an hour each day, but also suggested they visualize giving the speech before doing so. If the students were then rated as being better public speakers, there would be no way of knowing which of the two variables (practice or visualization) was responsible for the effect (better public speaking). These two actions likely had an effect on each other as well as on the dependent variable. Another commonly used example is as follows: imagine that you do a survey of various cities, and you measure two variables—crime incidence and ice cream consumption. You are going to discover that crime rates and ice cream consumption are strongly correlated. In this example, what are the dependent and independent variables? Do either one of these make sense to be dependent or independent? So, why is there a relationship between these two variables? The reason these are related variables in this instance is because both ice cream consumption and crime rates are dependent upon a third variable. This third variable is heat—hot weather drives people toward more outdoor interaction (and thus greater likelihood of confrontation). It also drives ice cream consumption, since ice cream is a cool, delicious treat on a hot day. Therefore, heat is the confounding variable, as it *muddies* the ability to detect the effect of the independent variable on the dependent variable. The relationship between the two variables, which is due to some confounding variable, is called a spurious correlation. When you design a research project and identify your variable, you need to attempt to anticipate potential confounds and eliminate them in the design of the study.

Table 4.6. An Example of a Confounding Variable in "Much Ado about Nothing" from *The Simpson's*

> **Homer:** Not a bear in sight. The Bear Patrol must be working like a charm.
>
> **Lisa:** That's specious reasoning, Dad.
>
> **Homer:** Thank you, dear.
>
> **Lisa:** By your logic I could claim that this rock keeps tigers away.
>
> **Homer:** Oh, how does it work?
>
> **Lisa:** It doesn't work.
>
> **Homer:** Uh-huh.
>
> **Lisa:** It's just a stupid rock.
>
> **Homer:** Uh-huh.
>
> **Lisa:** But I don't see any tigers around, do you?
>
> *[Homer thinks of this, then pulls out some money.]*
>
> **Homer:** Lisa, I want to buy your rock.
>
> *[Lisa refuses at first, then takes the exchange.]*

One of our favorite examples of a confounding variable is found in a newspaper article from June 11, 1984. The article, titled, "Ethel May Not Be Sexy, but She'll Do Better in Business than Cheryl," by Gary Dessler, reports on a master's thesis by Dorothy Linville. In this study, the author considered the question of whether the name of a woman would prevent her from landing management level positions. This particular research project utilized an experimental design. First, students rated the sexiness of 255 women's names on a scale of one to seven, with higher scores representing sexier names. Eight names receiving the highest scores were considered sexy, whereas the seven lowest scoring names were considered the least sexy. Keeping in mind that this study was done in the early 1980s, the sexy names were: Christine ($M = 5.08$), Candice ($M = 4.92$), Cheryl and Melanie ($M = 4.91$), Dawn, Heather, Jennifer, and Susan ($M = 4.83$). The least sexy names were as follows: Ethel ($M = 1.00$), Alma ($M = 1.08$), Zelda ($M = 1.16$), Florence, Mildred, Myrtle, and Esther ($M = 1.15$).

In the actual study, 100 college seniors and graduate students were asked to imagine being in the role of personnel managers. They received résumés of eight equally qualified women and were asked to rate them for management positions. Four of the résumés had unsexy names: Ethel, Myrtle, Mildred, and Esther; while four had high sexy names: Cheryl, Dawn, Jennifer, and Michelle. The results of this study indicated that men preferred hiring women with less sexy names for the management positions than did women. In fact, the article stated, "A new study finds that men are more likely to hire women with names they perceive as nonsexy for managerial positions, and give these women higher salaries. Women hiring other women are less influenced by the sound of a name" (Dessler, 1984). Is this really the conclusion one can draw based on the study as we have described it to you? Think for a minute about who you know with a name like Cheryl, Dawn, Jennifer, or Michelle. Then consider Ethel, Myrtle, Mildred, and Esther. Is it likely that these two groups of names come from two different generations? Therefore, there's a third variable going on here: perceived age of the applicant. Thus, it's highly possible that this is in fact age discrimination, not name discrimination. The key is that in this case there was another variable besides the sexiness of the name; therefore, it is incorrect to attribute the results to the sexiness of the woman's name.

There are two other types of variables that also have an effect on the dependent variable: mediating variables and moderating variables. These differ from extraneous variables in that they are typically predicted and controlled by the researcher.

Mediating Variables. With a mediating variable, instead of hypothesizing that A causes B directly, you might hypothesize that A causes M (mediating variable), which in turn causes B. An example of this might be that low communication apprehension (A) might cause a student to speak out more in class (M), which in turn might cause the student to get a better grade in class (B). Thus, while it may appear that low communication apprehension causes the student to get a better grade, it's only because of the mediating effect of speaking out more in class.

Moderating Variables. A moderating variable is a third variable that has an effect on both A and B. An example of this might be that an individual's overall health (M, moderating variable) affects both the individual's communication competence with his or her health-care provider (A) and the individual's satisfaction with his or her health care (B). Thus, it may appear that the individual's communication competence with his or her health-care provider causes the individual to be more satisfied with his or her health care, but it's actually that the individual's overall health affects both. We know that mediating and moderating variables sound similar to a confounding variable, but here's the primary difference—in the experiment, the researcher controls for the mediating and moderating variables and does not control for a confounding variable.

The Different Types of Relationships between Variables

In Chapter 5, we discussed how variables might have associational or causal, and directional or nondirectional, relationships with each other. As you have a better grasp on understanding the relationships between independent variables and dependent variables, and even how to look out for confounding variables, you must now consider the different types of relationships between the variables within the hypotheses you read and write.

Reversible and Irreversible Relationships

First, relationships between variables can be reversible or irreversible. **Reversible relationships** can go either way. For example, think about the pot-smoking example. Which comes first: pot smoking or grades? As you saw earlier, that relationship could go in either direction, thus it is a reversible relationship. Some are **irreversible relationships**, meaning the direction can only go one way. Think about the lung cancer and number of cigarettes smoked relationship. Can it go either way? No, thus it is an irreversible relationship.

reversible relationships
Relationships that can go in either direction or either way.

irreversible relationships
Relationships that can only go in one direction or one way.

Deterministic and Stochastic Relationships

Second, relationships between variables can be deterministic or stochastic. Relationships that are **deterministic** occur when the dependent variable must result from the independent variable. In communication studies, few relationships are deterministic; most are **stochastic**, which means probable. Again, think about the relationship between lung cancer and smoking. In fact, ask almost any smoker you know and he will tell you a tale of someone he knows who smoked like a fiend and died peacefully at an ancient age without ever getting lung cancer. That is because it is a probabilistic (stochastic) relationship, not deterministic. In other words, if a person smokes, she is more *likely* to get lung cancer (more probable), but smoking does not guarantee (determine 100%) lung cancer.

deterministic relationships
Relationships that occur when the dependent variable must result from the independent variable.

stochastic relationships
Relationships that are probable.

The above example is a classic case of what is sometimes referred to as an *individualistic fallacy*. When people fail to recognize the differences between stochastic and deterministic relationships, they may make inaccurate assumptions about the relationships between variables. It may very well be the case that the person in the example above knows someone who smoked his entire life and lived into old age in good health. There are always exceptions to rules. But in the aggregate, smoking will still damage your health and shorten your life. Rejecting this notion is an example of individualistic fallacy, rejecting a stochastic relationship based on a single observation.

Sequential and Coextensive Relationships

Third, relationships between variables can be sequential or coextensive. In **sequential relationships**, the ordering of the variables is important and must occur sequentially, meaning chronologically or in order. The Bobo doll experiments are an example of relationships between variables that occur sequentially (Bandura, Ross, & Ross, 1961). The researchers exposed children to violent or nonviolent cartoons, then allowed them the opportunity to play in a room complete with Bobo dolls as a measure of violent behavior. Here the relationship between viewing violence and violent behavior is sequential. On the other hand, if they are **coextensive relationships**, the variables within the relationship co-occur or happen simultaneously. For example, if we feel happy, we will also be smiling. Marital dissatisfaction and depression often co-occur within distressed marriages.

Sufficient and Contingent Relationships

Fourth, relationships between variables can be sufficient or contingent. In **sufficient relationships**, one variable is enough to bring about a second variable, whereas, if a third variable is needed, those are considered **contingent relationships**. Consider the following example: Is viewing violent television sufficient to cause violence or does viewing violent television cause violent behavior when drugs are present, weapons are present, and violence is in the living environment? If other factors are involved, then the relationship is contingent. If other factors are not involved, the relationship between variables is sufficient.

Necessary and Substitutable Relationships

Fifth, relationships between variables can be necessary or substitutable. When one variable must be present for the second variable to be present, you have **necessary relationships**. If other forces might bring about the same effect, you have **substitutable relationships**. As you think about the following question, consider whether it is a necessary or substitutable

---

sequential relationships
Relationships where the ordering of the variables is important and must occur sequentially, meaning chronologically or in order.

coextensive relationships
Relationships where the variables co-occur or happen simultaneously.

sufficient relationships
Relationships where the presence of or a change in one variable is enough to bring about a change in a second variable.

contingent relationships
Relationships where one variable is enough to bring about a third variable, if needed.

necessary relationships
Relationships where one variable must be present for a second variable to be present.

substitutable relationships
Relationships where other forces might bring about the same effect as a necessary relationship.

relationship: Is unprotected sexual behavior necessary to contract human immunodeficiency virus (HIV)? No, HIV can be transmitted by other means, such as intravenous drug use; thus, it is a substitutable relationship. However, fire cannot occur without oxygen; therefore, the relationship between fire and oxygen is a necessary relationship. As communication scholars study human beings, it is highly unlikely that many of the variables you study will constitute a necessary relationship; rather, most of the variables you study in communication are substitutable relationships.

The Dimensions of Variables

Variables are concepts that can be described and understood from one dimension or more than one dimension. We're talking here about the complexity of the item you're measuring. Some items are not complex at all, and require only one question or series of questions to address. These are called unidimensional concepts. Other concepts require many different questions or ways to look at them. They are called multidimensional concepts.

Unidimensional Concepts

Some variables are **unidimensional concepts**; they contain only one dimension. A simple example of a unidimensional concept is education: What's the highest grade you've completed in school? An example of a unidimensional scale is Neuliep and McCroskey (1997)'s classic Intercultural Communication Apprehension Scale, which measures cultural and ethnic communication apprehension on one dimension: the fear and anxiety a person associates with interacting with people from cultural or ethnic groups that differ from their own.

unidimensional concepts
Variables containing only one dimension.

Multidimensional Concepts

On the other hand, **multidimensional concepts** are complex variables embodying more than one component or dimension. We're sure you're familiar with the concept of self-disclosure as a multidimensional concept (breadth and depth). Another example of a multidimensional concept is the SAT Reasoning Test (formerly Scholastic Aptitude Test and Scholastic Assessment Test). A college entrance exam testing writing, mathematics, and critical reading skills, each construct of the SAT is measured through more than one measure and then a composite score is created from the combination of the three area scores. The variable sensation-seeking is also a multidimensional concept, including boredom susceptibility, disinhibition, experience seeking, and thrill seeking.

multidimensional concepts
Complex variables embodying more than one component or dimension.

So What?

This chapter has considered variables from every possible angle. Beginning with independent and dependent variables, we revisited the importance of the significance of how you choose and define your variables within research. We also considered some important variables to watch for: confounding variables. We explored the typology of relationships between variables. Considering measurement theory, you must remember that measurement levels determine the type of statistical analysis that you can conduct. We discussed the difference between whether variables are unidimensional or multidimensional. Our goal in this chapter is to continue reinforcing the idea that within the research process, the decisions you make—from the variables you choose, define, and measure—determine the path you take, guiding the subsequent research methodology you choose from your toolbox.

Glossary

Coextensive relationships
Relationships where the variables co-occur or happen simultaneously.

Conceptual fit
How closely your operational definition matches your conceptual definition.

Confounding variable
An extraneous variable that muddies the relationship between the independent and dependent variable.

Contingent relationships
Relationships where one variable is enough to bring about a third variable, if needed.

Dependent variable
The variable that is assumed to depend on or be caused by another variable.

Deterministic relationships
Relationships that occur when the dependent variable must result from the independent variable.

Hawthorne effect
An effect where people alter their behavior because they know they're being observed.

Independent variable
The variable that causes or determines the value in another variable.

Interval level measurement
This type of measurement specifies relative position and also establishes standard, equal distances between points on the scale.

Irreversible relationships
Relationships that can only go in one direction or one way.

Measurement
A process of determining the characteristics and/or quantity of a variable through systematic recording and organization of observations.

Multidimensional concepts
Complex variables embodying more than one component or dimension.

Necessary relationships
Relationships where one variable must be present for a second variable to be present.

Nominal level measurement
This type of measurement makes use of unordered categories, classifying the variable into qualitatively different and unique categories. These categories do not indicate any type of order or intensity of the degree to which a characteristic exists but represent the potential categories of some variable of interest.

Ordinal level measurement
  This type of measurement has ordered categories or rank, and it can be determined whether an observation is greater than, less than, or equal to other observations. However, this type of measurement does not indicate how much the difference is; the amount separating levels is not known.

Ratio level measurement
  As the most specific type of measurement, it has all of the characteristics of an interval scale, but also a true, meaningful zero point.

Reversible relationships
  Relationships that can go in either direction or either way.

Self-report
  This procedure is good at measuring individual's beliefs, attitudes, and values, or in finding out about behaviors we might not be able to observe directly.

Sequential relationships
  Relationships where the ordering of the variables is important and must occur sequentially, meaning chronologically or in order.

Social desirability
  The idea that if participants are asked to answer questions that are sensitive in nature, people will undoubtedly feel swayed to present themselves in a particular light, regardless of whether it is indeed true.

Stochastic relationships
  Relationships that are probable.

Substitutable relationships
  Relationships where other forces might bring about the same effect as a necessary relationship.

Sufficient relationships
  Relationships where the presence of or a change in one variable is enough to bring about a change in a second variable.

Unidimensional concepts
  Variables containing only one dimension.

References

Baccigalupo, C., Plaza, E., & Donaldson, J. (2008). *Uncovering affinity of artists to multiple genres from social behavior data*. Presented at the International Conference on Music Information Retrieval, Philadelphia, PA.

Bandura, A., Ross, D., & Ross, S. A. (1961). Transmission of aggressions through imitation of aggressive models. *Journal of Abnormal and Social Psychology, 63*(3), 575–582.

Bandura, A., Ross, D., & Ross, S. A. (1963). Imitation of film-mediated aggressive models. *Journal of Abnormal and Social Psychology, 66*, 3–11.

Beck, A. T., Ward, C. H., Mendelson, M., Mock, J., & Erbaugh, J. (1961). An inventory for measuring depression. *Archives of General Psychiatry, 4*, 53–63.

Dessler, G. (1984, June 11). Ethel may not be sexy, but she'll do better in business than Cheryl. *Miami Herald*. Retrieved September 16, 2008, from News Bank on-line database (America's Newspapers) on the website: http://infoweb.newsbank.com

Friedlander, F. (1966). Performance and interactional dimensions of organizational work groups. *Journal of Applied Psychology, 50*, 257–265.

Grey, S. H. (2002). Writing redemption: Trauma and the authentication of the moral order in *Hibakusha* literature. *Text and Performance Quarterly, 22*(1), 1–23.

Lachlan, K.A., & Spence, P.R. (2010). Communicating risks: Examining hazard and outrage in multiple contexts. *Risk Analysis, 30* (12), 1872–1886.

Likert, R. (1932). A technique for the measurement of attitudes. *Archives of Psychology, 140*, 1–55.

Lindlof, T. R., & Taylor, B. C. (2002). *Qualitative communication research methods*. Thousand Oaks, CA: Sage.

Neuliep, J. W., & McCroskey, J. C. (1997). The development of a U.S. and generalized ethnocentrism scale. *Communication Research Reports, 14*(4), 385–398.

Oliver, M. B., & Hyde, J. S. (1993). Gender differences in sexuality: A meta-analysis. *Psychological Bulletin, 114*, 29–51.

Osgood, C. E., Suci, G., & Tannenbaum, P. (1957). *The measurement of meaning.* Urbana, IL: University of Illinois Press.

Powell, H. L., & Segrin, C. (2004). The effect of family and peer communication on college students' communication with dating partners about HIV and AIDS. *Health Communication, 16*, 427–449.

Rogelberg, S. G., Allen, J. A., Shanock, L., Scott, C., & Shuffler, M. (2010). Employee satisfaction with meetings: A contemporary facet of job satisfaction. *Human Resource Management, 49*, 149–172.

Stephens, K. K., & Davis, J. (2009). The social influences on electronic multitasking in organizational meetings. *Management Communication Quarterly, 23*, 63–83.

Thurstone, L. L. (1928). Attitudes can be measured. *American Journal of Sociology, 33*, 529–554.

Uhlmann, E., & Swanson, J. (2004). Exposure to violent video games increases automatic aggressiveness. *Journal of Adolescence, 27*, 41–52.

Warren, J. T., & Kilgard, A. K. (2001). Staging stain upon the snow: Performance as a critical enfleshment of whiteness. *Text and Performance Quarterly, 21*(4), 261–276.

Weaver, J., III. (1991, Summer). Are "slasher" horror films sexually violent? A content analysis. *Journal of Broadcasting & Electronic Media, 35*(3), 385. Retrieved August 28, 2008, from Communication & Mass Media Complete Database.

UNDERSTANDING SAMPLING

CHAPTER OUTLINE

1. How Important Is Sampling?
2. Sampling Theory
   a. Generalizability and Representation
   b. Sampling Frame
   c. Unit of Analysis or Sampling Units
3. Sampling in Quantitative Research
   a. Sampling Methods
      i. Random Sampling
         A. Simple Random Sample
         B. Systematic random sample
         C. Stratified Sample
         D. Proportional Stratified Sample
         E. Cluster Sampling
      ii. Nonrandom Sampling
         A. Convenience Sample
         B. Volunteer Sample
         C. Snowball Sampling
         D. Network Sampling
         E. Advantages and Disadvantages
   b. Response Rate and Refusal Rate
   c. Sample Size and Power
4. Sampling in Qualitative Research
   a. Sampling Methods
      i. Purposive Sampling
      ii. Quota Sampling
      iii. Maximum Variation Sampling
      iv. Theoretical Construct Sampling
      v. Typical and Extreme Instance Sampling
   b. Sample Size and Data Saturation
5. So What?

KEY TERMS

Cluster sampling
Convenience sample
Data saturation
Extreme instance sampling
Generalizability
Maximum variation sampling
Network sampling
Nonrandom sampling

Proportional stratified sample
Purposive samples
Quota sampling
Random sampling
Refusal rate
Response rate
Sample size
Sampling frame

Simple random sample
Snowball sampling
Statistical power
Stratified sample
Theoretical construct sampling
Typical instance sampling
Unit of analysis
Volunteer sample

67

CHAPTER OBJECTIVES

1. To understand how we select the participants we include in our research
2. To know how to design the sample for a research study that is valid and representative
3. To be able to critique how representative a given sample is

How Important Is Sampling?

We cannot overstate how important sampling is to the quality, validity, and credibility of your research. You may have a solid study design, well written survey instrument or study protocol, and do an outstanding job in coding or statistical analysis, but if all that effort is devoted to a bad sample you are simply wasting your time. Proper sampling ensures that you are appropriately representing whomever you claim you're representing (we'll talk more about this in a minute). By the way, this is called *external validity*—are your findings valid among the population you're studying? For now, just know that *whom* you study is just as important as *how* you study them.

This chapter will give you an overview of the theory behind sampling and will help you connect sampling strategies to different metatheories and research paradigms. We'll also talk about the basic concepts behind appropriate sampling, then we'll show you how sampling is done in both quantitative and qualitative research. We'll also discuss issues such as sample size and statistical power.

Sampling Theory

Generalizability and Representation

First, let's explain a basic concept behind research design. In research, a *sample* of people is chosen to be included in the study as participants. This *sample* is expected to be *representative* of the entire *population* under study. Your *population* is the body of people you are claiming to generalize toward based on the sample. Populations can vary greatly in terms of breadth, though it should be noted that as scientists we seldom attempt to generalize to a population of *all* people. It is much more likely that we attempt to generalize to a populations specific to our research needs, such as "college students enrolled in a public speaking course," "elderly individuals in assisted care facilities," etc. If you carefully choose a *representative sample of one of these*

generalizability
Ensuring that a researcher's findings will apply to other people and situations that a study's sample supposedly represents.

groups, you can find out information about the *population* without having to interview the entire *population*.

Maybe you're asking, what's wrong with interviewing the entire population? Do you know what it is called when you actually interview an entire population? It's a *census*. It's so difficult to do that the federal government only does it once every ten years. Few researchers can afford to take a census of their entire population, and equally accurate data can be collected from a smaller sample when done correctly.

Unless you have an extremely small population, you would want to research a sample of your population. However, there is a trade-off in researching only a sample of your population: how well does that sample represent your population? Since you are not going to include everyone, the people you do include act as spokespersons for everyone else. In quantitative research, especially, this issue of representation is quite salient, as each study participant potentially represents the ideas or opinions of thousands of people. And in quantitative research, you are measuring and making predictions about those measurements, projecting them to your population. Obviously, if you are going to make predictions about your population based on the research you do of your sample, you want your sample to represent your population in a measurably accurate way. Representation is important in qualitative research also, by the way, but in a different way. We'll discuss that shortly.

So, let's talk about representation—how much of a problem is this? Wouldn't any group of people from your population represent your population? And how large should this group be? Five percent of the population? Fifty percent?

Let's look at an example. When your author Christine Davis was growing up, her parents had fairly conservative beliefs, while she and her sisters had fairly liberal beliefs. Suppose you wanted to survey them to determine how we felt about 10:00 PM Friday night curfews. Further, suppose you said her parents should represent their family—after all, they are the parents.

If you interviewed Christine's parents, you would be talking to 40 percent of her family. Surely this is a large enough sample to be representative, right? Wrong!

If you had sampled Christine's parents about their attitudes toward the curfew, you would probably have gotten 100 percent responses in favor of the curfew. Is this representative of the population? Let's take a census and compare:

- Mom—For
- Dad—For
- Cris—Against
- Kathy—Against
- Kelly—Against

The results of the census show that, in the population, only 40 percent were for the curfew, and 60 percent were against it.

Since that's the case, why did the sample differ so much from the census? Why wasn't interviewing 40 percent of the population enough?

It might have been, *if* it had been a representative sample.

In both quantitative and qualitative research, in order to derive a representative sample, there are several steps you would take.

You would first define your population. Your population may be as broad as all adults over the age of 18, but you still need to state the definition. More likely, your population will have some parameters, such as Communication undergraduates at your university (that's a pretty narrow definition), or all young adults between the ages of 18 and 24 (that's a fairly broad definition). If you're a rhetorical scholar, perhaps you study African American oratory. That's pretty broad. In order to conduct a research project, you would need to define which orators, which years, which speeches you plan to study, and so on. Perhaps you're an ethnographer, and you want to understand how a particular mental health treatment team interacts (see Davis, 2006), or how a specific street gang communicates (see Siegel & Conquergood, 1990). That mental health team or street gang would be your population, but then your sampling would be more concerned with representing their meetings or interactions. For example, you might want to observe student activities on campus; in this case, you're not sampling people, you're sampling observations (times of day, weeks, months, year, variety of locations, etc.). For example, you wouldn't only observe the library on Saturday morning during summer session—this likely is not representative of all student activities, and will likely produce very different data than observing the student center at lunchtime during fall semester. For your sample to be representative, you'd want to observe both, and probably more (more times, places, etc.).

Sampling Frame

Once you have defined your population, you have to determine how you will access them. The units to which you have access to are called your **sampling frame**. For example, if your population consists of all Communication undergraduates at your university, you might define your sampling frame as all Communication majors currently enrolled in classes. This will capture most of your population, but not all (for instance, there may be freshmen who intend to major in Communication, but have not yet taken coursework in the major). The sampling frame can be thought of as the realistic version of your population—the ones you can identify and access. Perhaps you want to study newspaper accounts of a particular event. You might define your sampling frame as the news stories available through the Lexis-Nexis database. If you're studying that medical team or street gang, your sampling frame might be the meetings or interactions you can access.

sampling frame
A realistic version of your population; the ones you can identify and access.

Unit of Analysis or Sampling Units

Your next step will be to define your **unit of analysis** or sampling units. For social researchers, more often than not the unit of analysis will be individuals— such as the individual students in our example above. Sometimes, however, your unit of analysis will be something other than individuals. For example, if you are studying couples' communication, your unit of analysis may be marital (or relational) dyads. If you are studying patient–provider communication, your unit of analysis may be patient–provider dyads. If you are studying group communication, your unit of analysis may be meetings, or groups themselves. Other units of analysis or sampling units might consist of sites, activities or events, times, or artifacts (documents, diaries, or texts). In a participatory action research study examining narrative as a method of transformation within emergency medicine, Eisenberg, Baglia, and Pynes (2006) defined their unit of analysis as an entire emergency department of an urban hospital.

unit of analysis
Sampling units.

Sampling in Quantitative Research

Sampling Methods

You have now identified your population by defining it, by identifying your sampling frame, and by defining your unit of analysis. Now you need to determine what sampling method you will use to represent your population. The sampling method you choose depends a lot on your study objectives, hypothesis, or research questions. Let's define the different types of samples used in quantitative research.

Random Sampling. In quantitative research, in order to ensure that you have a representative sample, you sample *randomly*. This means that each person in the sampling frame has an equal chance of being interviewed as each other person. The laws of statistics and probability insure that, if you have a true random sample, it will be representative of your population. Random sampling is typically used by research in the positivist paradigm, because it helps ensure the objective reality being measured is being measured accurately. By the way, random samples are also called probability samples, because, based on probability theory, there is a measurable probability that the sample represents the population. Therefore, nonrandom samples are also called nonprobability samples.

Simple Random Sample. The first sampling method, therefore, is called a **simple random sample**. Professional researchers (such as market researchers) who have sophisticated data collection technology do this by creating computer-generated random telephone numbers. A computer generates random seven-digit combinations of numbers, and these numbers

simple random sample
A basic sampling method where a group of subjects (sample) are selected for study from a larger group (population), and each member of the population has an equal chance of being chosen at any point during the sampling process.

are called. This allows an equal chance that people with unlisted numbers will be called, as well as those with listed numbers. Another alternative is to generate a list of random numbers through your computer (e.g., Excel has a function to do this). Number your sampling frame, giving the first name on the list a number of one, and so on. If you want a sample size of 100, generate a list of 100 random numbers. Choose the 100 people from your sampling frame who correspond to the random numbers.

Here's an example of how this works in real-life research. Mannion (2008) studied the effects of caring for people with Alzheimer's disease on informal caregivers. She used a:

> ... *random representative group of caregivers registered with the Alzheimer Society of Ireland, Galway, or the Western Alzheimer's Foundation. The sampling frame was the list of caregivers registered with these organizations. The technique for the study was simple random sampling, which involved an employee from both voluntary organizations randomly selecting numbers from the list of registered caregivers until the required number of subjects was chosen. (p. 33)*

SYSTEMATIC RANDOM SAMPLE. A variation on random sampling is known as the **systematic random sample**. In this type of sampling, a list of the entire sampling frame is assembled, and some seed number is chosen to make selections off of the list. For some reason, social scientists are fond of the numbers 7 and 11 (perhaps because they are prime numbers). If 7 is chosen, then you would choose every 7th person on the list for inclusion in the sample—so person 7, person 14, 21, 28, etc. You would repeat this process until you attained a sample size appropriate for the study, which we will discuss in a few pages.

You can approximate this method yourself. Get a list of your sampling frame, perhaps a telephone book, or a list of every Communication major, or a course registration list. Pick every fifth name (or tenth, or twentieth, depending on the sample size you desire). Make sure you call people from the beginning of the book, the middle of the book, and the end of the book. You don't want Jonathan Abernatny to have a greater chance of being called than Benny Zimmerman.

Stratified Sample. Sometimes you want more detail by subgroup than simple random sampling provides. Let's say you're not just interested in Communication Studies students in general, but you want to be able to compare students in Interpersonal Communication classes with students in Public Speaking classes, and students in Mass Media classes. You would choose to use a **stratified sample**.

---

systematic random sample
A variation on random sampling in which a list of the entire sampling frame is assembled, a seed number is chosen, and participants are selected based on multiples of that seed number (for example, every 7th person on the list is selected).

stratified sample
A type of sampling that uses a technique in which different subcategories of the sample are identified and then randomly selected.

Interpersonal Communication students would be one stratum, Public Speaking students would be another stratum, and Mass Media students would be a third stratum. In this case, rather than sampling 100 students randomly, you might randomly sample 33 students in the first stratum, 33 in the second stratum, and 33 in the third stratum. In instances in which you want to make comparisons between or across groups, it may be wise to have equal proportions of individuals who fall into those groups.

Stratified samples are fairly common in content analytic research too. In a content analysis of newspaper radio schedules from 1930 to 1939 in three major Canadian cities to determine what percentage of the programming originated from the United States as opposed to Canada, MacLennan (2005) used a stratified random sample—taking three weeks' programming from each year. She had ten strata—each year was a stratum, and the strata had equal sample sizes (three weeks' programming in each).

Proportional Stratified Sample. Let's say you want to represent students from Interpersonal Communication, Public Speaking, and Mass Media, but you want to represent them proportionally to their occurrence in the population. For example, perhaps 40 percent of your students are Interpersonal Communication students, while 45 percent are Public Speaking students, and 15 percent are Mass Media students. In this case, you would take a **proportional stratified sample**. Since 40 percent of the students are Interpersonal Communication students, then 40 percent of your sample (out of your sample of 100, or 40 students) would be Interpersonal Communication students; 45 percent (or 45 out of 100) would be Public Speaking students; and 15 percent (or 15 out of 100) would be Mass Media students. Of course, this strategy is contingent on knowing what the proportions are across these categories in the population.

For example, in order to study the optimal channel distribution (theaters, home video, video on demand) of movies and media, Hennig-Thurau, Henning, Sattler, Eggers, and Houston (2007) used a proportional stratified random sample to represent movie consumers in three major movie markets: the United States, Japan, and Germany. They drew three random samples of a total of 5,094 consumers in the United States (n = 1,701), Japan (n = 1,802), and Germany (n = 1,591). Within each of these samples, they made sure that they had even gender distributions, and that the age breakdown for each sample was consistent with the population statistics for the country in which the data was collected.

Cluster Sampling. What if you can't get a sampling frame for your entire population? Let's say that you have defined your population as Communication Studies majors, but you can't access a list of all majors. You can, however, get several instructors to give you access to their class

proportional stratified sample
A type of sampling that uses a technique in which different subcategories of the sample are identified and then selected proportionate to their occurrence in the population.

cluster sampling
A type of sampling method in which clusters, or groups (subsets of a population), are identified that are representative of the entire population, and are then sampled randomly within each cluster, letting each cluster represent the population.

rosters. You could conduct what's called **cluster sampling**. In cluster sampling, you identify clusters, or groups (subsets of your population), that you think are representative of the entire population and sample randomly within each cluster, letting each cluster represent the population. In the example, you could use Dr. Smith's Public Speaking class as one cluster, and Dr. Jones' Interpersonal Communication class as another cluster. The trade-off for this method is obvious—if you cannot ensure that the clusters truly represent the population, you do not have a representative sample.

Hilari and Northcott (2006) used cluster sampling to understand the role of social support in communication difficulties (called *aphasia*) after a stroke. Their clusters were three different speech therapy and rehabilitation sites, and they sampled randomly within each cluster.

Sarrafzadegan et al. (2009) evaluated the effects of a lifestyle intervention on diet, physical activity, and smoking in communities in Iran. They used cluster sampling in which they targeted three cities, and randomly sampled within each city. The cities each served as a cluster.

Nonrandom Sampling. Sometimes, for logistical or convenience reasons, researchers use **nonrandom sampling** techniques. The most commonly used nonrandom samples in quantitative research are: convenience samples, volunteer samples, and snowball samples. While nonrandom sampling is often used by researchers with a positivist bent, the samples are used with an acknowledgment of the accuracy they're giving up by not using a random sample. Researchers from an interpretivist metatheoretical bent might be more comfortable with samples that are representative in ways that are different from orderly, fixed, predictable measurements.

nonrandom sampling
Sample that is not generalizable to the population; sample that is not a random sample.

Convenience Sample. A **convenience sample** is, simply, a group of people that is convenient to access—a Communication Studies class, for example, or patients of a particular doctor or medical clinic, or employees of a particular organization.

Samp and Haunani Solomon (2005) sampled 106 dating couples to analyze their dyadic communication before and after they received certain types of problematic messages. This is clearly an experimental design, though the authors used a convenience sample of students solicited from "undergraduate communication courses at a large Midwestern university" (p. 30). Students were given extra credit or $10 to participate. Samp and Solomon's analysis does not discuss the limitations of their sample choice, but we can think of several. First, their sample is only representative of those 106 dyads. It's not necessarily representative of all communication students in that university, because students who participated may be different than students who didn't. Even if that wasn't an issue, it's also only representative of couples with the same demographics as the people in their sample—18 to 31 years old, and in relationships from 1 to 70 months.

convenience sample
A group of people that is convenient to access.

What other limitations to the sample can you think of? Nonetheless, it's published in a key communication journal (*Communication Monographs*), and this method of sampling is common in academic studies.

Volunteer Sample. A **volunteer sample** is similar to convenience sampling—it consists of people who are willing to volunteer for a study, perhaps people who respond to a flyer you send out or post. Wilson, Morgan, Hayes, Bylund, and Herman (2004), for example, used a volunteer sample in a study to categorize mothers' child abuse potential based on observation of playtime interactions between mothers and children. They posted flyers advertising the study at two social service agencies, and when clients indicated an interest in participating, the researchers contacted them.

volunteer sample
Consists of people who are willing to volunteer for a study.

Snowball Sampling. **Snowball sampling** is the method of asking study participants to make referrals to other potential participants, who in turn make referrals to other participants, and so on.

Doerfel and Taylor (2004), for example, conducted a social network analysis (analysis of social networks) of Croatian organizations to understand how organizations and media in Croatia work together. They used snowball sampling to identify organizations to include in their sample. In their paper, they state:

> *Organizations for inclusion ... were identified through interviews with USAID, IREX Pro-Media (1999), Soros, and the British Fund. These international donors identified active organizations in the 2000 parliamentary campaign that were also continuing to work on civil-society projects. (p. 381)*

snowball sampling
This sampling method asks study participants to make referrals to other potential participants, who in turn make referrals to other participants, and so on.

Snowball samples can be useful in that they tend to generate a lot of data very quickly. Even with a fairly low response rate, if everyone who agrees to participate then recruits additional participants, the sample size will grow multiplicatively. They are also useful for getting data from organizations or groups that may be difficult to access—once a member of the organization participates, he or she can recruit additional individuals.

The major tradeoff, however, is a lack of control. You have no way of knowing who the individuals are who are being recruited, nor can you determine if they are representative of the population. In instances in which perfect generalizability is less important to the researcher than is generating a lot of data fast, or infiltrating a particular group, snowball samples work. If you are primarily concerned with perfect representativeness, they may not be the best solution.

NETWORK SAMPLING. **Network sampling** is using social or other networks (workplace, organizations, support groups, etc.) to locate and recruit participants.

Smith et al. (2008) sampled agricultural workers to assess brochures designed to inform them about the threat of hearing loss in their profession. They recruited participants through "seminars sponsored by the Michigan

network sampling
Using social networks to locate or recruit study participants.

Farm Bureau . . . [and] through a pesticide certification meeting and by contacting the landscape departments of large organizations and local firms" (p. 204). This was network sampling—the networks being the Michigan Farm Bureau, the pesticide meeting, and the organizations and firms.

Research exploring the unique communication processes surrounding adoption within a family system requires creative use of both snowball and network sampling. Specifically, Harrigan and Braithwaite (2010) were interested in adoptions wherein it would be obvious to outsiders that an adoption had taken place due to differences in racial characteristics, a visible adoption. Here they describe their sampling decision:

> *We used both network and snowball sampling procedures. Participants met three specific criteria. First, they were the age of majority in the state in which they resided. Second, they parented a visibly adopted child. Third, they self-identified as heterosexual. It is important to note that we do not deny the need for understanding salient communication in same sex families; instead adding this last criterion allowed us to focus on parents' communication regarding adoption and visible differences rather than same sex parenting. (p. 130)*

ADVANTAGES AND DISADVANTAGES. The advantages of nonrandom samples are obvious—they are easier (and often less expensive) to obtain than random samples, so research projects can be facilitated. The dangers to such samples are many, however. Research that gives a great deal of information about a nonrepresentative sample can be useless or at least misleading. It's important to know who or what your sample is representative *of*, and limit your conclusions to that population. Use of all samples must be done with the full knowledge of the limitations of the study.

Response Rate and Refusal Rate

Another factor in determining the representativeness of your sample is the **response rate**. The response rate is the proportion of people actually included in your sample, relative to the number of people you attempted to include. In other words, it's the number of people who agreed to participate, versus the number of people who refused participation (called the **refusal rate**). The higher the response rate, the better, and ideally you would want your response rate to be 60 percent or better (though this is quite rare). The problem with low response rates is that, if a lot of people are refusing to take part in your study, people who agree may be different in some way than people who refuse. In other words, there may be something consistent about the people who choose to respond that renders the obtained sample non-representative.

There are several things you can do about low response rates. The first set of suggestions involves ways to improve your response rate: Offer an incentive of some kind to get more people to agree to participate; follow

---

response rate
The proportion of people actually included in a sample, relative to the number of people who were attempted to be included.

refusal rate
The number of people who refuse participation in a study.

up with people who refuse to participate to ask them again, hoping they'll change their mind the second time you ask; make your study easy to participate in (shorter surveys, for example), so they'll be less likely to refuse. The second suggestion is to determine if people who refused to participate have similar attitudes or characteristics than people who agreed. The only way to do this is to re-contact a sample of those who refused and try to get them to answer a few questions from the original survey, so that you can compare their responses with people who completed the entire study.

Sample Size and Power

Now that you know who to talk to, how many of them do you talk to? How many is enough to represent your population?

Let's do an experiment. You can do this yourself. Take a jar of marbles—some are black and some are white. You want to know how many black marbles are in this jar. You don't want to take the time to count them, so you take a sample.

Let's also say that you can draw out random handfuls of marbles.

In the first handful, you pull out five marbles—two of them are black (40%). You put them back and shake up the jar. Now, you pull out ten marbles—five of them are black (50%). You put them back and shake up the jar. Now, you pull out twenty marbles—eleven are black (55%).

Each time you increase your sample size, the number of black marbles you find in your sample is closer to what the actual number really is in your population. (Because you counted the marbles before you started the experiment, you know that 60% of the marbles are black).

The larger the sample you take, the more representative that sample is of the population. This is the "Law of Large Numbers."

So, you might wonder, what is large enough? That depends on what you want to do with the information after you get it.

Let's define two more terms: *confidence levels* and *margins of error*. You may have heard a television newscaster quote a political poll and say it had a 5 percent margin of error at a 95 percent confidence level. Statisticians talk about confidence levels of 80 percent, 90 percent, and 95 percent.

A confidence level of 95 percent means that, if you take 100 handfuls of marbles, 95 of those times you will come up with the same number of black marbles that are actually in the jar, within a margin of error, which we will define in a minute.

In other words, there is a 95 percent probability that your answer is pretty close to correct.

How close you are to correct is the margin of error. If you have a 5 percent margin of error, that means that your answer is within -5 or $+5$ percentage points of the true answer in the population.

In the case of your marbles, if you have a 5 percent margin of error, that means you count out between 55 percent and 65 percent black marbles.

If we tell you that at a 95 percent confidence level and a 5 percent margin of error, there are 60 percent black marbles in the jar, we are telling you that there is a 95 percent probability that there are between 55 percent and 65 percent black marbles in the jar.

Using a more real-life example, if we tell you that at a 95 percent confidence level and a 5 percent margin of error, your advertisement has 80 percent consumer recall, we are telling you that there is a 95 percent probability that your advertisement has consumer recall somewhere from 75 percent to 85 percent.

If you're right 95 percent of the time, that's not bad odds, is it? What confidence level you choose to use depends on what you are going to do with the information. For example, if your doctor is choosing a medicine to treat you for cancer, you surely want your doctor to choose a drug that was tested with a pretty high confidence level—99 percent, preferably (100% is impossible). If you are making a go/no-go decision on spending your life savings to open a business, you would probably want a fairly high confidence level. Other decisions only warrant an 80 percent confidence level—being right 80 percent of the time isn't always bad. In social science research, like the quantitative research Communication Studies scholars conduct, most studies are conducted at the threshold of 95 percent confidence level with a desired margin of error at ±5 percent.

So, you may ask: What does all this have to do with sample size? There are many factors that enter into the statistics of sample size, and they have to do primarily with the statistical power you want for your study. We'll talk a lot more about this in later chapters when we discuss statistics, but for now, you need to understand what statistical power has to do with **sample size**. **Statistical power** is defined as the probability your research will identify a statistical effect when it does, in fact, occur in the population. You want your sample size to be large enough to give your study the ability to do just that—to detect a statistical effect when it actually occurs. Statistical power is determined by a combination of sample size, confidence level, margin of error, and the data itself resulting from the research. The sensitivity of your research to identify this statistical effect can be increased by increasing your sample size. In other words, the larger your sample, the more statistical power your study has. However, there's a limit as to how large you can make your sample. For cost and other practical considerations, you want your sample to be just large enough to have the statistical power you need. To determine what that is, you can conduct an *a priori* power analysis; to do this, you need to know your desired confidence level, your desired margin of error, and the data proportions (e.g., effect size) you expect to find in your study. Since you often won't know the data results you expect ahead of

sample size
The number of data sources that are selected from a total population.

statistical power
The probability that research will identify a statistical effect when it occurs.

time, researchers use a general rule to calculate power and sample size. This rule assumes the largest sample size necessary to detect effect size. **Table 5.1** below gives what that sample size rule would be for each of several combinations of confidence level and margin of error. For example, if you are conducting a study and plan to set a confidence level of 95 percent and want to be able to detect differences at an error factor of ±5 percent, you would want to have a sample size of 400. If you are content with detecting differences at an error factor of ±8 percent, you can lower your sample size to 150.

Table 5.1. Sample Size Rules

	At a confidence level of:			
	80%	90%	95%	99%
With an error factor of:	Your sample size should be:			
± 5%	160	275	400	665
8%	64	100	150	260
±10%	40	70	100	170

For you math lovers in the class (yes, we know there are a few!), the formula for determining these sample sizes is:

$$n = \frac{(s^2)pq}{B^2}$$

In this formula, p and q are the two proportions (percentages) you'll be conducting your study to determine. Thus, this really contains circular reasoning, since you need to know what those proportions will be to determine your sample size, but you don't know what they are until you conduct your study. You can be more precise in determining sample size if you base these numbers on a pilot study or on previous research. However, for the purposes of the chart above, we used the most conservative estimate of proportions—we estimated that the proportions would end up being 50–50. B refers to the error factor (±5%, etc.), and s refers to the number of standard deviations from the mean your confidence intervals are. We haven't discussed this yet and won't until we get into statistics later, but for now know that (**Table 5.2**):

Table 5.2. Confidence Levels and Standard Deviations

A confidence level of	Is this many standard deviations from the mean
80	1.28
90	1.645
95	1.96
99	2.58

So, if you want to determine the sample size for an error factor of 5 percent, a confidence level of 95 percent, and proportions that are 50–50, your formula would be:

$$n = \frac{(1.96^2)(.5)(.5)}{.05^2}$$

$$n =$$

If you do the math, it comes to 384. We round to 400.

We said previously that there are many factors that enter into deciding the sample size. Strangely enough, the size of the population is *not* one of the factors that impacts the necessary sample size. Generally speaking, the size of your population is irrelevant to your desired sample size.

The only time the population size is important is if it is extremely small—so small that your sample size would be 5 percent or more of your population size (or when your population is less than 20 times larger than your sample). Then, there is a statistical correction for a small population. However, even this correction doesn't make much of a difference.

Again, for you math lovers, here's the formula for the correction:

$$\sqrt{1 - \frac{n}{N}}$$

You may remember from your statistics class that small *n* refers to your sample size and large *N* refers to your population size. So, let's say the earlier formula said you should have a sample size of 400, but your population size is only 4,000. If you apply those numbers to this formula for the small population correction, you'll end up with .95, which is the correction you should make to the sample size. Thus, .95 * 400 (the original sample size) is 380—and that's the sample size correction you would make.

You may have noticed that you can't use this formula if your population is smaller than your sample size, because you'll be trying to get the square root of a negative number and you can't do that. That's okay. First of all, if your population is that small, you may want to reconsider your desired confidence level and error factor, conduct a census, redefine your population, or consider a qualitative or case study method. Otherwise, you may feel better to note that Hamburg (1970), in his classic statistics textbook, states that "so long as the population is large relative to the sample, sampling precision becomes a function of sample size alone and does not depend on the relative proportion of the population sampled" (p. 290). In other words, it's what we said earlier—the size of your population is somewhat irrelevant to your desired sample size. Hamburg also notes that in the early days of statistics, researchers just arbitrarily sampled a percentage of their population—10 percent, for example. We don't generally recommend that, but you'll have to make some concession if your population is that small.

You may find it odd that population size is irrelevant to your desired sample size. The reason for this is that all populations, regardless of their size, fall into what is called a *normal distribution*. This means that, in any population, 95 percent of the responses will cluster around the average response, with a certain variability.

This is true if the population is 100 people or one million people. Since the sample is attempting to represent this cluster of responses, it doesn't matter how large the population is. We are only interested in sampling enough people to represent the curve of responses, regardless of the size of the population.

Sampling in Qualitative Research

Sampling Methods

In qualitative research, you are also sampling to represent the population. However, you don't want to represent the population numerically or in a way that you can predict numbers or proportions. You want to represent the sample behaviorally, or in a way that you can describe or understand the population. While quantitative research typically involves large samples so you can make accurate predictions mathematically (little information about a lot of people), qualitative research typically involves small samples that you study in-depth (a lot of information about a few people). Qualitative researchers frequently also use convenience and volunteer samples, snowball and network sampling, but they also use other types of sampling methods.

Purposive Sampling. Qualitative samples are often **purposive samples**—samples chosen for a particular purpose. For example, in health-care research, you might want to conduct a focus group among residents of a battered women's shelter who have been receiving services

purposive samples
Samples chosen for a particular purpose.

for at least six months, so you would specifically choose people who meet that purpose or criteria. You might purposely choose people because they can serve as *informants*—people who can give you inside information about the group you're studying.

Karen Tracy (2007), for example, used a purposive sample in her case study of crisis communication in school board meetings. She studied meetings from one school board, but her unit of analysis was not school boards, it was meetings. Therefore, we need to see how she chose the meetings to analyze. She did not analyze all the meetings, but she analyzed three specific meetings, chosen because they "were the center of public attention" (p. 438). She also analyzed documents downloaded from the school board's website, as well as all relevant stories in the local newspapers during the time period under study. She determined relevance of documents and news stories based on whether they discussed the crisis issue.

In order to examine the question of what men think about gender roles and issues surrounding work-life, Tracy and Rivera (2010) recruited thirteen male executive gatekeepers to interview. Other forms of sampling simply wouldn't have been appropriate to answer this question. Remember that your questions should help determine your methods, including the best choices for sampling.

Martin (2004) also observed meetings—workplace meetings—to investigate the use of humor among women in middle management positions. She conducted research at one field site (a zoo) and sampled women who fit the desired characteristics (they were middle managers). She also studied the people who report to them and their male peers as informants. Her paper clearly states the limitations of this sampling method:

> It is important to realize that the findings from this study are limited to the site and informants from which they are derived. For example, the behaviors exhibited by managers at The Zoo cannot be assumed to apply to non-white women, who may confront additional or very different constraints around humor usage and who may face entirely different forms of organizational paradox. (p. 153)

Yet, even though the findings may not be generalizable in a positivist sense, how might an interpretivist feel about the representativeness of the sample?

Quota Sampling. Perhaps you want to talk to people who have been receiving services at the battered women's shelter for less than six months and people who have been receiving services for more than six months. You might conduct five in-depth interviews among people who meet each of those criteria. If you did this, you would be doing **quota sampling**—assigning quotas of interviews/focus groups to different groups. You'll notice that quota sampling is similar to stratified sampling, but stratified sampling is a random sampling method while quota sampling is conducted with nonrandom samples.

For example, Duke and Ames (2008) conducted a study to understand unplanned pregnancies among women enlisted in the U.S. Navy. They

---

quota sampling
A nonprobability (nonrandom) sampling technique that sets quotas for key categories to identify how many members of the sample should be put into those categories.

conducted fifty-two in-depth interviews at seven naval facilities. They used quota sampling, and in order to represent the different viewpoints adequately, they assigned quotas by gender, occupation (sailors versus other personnel), and location.

Maximum Variation Sampling. Qualitative researchers also use several other sampling methods to ensure that their samples represent their populations in ways that meet their study objectives. **Maximum variation sampling** is a method that selects study participants to find examples that represent a wide range of characteristics that are present in the population and are of interest to the research. This sampling method is based on the "law of requisite variety," which says that any research study should represent the variety of characteristics present in the population. If you're studying street gang interactions, you might want to observe a range of different types of meetings or interactions.

Tracy (2004), for example, observed and interviewed correctional officers and staff to analyze organizational discourse. She "studied both male and female officers who worked 8- and 12-hour shifts and who represented a variety of ethnic backgrounds but were primarily white, black, and Hispanic" (p. 126). Assuming these characteristics represent the range of characteristics at the correctional facility, she used maximum variation sampling.

Theoretical Construct Sampling. **Theoretical construct sampling** selects study participants who have characteristics that represent theories on which the study is based. For example, a researcher might wish to study medical teams through the lens of systems theory, and might select such teams based on their systemic properties (e.g., teams that interact with each other a great deal).

Klossner (2008) conducted a study to understand socialization among students in an athletic training program. She used theoretical sampling, specifically recruiting second-year students because they were in the middle of their educational experience, and she theorized that they would be at the third phase of professional socialization and their point of enrollment would enable them to have reciprocal social interaction.

Typical and Extreme Instance Sampling. **Typical instance sampling** would consist of sampling units (e.g., participants or meetings) who have characteristics typical of the population (e.g., a typical meeting), while **extreme instance sampling** would consist of sampling units who have characteristics quite different from the rest of the population (e.g., unusual interactions).

Davis (2009), in her ethnographic study of a hospice interdisciplinary team, sampled typical interactions between team members by attending various normal team meetings and health care visits.

Manatu-Rupert (2000), for example, used extreme instance sampling when she conducted a textual analysis of the depiction of black women in films

maximum variation sampling
A sampling method that selects study participants who represent a wide range of characteristics that are present in the population and are of interest to the research.

theoretical construct sampling
The selection of study participants who have characteristics representing theories on which a study is based.

typical instance sampling
Consists of sampling units who have characteristics typical of a population.

extreme instance sample
Consists of sampling units that have characteristics quite different from the rest of a population.

by African American and non–African American filmmakers. She analyzed two films—Spike Lee's *She's Gotta Have It* and *Lethal Weapon*—chosen for their controversial representation of black women.

Sample Size and Data Saturation

Determining sample sizes for qualitative research is quite different than for quantitative research. Remember, again, you're not trying to measure or predict anything with qualitative samples; you're trying to understand, explain, or describe. For that reason, qualitative researchers are more concerned with the *level of depth* of information than the number of participants about whom they're getting the information. Qualitative researchers sample until they reach what is called **data saturation**—until no new information emerges. Researchers typically begin with a planned sample size (maybe ten to twenty-five interviews, maybe monthly meetings over twelve months, maybe six to twelve months of field observations), then adjust this size as they collect the data, adjusting the size up if they determine they need more information, and adjusting down if they determine they are reaching saturation earlier than expected.

Guest, Bunce, and Johnson (2006) conducted a project about social desirability bias in health research among women from two West African countries, in which they attempted to determine the ideal sample size required for saturation to occur. Their study yielded thematic saturation at twelve interviews, but this may or may not hold for other dissimilar studies. Recommended sample sizes vary depending on the type of qualitative research conducted.

data saturation
Sampling until no new information emerges.

So What?

Whether you're conducting qualitative or quantitative research, whether you're approaching your research from a positivist or an interpretivist paradigm, your sample will be representative of something, and as a good researcher, it's your job to make sure it's representative of what you intend to study. Sampling procedures range from random, parametric samples that are representative of the population in a measurable, predictive sense to nonrandom, nonparametric samples that are representative of theories, behaviors, descriptions, or viewpoints. We'll talk later in the book about issues of validity, reliability, and credibility, but for now, know that a study is not valid, reliable, or credible if it doesn't represent whomever or whatever it's supposed to represent.

Glossary

Cluster sampling
A type of sampling method in which clusters, or groups (subsets of a population), are identified that are representative of the entire population, and are then sampled randomly within each cluster, letting each cluster represent the population.

Convenience sample
A group of people that is convenient to access.

Data saturation
Sampling until no new information emerges.

Extreme instance sample
Consists of sampling units that have characteristics quite different from the rest of a population.

Generalizability
Ensuring that a researcher's findings will apply to other people and situations that a study's sample supposedly represents.

Maximum variation sampling
A sampling method that selects study participants who represent a wide range of characteristics that are present in the population and are of interest to the research.

Network sampling
Using social networks to locate or recruit study participants.

Nonrandom sampling
Sample that is not generalizable to the population; sample that is not a random sample.

Proportional stratified sample
A type of sampling that uses a technique in which different subcategories of the sample are identified and then selected proportionate to their occurrence in the population.

Purposive samples
Samples chosen for a particular purpose.

Quota sampling
A nonprobability (nonrandom) sampling technique that sets quotas for key categories to identify how many members of the sample should be put into those categories.

Refusal rate
The number of people who refuse participation in a study.

Response rate
The proportion of people actually included in a sample, relative to the number of people who were attempted to be included.

Sample size
The number of data sources that are selected from a total population.

Sampling frame
A realistic version of your population; the ones you can identify and access.

Simple random sample
A basic sampling method where a group of subjects (sample) are selected for study from a larger group (population), and each member of the population has an equal chance of being chosen at any point during the sampling process.

Systematic random sample
A variation on random sampling in which a list of the entire sampling frame is assembled, a seed number is chosen, and participants are selected based on multiples of that seed number (for example, every 7th person on the list is selected).

Snowball sampling
This sampling method asks study participants to make referrals to other potential participants, who in turn make referrals to other participants, and so on.

Statistical power
The probability that research will identify a statistical effect when it occurs.

Stratified sample
A type of sampling that uses a technique in which different subcategories of the sample are identified and then randomly selected.

Theoretical construct sampling
The selection of study participants who have characteristics representing theories on which a study is based.

Typical instance sampling
Consists of sampling units who have characteristics typical of a population.

Unit of analysis
Sampling units.

Volunteer sample
Consists of people who are willing to volunteer for a study.

References

Davis, C. S. (2006). Sylvia's story: Narrative, storytelling, and power in a children's community mental health system of care. *Qualitative Inquiry, 12*(6), 1–24.

Davis, C. S. (2009). *Death: The beginning of a relationship.* Cresskill, NJ: Hampton Press.

Doerfel, M. L., & Taylor, M. (2004). Network dynamics of interorganizational cooperation: The Croatian Civil Society movement. *Communication Monographs, 71*(4), 373–394.

Duke, M., & Ames, G. (2008). Challenges of contraceptive use and pregnancy prevention among women in the U.S. Navy. *Journal of Qualitative Health Research, 18*, 244–253.

Eisenberg, E. M., Baglia, J., & Pynes, J. E. (2006). Transforming emergency medicine through narrative: Qualitative action research at a community hospital. *Health Communication, 19*, 197–208.

Guest, G., Bunce, A., & Johnson, L. (2006). How many interviews are enough? An experiment with data saturation and variability. *Field Methods, 18*(1), 59–82.

Hamburg, M. (1970). *Statistical analysis for decision making.* New York: Harcourt, Brace, & World.

Harrigan, M. M., & Braithwaite, D. O. (2010). Discursive struggles in families formed through visible adoption. *Journal of Applied Communication Research, 38*, 127–144.

Hennig-Thurau, T., Henning, V., Sattler, H., Eggers, F., & Houston, M. B. (2007). The last picture show? Timing and order of movie distribution channels. *Journal of Marketing, 71*, 63–83.

Hilari, K., & Northcott, S. (2006). Social support in people with chronic aphasia. *Aphasiology, 20*(1), 17–36.

Klossner, J. (2008). The role of legitimation in the professional socialization of second-year undergraduate athletic training students. *Journal of Athletic Training, 43*(4), 379–385.

MacLennan, A. F. (2005). American network broadcasting, the CBC, and Canadian radio stations during the 1930s: A content analysis. *Journal of Radio Studies, 12*(1), 85–103.

Manatu-Rupert, N. (2000). The filmic conception of the black female. *Qualitative Research Reports in Communication, 1*(3), 45–50.

Mannion, E. (2008). Alzheimer's disease: The psychological and physical effects of the caregiver's role. Part 2. *Nursing Older People, 20*(4), 33–38.

Martin, D. M. (2004). Humor in middle management: Women negotiating the paradoxes of organizational life. *Journal of Applied Communication Research, 32*(2), 147–170.

Samp, J. A., & Haunani Solomon, D. (2005). Toward a theoretical account of goal characteristics in micro-level message features. *Communication Monographs, 72*(1), 22–45.

Sarrafzadegan, N., Kelishadi, R., Esmaillzadeh, A., Mohammadifard, N., Rabei, K., Roohafza, H., Azadbakht, L., Bahonar, A.,
Sadri, G., Amani, A., Heidari, S., Malekafzali, H. (2009). Do lifestyle interventions work in developing countries? Findings from the Isfahan Healthy Heart Program in the Islamic Republic of Iran. *Bulletin of the World Health Organization, 87*, 39–50.

Siegel, T. (Producer), & Conquergood, D. (Director). (1990). [DVD]. *The heart broken in half.* Portland, OR: Collective Eye.

Smith, S. W., Rosenman, K. D., Kotowski, M. R., Glazer, E., McFeters, C., Keesecker, N. M., & Law, A. (2008). Using the EPPM to create and evaluate the effectiveness of brochures to increase the use of hearing protection in farmers and landscape workers. *Journal of Applied Communication Research, 36*(2), 200–218.

Tracy, K. (2007). The discourse of crisis in public meetings: Case study of a school district's multimillion dollar error. *Journal of Applied Communication Research, 35*(4), 418–441.

Tracy, S. J. (2004). Dialectic, contradiction, or double bind? Analyzing and theorizing employee reactions to organizational tension. *Journal of Applied Communication Research, 32*(2), 119–146.

Tracy, S. J., & Rivera, K. D. (2010). Endorsing equity and applauding stay-at-home moms: How male voices on work-life reveal aversive sexism and flickers of transformation. *Management Communication Quarterly, 24*, 3–43.

Wilson, S. R., Morgan, W. M., Hayes, J., Bylund, C., & Herman, A. (2004). Mothers' child abuse potential as a predictor of maternal and child behaviors during play-time interactions. *Communication Monographs, 71*(4), 395–421.

SURVEY RESEARCH

Chapter Outline

1. Why Surveys?
2. Survey Research
   a. Applications of Survey Research
      i. Survey Research Measuring Attitudes
      ii. Survey Research Measuring Retrospective Behaviors
      iii. Political Polls
      iv. Evaluation Research
      v. Market Research
   b. Design Concerns
      i. Sampling
      ii. Cross-Sectional Design
      iii. Longitudinal Design
         A. Trend Study
         B. Cohort Study
         C. Panel Study
   c. Measurement Techniques
3. Constructing a Survey Questionnaire
   a. Writing Survey Questions
      i. Strategies for Questions
   b. Types of Questions
   c. Structure and Arrangement of Questions
      i. Tunnel Format
      ii. Funnel Format
      iii. Inverted Funnel Format
      iv. How to Choose the Right Format
   d. Survey Administration
      i. Researcher-Administered
      ii. Self-Administered
      iii. Interviews
4. So What?

Key Terms

Cohort study
Cross-sectional survey
Evaluation research
Funnel format
Interview
Inverted funnel format

Longitudinal survey design
Market research
Panel study
Political polls
Researcher-administered questionnaires

Self-administered questionnaires
Survey design
Trend study
Tunnel format

CHAPTER OBJECTIVES

1. To become familiar with survey research
2. To understand survey measurement techniques
3. To examine common types of research design
4. To explore the advantages and disadvantages of interviews and questionnaires

Why Surveys?

Comedian Dave Barry once quipped, "If you surveyed a hundred typical middle-aged Americans, I bet you'd find that only two of them could tell you their blood types, but every last one of them would know the theme song from 'The Beverly Hillbillies'" (*The Quote Garden*, n.d.). *Late Night* host David Letterman said, "*USA Today* has come out with a new survey—apparently, three out of every four people make up 75% of the population" (*The Quotations Page*, n.d.). No doubt about it—survey research is popular in everyday society. In this chapter, we consider one of the most common types of research methodologies: surveys. We will consider why surveys are immensely popular; examine common survey research designs; explore survey measurement techniques, including questionnaire design; and scrutinize the pros and cons of different ways of administering surveys.

Survey Research

survey design
A method of asking research participants questions that provides researchers with a method of information gathering from a large number of people over a relatively short period of time.

For most of us, **survey design** is perhaps the most familiar research method, and may be the first method that comes to mind when we think about social research. When you fill out a teacher's evaluation at the end of the semester, a comment card at a restaurant, or even a profile on a dating website, you are completing a survey of one type or another. Surveys are popular in both proprietary and scholarly research for a variety of reasons. First, survey design provides researchers with a method of information gathering from a large number of people in a relatively short period of time. This allows you to gather a representative sample from a population of interest to you. Second, surveys are relatively inexpensive to administer. With Web-based applications, such as Survey Monkey (www.surveymonkey.com), Survey Share (www.surveyshare.com), and Qualtrics (www.qualtrics.com), the survey creation process has become even easier and more accessible. Third, this methodology involves a relatively straightforward research strategy. You ask people questions and analyze their answers. Fourth, surveys can include both quantitative questions and qualitative (open-ended) questions. Finally, since you can easily provide and administer identical questions to many participants, a well-written survey questionnaire is a reliable measurement technique.

Applications of Survey Research

Surveys have been widely used in communication research in many different ways. Macias, Springston, Lariscy, and Neustifer (2008) conducted a content analysis of 54 communication-related journals published from 1990 to 2002, and found that 565 studies used a survey methodology. Most survey research they found was conducted in the subfields of public relations, marketing, public opinion, advertising, and mass communication journals; however, 85 percent of the journals investigated had some survey research in them, indicating that most segments of our field use survey research at least some of the time.

You can use surveys to describe communication characteristics of participants for the purpose of theory building, or for generalizing about the population they represent. Other times, you utilize survey research to test theoretical predictions about the relationships between communication variables and other variables in a population of interest. In addition, a lot of communication research uses surveys to assess participants' attitudes, beliefs, and opinions, and to let participants retrospectively replay incidents, behaviors, and meanings. Market research surveys, political polls, customer satisfaction surveys, employee feedback surveys, and surveys designed to measure product perceptions and market position are all examples of ways surveys are used in business and industry.

Survey Research Measuring Attitudes. If you're designing a communication campaign to promote a product, service, or behavior, you're going to want to do an audience analysis—to determine what your potential audience already thinks, feels, or believes about your topic. You'd likely conduct a survey to find that out—it would give you a baseline understanding of where your audience stands at one point in time. Communication researchers also assess attitudes in surveys to develop, test, or apply theoretical concepts for both applied and scholarly research.

For example, Salmon, Park, and Wrigley (2003) conducted a survey research study among corporate spokespersons from 100 public companies to understand their perceptions of risk and bias toward optimism about the possibility of bioterrorism among corporate spokespersons. They tested five hypotheses:

H_1: Corporate spokespersons will tend to estimate their own organization's risk to be less than that of other organizations similar to their own.

H_2: Optimistic bias will be greater for referents that are more distant (e.g., other corporations in the United States) than for those that are proximate (other corporations in the state).

H_3: Corporate spokespersons who perceive their own organizations as low in vulnerability tend to show high optimistic bias.

H_4: Corporate spokespersons who perceive high severity of bioterrorism tend to show high optimistic bias.

H_5: Corporate spokespersons who perceive that their own organizations can control external events tend to show high optimistic bias.

A survey method was appropriate for these hypotheses because they were measuring participants' attitudes, beliefs, and perceptions. Salmon and colleagues (2003) used a purposive sampling method. They got a list (sampling frame) of the 100 largest privately and publicly held companies in the state from the Harris Michigan Industrial Directory (Carlsen, 2010). They called each company and got a list of 142 names of corporate spokespersons. They mailed out an introductory letter, then called each potential participant. If a participant refused, they called a second time five days later to see if the person had changed his or her mind. They ended up with a sample size of 72, which represents a 51 percent response rate.

Applying Weistein's concept of optimistic bias to risk perception, Salmon and colleagues (2003) designed their own measurements of bioterrorism awareness, perceived vulnerability, perceived severity, and perceived controllability using Likert-type scales. They used Weinstein's own measure of optimistic bias. Based on their statistical analysis, Salmon et al. (2003) determined that there is a relationship between optimistic bias and perceived vulnerability and perceived severity, but not between optimistic bias and perceived control. What do you think are the pros and cons to their use of the survey method? What internal validity issues might they need to consider? How about external validity issues? How about ecological validity issues? How can they address these validity issues in future research? What can they do with this information?

Survey Research Measuring Retrospective Behaviors. Some researchers use surveys to ask participants to report on retrospective, or past, behaviors. While asking participants to remember past events raises concerns about the accuracy of memory, this method does have the advantage of obtaining a recollection of an incident from the point of view of a participant. Here's an example of this use of surveys: Botta and Dumlao (2002) wanted to see if there was a relationship between conflict communication styles between fathers and daughters and eating disorders in the daughters. They had numerous hypotheses and research questions, all pertaining to that general topic (conversation orientation, conformity orientation, pluralistic, laissez-faire, and protective all referring to family communication styles; compromising, collaborating, avoiding, accommodating, confronting, and avoiding all referring to conflict styles):

H_1: Conversation orientation as encouraged by the father will be a significant negative predictor of anorexic and bulimic behaviors.

H_2: Conformity orientation as encouraged by the father will be a significant positive predictor of anorexic and bulimic behaviors.

H_3: Being raised by a pluralistic father will be a significant negative predictor of anorexic and bulimic behaviors.

H_4: Being raised by a protective father will be a significant positive predictor of anorexic behaviors.

H_5: Compromising as a way to respond to conflict will be a significant negative predictor of anorexic behaviors and a significant negative predictor of bulimic behaviors.

H_6: Collaborating as a way to respond to conflict will be a significant negative predictor of anorexic behaviors and a significant negative predictor of bulimic behaviors.

H_7: Avoiding as a way to respond to conflict will be a significant positive predictor of anorexic behaviors.

H_8: Accommodating as a way to respond to conflict will be a significant positive predictor of anorexic behaviors.

H_9: Confronting as a means of responding to conflict will be a significant positive predictor of bulimic behaviors.

H_{10}: Avoiding as a means of responding to conflict will be a significant negative predictor of bulimic behaviors.

RQ_1: Is being raised by a protective father, a laissez-faire father, or a consensual father a significant predictor of bulimic behaviors?

RQ_2: To what extent do family communication styles as encouraged by the father moderate the influence of a strong drive to be thin on anorexic and bulimic behaviors?

RQ_3: To what extent do conflict resolution styles between father and daughter moderate the influence of a strong drive to be thin on anorexic and bulimic behaviors?

To measure family communication patterns, Botta and Dumlao (2002) used Ritchie's 1991 Revised Family Communication Patterns (RFCP) instrument, a multidimensional Likert scale that has been shown to have high reliability—Cronbach's Alpha for conversation orientation was .91, and for conformity orientation was .86. To measure conflict styles, they used Rahim's Organization Conflict Inventory, a multidimensional Likert scale that also has been shown to have high reliability—avoidance conflict style (α = .85), collaborating conflict style (α = .89), compromising conflict style (α = .74), confronting conflict style (α = .80), and accommodating conflict style (α = .81). They measured eating disorders using two scales: Garner and Olmsted's Eating Disorder Inventory and the Eating Attitudes Test, two Likert-type scales, both of which they report have high validity and reliability.

What are other methods they could have used to collect their information and address their hypotheses and research questions? Why do you think they chose surveys over other methods such as ethnography or experiments?

There are three additional applications of survey research we should also consider: political polls, evaluation research, and market research.

Political Polls. One of the most common and readily available uses of surveys in the world today is in the form of **political polls**. It seems that every day leading up to an election, we are bombarded with a detailed account of who is leading whom in the run for a particular office. In fact, we have become so bombarded with polling data that data aggregation sites, such as Nate Silver's 538 (www.fivethirtyeight.com), have become popular resources for summary statements about what we can glean from the polls when taken together.

Oftentimes political poll surveys are conducted over the phone. The key to political polls and the validity of their findings rests upon the basic research method strategies used, the quality of sampling and sample size, the response rate, and as we will see shortly, even the types of questions asked.

Evaluation Research. Another type of survey research that many of you are already familiar with is the use of survey data in **evaluation research**. Evaluation research is designed to assess the effectiveness of campaigns, programs, or products either before (or while) they are being developed, or after their completion. The use of evaluation research for campaigns and programs allows practitioners and managers to develop more effective communication programs. A good example of evaluation research in organizational communication would be research designed to assess a new training program put in place in the organization. If you are a participant in the training, you might be asked to fill out a survey at the conclusion of the program, so the trainer can assess his or her success. In health communication, you might be interested in evaluating the relative success of a smoking cessation program or a new exercise regimen. You could even evaluate the success of a nutrition campaign such as the "5 a day" campaign that encourages Americans to eat five fruits and vegetables a day. This type of evaluation research is often called *summative research*, as it traditionally takes place after the program has run its course or the campaign is ending (Center & Broom, 1983).

Another type of evaluation research is known as *formative research*; this is simply evaluation research that helps the campaign or program manager develop a campaign or program, or evaluate it while it is ongoing (Atkin & Freimuth, 2000; Center & Broom, 1983).

---

political polls
One of the most common and readily available uses of surveys. They provide a detailed account of who is leading whom in the run for a particular office during an election.

evaluation research
Research that is designed to assess the effectiveness of programs or products during development or after their completion.

The benefit of these types of evaluation research is that they allow you to identify ways in which the program or campaign can be refined and improved. The third type of evaluation research, *needs analysis*, is a mechanism for identifying problems experienced by a group of people by comparing what exists with what study participants want. For example, organizational employees might fill out a needs assessment survey to help management develop a new training program by comparing what existing training programs offer versus what employees want or need in a training program. This data is often used to guide in the development of communication interventions, such as skill training. Finally, the fourth type of evaluation research, *organizational feedback*, also utilizes survey design. Here, organizational members are asked to report on practices within the organization. You might be interested in surveying national insurance companies about the communication practices within their organization. You could use surveys to ask them about the use of different channels of communication, the quality of information provided, and even their preferred method of communication. The results can then be used for organizational improvement.

Market Research. Another common example of survey design comes in the form of **market research**. This is research designed to study consumer behavior, preferences, and opinions. The idea behind market research is that if you can determine what people consume, how often, and why, then you can predict future consumption (or at least market researchers can). Market research may question consumer reactions to a new product, interest in new products, and preferences for products and services. This type of research evaluates how satisfied consumers are with products and services, as well as explores persuasive strategies for advertising, product pricing, and even packaging. The most obvious example of market research in your world is likely to be a discount or frequent shopper card on your key ring, or the survey invitations issued to you on the receipt you receive from a local discount store. It seems marketers have many opportunities to gather data about your consumer behaviors. Did you really think the shopper card is to help you save money? What types of information do companies gather from your frequent shopper card? What marketing decisions could they make with it?

market research
Research that is designed to study consumer behavior.

Design Concerns

Sampling. We discussed sampling in detail a bit later in the text, but let's review the types of sampling that are done in survey research. Because of the techniques used in administering surveys, researchers have the ability to conduct a truly random and representative sample if they have the necessary resources. Regardless of the type of survey you are designing, your design concerns are similar. One of your first concerns related to survey research design is selecting survey participants. To do this, you must have a sampling frame. Recall that a sampling frame is ideally a list of all members of a population, or at least it is the list you let stand in for your population. In some instances, an actual list of the population may be impossible to come by. At one time, telephone directories might have been a good choice; in today's world, this would be an incomplete sampling frame at best, because so many people use telephone numbers—cell phones, for example—that are not listed in directories. In fact, these days, we might argue that using a list of numbers from a telephone directory is only representative of, perhaps, older, less technologically savvy people, and there is evidence that the samples derived from telephone directories tend to skew toward older audiences. This is why many survey researchers are moving to random digit dialing—letting a computer randomly generate telephone numbers within an area code and exchange. Using random digit dialing, you're not limited to listed or land-line numbers, and, if you're looking for an overall population sample, your sample should be more representative. However you decide to sample, remember that your sample should represent your population as closely as possible. If you were interested in studying dating behaviors of college students at UCONN and UNC–Charlotte, you could likely contact the registrars of each of the schools and obtain a list of potential participants (with Institutional Research Board approval, of course). This list would be your sampling frame. If you're interested in why people voted for a particular candidate in an election, it would not make sense to poll people who didn't vote. Therefore, a sampling frame of all people—regardless of whether they voted—would not be very representative of the population you're interested in studying. You'd be better off using a list of registered voters, at least eliminating those who definitely couldn't have voted.

Many types of sampling can be used with survey design: random sampling, cluster sampling, stratified sampling, purposive samples, and even volunteer samples. What defines the best choice for a particular study? That's right, it's the research question. The question(s) and/or hypothesis(es) determine the technique you choose.

Cross-Sectional Design. Another consideration and decision you must make early in the survey research design process is whether a cross-sectional or longitudinal design is best for your study. A **cross-sectional survey** describes the characteristics of a sample representing a population at one point in time. Think of it as a picture, or a snapshot. Researchers frequently utilize cross-sectional survey research because it's easy to collect data from a large number of people, in a short period of time, at a single time point. One researcher we know has, at times, been able to sample from the local jury pool. In just one afternoon, he collected nearly 500 surveys

cross-sectional survey
A survey design that describes the characteristics of a sample representing a population at one point in time.

of a very wide sample of people who were appropriate for his research question. The Salmon et al. (2003) study mentioned earlier is an example of a cross-sectional study.

A cross-sectional design is great for describing the status quo—how things are right at one particular time point. However, there are some cautions to keep in mind. First, it is important to keep in mind the particular point in time when the survey was conducted. A friend of ours went through the Institutional Research Board and was approved to collect data on her project late one September. She was interested in studying different types of messages on brochures regarding breast self-exams. As she began her project, she realized that October, when she collected the majority of her data, happens to be Breast Cancer Awareness Month. Is there any chance that this particular month for data collection affected the outcome of her study? Absolutely. Data can be misleading if the survey is conducted at an unrepresentative time.

An interesting example of the use of cross-sectional survey design comes from Lim and Teo (2009) who studied e-manners, or the level of respect communicated via e-mail communication in the workplace. They measured 192 employees in the financial services industry in Singapore at just one point in time. However, they caution that their results limit their ability to determine cause and effect despite some significant relationships between variables.

Cross-sectional surveys assume the variables and processes being studied have reached stability, but many variables and processes are constantly changing. For example, marital satisfaction, television viewing behavior, and communication apprehension are variables that have the potential to change over time. By the same token, you can't take one measurement at one point in time and assume causality. Consider the hypothesis that video game violence leads to an increase in aggressive behavior. If you measure both of these variables and find a positive correlation between them, can you conclude that video game violence caused aggressive behavior in your sample? No, you cannot. *Causal conclusions can never be drawn from cross-sectional data.* It is a lot like the question of which came first—the chicken or the egg. Do you know whether exposure to video game violence came before or after exhibiting aggressive behavior? Not if you only measure at one point of time. While a reasonable person might likely argue that watching violence causes aggressive behavior, it is possible that individuals with aggressive tendencies could choose to play violent video games. It is also equally likely that some other variable, such as family discipline, affects both video game playing and aggressive behavior.

The above is an example of the problems sometimes associated with confounds, or third variables. Recall, a confounding variable is some third variable that explains the change in the dependent variable better than the independent variable. The independent and dependent variable may appear to be linked, while in reality they simply vary together because of some unmeasured confounding variable that is impacting both of them. You should always try to anticipate potential confounds and eliminate them from the study design. Keep in mind that in cross-sectional designs you cannot evaluate change over time, so it is possible to demonstrate correlation but not causality.

Longitudinal Design. In **longitudinal survey design**, you gather data from respondents at several points in time. This allows you to evaluate the impact of unusual or unique environmental events on a population, and assess whether a population's beliefs, attitudes, and/or behaviors are enduring or stable over time. One of the greatest strengths of longitudinal design is to allow you to examine causal relationships. You add this feature to survey research with a longitudinal design by determining whether A comes before B in time. You can only do this with a minimum of two measurements over some timeframe. There are three types of longitudinal research design: a trend study, a cohort study, and a panel study.

longitudinal survey design
A survey design that gathers data from respondents at several points in time.

TREND STUDY. In a **trend study**, measurement occurs at two or more points in time, from different samples selected from the same population. This type of study is designed to identify changes or trends (thus the name) in people's beliefs about the variable of interest, or in the correlations between variables at different time points. An example of a trend study is the Gallup polls used during a presidential election. The Gallup organization, a premier research firm in the United States, draws a sample from all eligible U.S. voters and asks whom they plan to vote for in the upcoming presidential election. Each week they poll another group of people (sample) from this population (all eligible voters). Remember, the samples Gallup is taking are not the same people; they are merely samples from the same population. Keep in mind, though, that as your goal is comparison over time, you should be sampling from the same general population, at least. What if you sample first from the Socialists of America, second from the Students for Democratic Government, and third from the Young Republicans? Clearly, you cannot compare how people's attitudes changed over time because your sample would be very different each time. To compare trends, you must have comparable representative samples. What do you think are the pros and cons to trend studies?

trend study
Measurement occurs at two or more points in time, from different samples selected from the same population. This type of study is designed to identify changes or trends in people's beliefs about a variable of interest.

COHORT STUDY. In a **cohort study,** responses from a specific subgroup of the population are identified and compared over time. In a cohort study, the key is that for some reason (relevant to your study) you are interested in studying a group of people that have some characteristic in common because of a historical marker of significance (i.e., lived through the Depression) or some other meaningful life event. For example, you

cohort study
A study in which responses from specific subgroups of a population are identified and compared over time.

might be interested in people born or graduated from high school in the same year. Simply put, a cohort is usually defined with respect to time or history.

Imagine for a moment you are interested in comparing how baby boomers talk about money and financial security over time. You decide to embark on a ten-year longitudinal study with a cohort design in which you measure attitudes and financial talk once every two years. You decide on a cohort study of baby boomers (individuals generally born from 1946 to 1964, who are currently between the ages 45 to 63). You sample persons 45 to 63 in 2009, another sample of individuals 47 to 65 in 2011, another sample of persons 49 to 67 in 2013, and so on. Although the *specific set of people* studied in each of these surveys would be different, each sample represents the cohort born between 1946 and 1964.

PANEL STUDY. In a **panel study**, responses are obtained from the exact same people over time. Essentially, you draw a sample from your population, and measure those same people or objects at multiple points in time. This is also known as repeated measures. The most significant advantage of using a panel study is that it allows for true tests of causality, as it allows the researcher to look at correlations over time and rule out confounding variables.

panel study
A study in which a sample is drawn from a population or universe and those same people or objects are measured at multiple points in time.

If panel studies allow for true causal analyses, then why are they not used all the time? While there are important advantages to this type of design, it is not without serious disadvantages that warrant consideration. One important disadvantage of a panel study is that as you continue taking measurements over time, you may lose subjects. This is known as a high attrition rate, or as an issue of mortality. It is unlikely that you will literally lose participants due to death when conducting Communication research. It's more likely that participants will drop out of school, change address or contact information, or just become impossible to track down to measure at a subsequent wave of measurement (particularly if the study extends over a period of months or even years). Another major concern with attrition or mortality in a panel study is that you may not end up with enough participants in your study, and/or participants that do participate in all points of measure may somehow differ from participants who drop out of the study. This is not unlike our earlier comments on response rate. If you lose a large number of participants, perhaps there is something systematic about those who remain that call the generalizability of the findings into question.

Consider Segrin and Flora's (2000) study of students transitioning to college. They measured social skills and psychosocial problems at two points in time: during the end of the senior year in high school (wave 1), and again at the end of the first semester in college (wave 2). They found that (1) social skills interacted with stressful life events to predict changes in depression and loneliness,

(2) people with lower social skills were predicted to make the transition to college with the worst psychosocial problems, and (3) people with lower social skills were more vulnerable to development of psychosocial problems than people with higher social skills. This all certainly makes sense and is a great use of a panel longitudinal survey method. However, what limitations can you identify with this method? What if the people with the poorest social skills dropped out by the second wave of interviewing? Would that make both waves of interviewing equivalent?

Consider another example of survey design. You might decide you are interested in studying family communication between children and their parents, paying particular attention to conflict. Your research question is this: Do parents believe conflict with their children increases as children move from elementary school through middle school and high school? How could you study this using a cross-sectional design? How could you study this same question using a longitudinal design? In a cross-sectional design, you would put together a questionnaire including a measure of conflict and ask parents of children in third, seventh, and eleventh grades to complete your survey. Or you could give one questionnaire to parents of eleventh-grade kids and ask them to fill out the questionnaire for their children when they were in third, seventh, and eleventh grades. In a longitudinal panel design, you could use the same questionnaire with the measure of conflict to assess parents with children currently in third grade, and then collect the same measurement again as their children entered seventh grade, and again four years later when their children were eleventh graders. What do you think are the pros and cons of each approach?

Measurement Techniques

Survey measurement techniques are what we call self-report. Typically, in a survey you are asking the participants to tell you what they think or feel, and they are reporting on themselves. Do you think this is a good strategy? The obvious answer is it depends upon what you want to know. We will first consider some strategies for enhancing the strength of self-report data, before considering the disadvantages of self-report techniques. Self-report data is perhaps most commonly used (at least in positivist research), and when utilizing tight procedures, it can provide a clear and valid picture of some phenomenon of interest to the researcher.

To enhance the likelihood of obtaining valid self-report data, it is important that you clearly delineate why the study is important. Most questionnaires or surveys will include a statement on their cover sheet and their consent form detailing at least an abbreviated version of the main purpose of the study. While it may not be desirable to tell participants everything about the study purpose, they need to be given at least a general idea of what you're doing; if the subjects are given incomplete information in order to mask the intention of the study, then that needs to be revealed in some kind of debriefing statement. It is also essential that participants be informed of whether their data will be kept in confidence or will be anonymous. As we discussed in Chapter 4, it is important that the data is protected as though it was the researcher's own private information. Participants should be encouraged to give complete and accurate information when possible. We will discuss questions at length later, but participants should not be asked to respond to items that are irrelevant to them or their situation. You should also ensure that you consider the audience of the questionnaire before writing the statements and/or questions.

Self-report surveys are great for recording self-perception, covert or hidden behavior, beliefs, attitudes, opinions, and values. They might also be useful for questions of a personal nature, anything that might be considered private information. Self-report is also a strong technique for recording emotion or feelings; however, keep in mind that these have to be conscious thoughts and feelings you are interested in measuring.

As research questions ultimately guide your methodological choices, it is helpful to know what self-report surveys are particularly unsuccessful at measuring. First, self-report is a poor choice for unconscious behaviors and feelings, difficult to remember events, and things that happened in the distant past. Surveys are also a weak choice as a method of gathering data about abilities, skills (think communication competence), and socially undesirable behaviors—as individuals are often unlikely to report their own shortcomings or behaviors they may perceive as social undesirable.

Constructing a Survey Questionnaire

Writing Survey Questions

In designing survey questionnaires, one concern is how best to construct the questions. The first issue is the type of questions you can ask in a survey, which in turn depends upon the research question asked and/or hypotheses stated. You can ask questions about experience or behavior: How often do you talk with your mother? You can ask questions about opinions or values: Is television too violent? You may ask questions about feelings or attitudes: Do you like your new research methods textbook? You might ask questions about factual knowledge: How many drinks can you consume before your blood alcohol level goes over .10? You can ask questions about background or demographics: How old are you? What is your major? Where are you from?

Strategies for Questions. While the initial criteria for writing and deciding upon what questions to ask in a research study come from the research questions or hypotheses, there are additional strategies for what questions work best. First, recent and important events are remembered more easily. For example, if you ask people to report on their television viewing behavior, asking them to report the previous day or week's behavior will produce more accurate data than asking about the distant past. People can recall past serious issues, but not past minor issues, and verbatim memory of minor issues can erode in as little as a few days. For example, you may not be able to recall whom you communicated with last Friday; yet most of you remember the first person you spoke with following the Boston Marathon bombings (which, at this writing, took place over three years ago). Another important strategy is that unpleasant and ego-threatening incidents tend to be reported inaccurately. In other words, parents underreport children's misbehavior, college students underreport unsafe sexual behavior, and almost no one admits to driving under the influence of alcohol (since it is both socially undesirable and a crime).

1. Questions should be clear.
    Creating good questions, at first glance, seems like an easy task; yet upon the first attempt, you will find this is a complex task and warrants much deliberation. Some guidelines can make the task easier. First and foremost, questions should be clear, using simple language participants can easily understand. Your word choice is dependent upon your audience. Just as you have been trained to consider your audience in public speaking, you need to give thought to your audience when writing a question for a survey. If you are surveying adolescents or engineers, the words you choose will differ. It is common for words to have multiple meanings, so you need to be sure that the interpretation you are thinking of is clear to the participants. For example, think about the word "drugs." Suppose you ask the question "Have you ever taken drugs?" What would people think you were asking about? On many research projects you might be talking about illegal substances, such as cocaine; however, in some health communication studies, you might be talking about prescription drugs. The key here is to be clear! If there is any doubt about what your question is asking, you need to write a better question.

2. Questions must be about only one issue.
    A second important guideline to follow when writing research questions is that the questions you write must be about only one issue. Questions that contain more than one issue are called *double-barreled* questions. Why should it matter if you ask questions containing more than one concept? Imagine that you ask the following question: "Do you like the education and social life at UNC–Charlotte?" In reality, a "Yes" tells you that the participant likes both the education and social life at

UNC–Charlotte, while a "No" tells you that the participant dislikes both the education and social life at UNC–Charlotte. However, are these the only two possible answers? No. One might like the education and dislike the social opportunities at UNC–Charlotte, or one might dislike the education and like the social life at UNC–Charlotte. In any event, if you ask a double-barreled question, you can never be certain what the participant intended when he or she answered the question, or if they give a lukewarm answer that is indicative of conflicted opinions on the question. This will affect both the reliability and validity of the survey, compromise the measure's integrity, and thus impact the overall study.

3. Questions should avoid biased wording.
   Another guideline for good question construction is to avoid using wording that leads participants to particular outcomes. The actual wording of the question can dramatically change the outcome. Some common examples of this include starting questions and/or statements with phrases like "Wouldn't you agree . . ." or "Isn't it true . . ." A related guideline for question construction is to avoid language that is emotionally charged, as this can bias answers. A great example of emotionally charged language can be seen in the abortion debate. Regardless of what side you identify with, the language both sides use to talk about their perspective is emotionally provocative. Let's consider the debate language. Pro-choice groups equate legal abortion with free choice and a woman's control over her own body. They talk about being *pro-choice*, while they see the other side as being *anti-choice*. Similarly, pro-life groups equate legal abortion with murder, using phrases such as *pro-life* and *pro-abortion*. All of these terms, regardless of your own personal beliefs, are emotionally charged, and if used in a survey will likely result in difficulty in getting an unbiased response.

4. Questions should avoid making assumptions.
   The fourth guideline for question construction is to avoid making assumptions about your participant. So, while we suggested earlier you need to consider your audience when writing questions, here you want to move a step beyond that by asking participants questions that are relevant to them, and asking questions only when participants are informed about the topic. Do you take your pet to the vet for yearly exams? This question assumes the person answering the question has a pet. What do you think of Proposition 301? This question assumes the person answering the question knows what Proposition 301 is. Neither

of these questions will provide accurate or reliable answers with the wrong participants. The solution to this problem often comes in the form of filter questions, which can assist in *filtering* out individuals who lack the appropriate knowledge or lack the appropriate conditions to answer the question at hand.

5. Questions should avoid offending participants if possible.
Be careful how you phrase sensitive questions. Examples of sensitive topics are age and income. Suppose you ask such questions as "How old are you?" and "How much money do you make?" You will probably get an answer like "None of your business!" The best way around this is to list groupings of ages and income levels to follow your questions, such as: "In which of the following age categories do you fit?" and "In which of the following categories was your total household income before taxes last year?" It is also wise to place questions like these (especially those regarding demographics) at the very end of a survey; not only does this minimize the risks associated with offending the respondent, but they are easy questions to answer, so fatigue is not much of an issue.

Types of Questions

Before we leave the discussion of questionnaire writing, let's talk briefly about different types of questions. There are basically two types of questions: *closed-ended* questions and *open-ended* questions. A closed-ended question is one where you only give the respondent certain possible answers that his response must fit into—for example, a "yes/no" question, or the question "In which of the following age categories do you fit? Under 21; 21–34; 35–49; 50–64; or 65 and over." Closed-ended questions are suited for eliminating interviewer interpretation, eliminating coding and editing interpretations, making recording of the data easier as the interview is being conducted, and ensuring consistency in interviewing. When you are using scales or similar measurement tools that we discussed earlier, you are usually using closed-ended questions.

However, sometimes closed-ended questions are not appropriate for the research questions that are being asked. What would happen with the closed-ended question "Do you believe the United States ought to enter into a treaty with Iran to eliminate long-range nuclear warheads?" Some people may simply say "yes" or "no." But others may wish to elaborate: "It depends on—if they will honor it, if they will allow independent inspections, and if they are willing to cease production now until the treaty is signed." In other words, "yes" and "no" may not be a sufficient choice of answers for some participants, and you'll need to allow for expanded answers. In this instance an open-ended question would make more sense.

Open-ended questions are suited when you need to measure a participant's level of knowledge, or playback of something, or detailed explanation of an opinion. Examples of open-ended questions are "Why do you say that?" and "What do you remember about ____?" and "What are your impressions of ____?"

Although we are not talking about *in-depth qualitative* interviewing, open-ended questions require some amount of probing and clarifying. A common weakness of inexperienced interviewers is poor probing. After the participant has seemingly finished what he or she is going to say, you would need to probe. For example, you may need to ask: "What do you mean by that?" or "What else do you remember?" or "Why do you say that?" A probe of "Do you remember anything else?" usually results in a "no." But if you ask, "What else do you remember?" often you will get more responses. It is also very important to probe for clarity. There is nothing more frustrating than reading over a questionnaire later and thinking, "I wonder what he or she meant by that." If you don't ask when he or she is there in front of you, you'll never know what he or she meant.

Structure and Arrangement of Questions

Of course, many researchers use already published and validated scales to build their questionnaires, instead of writing their own questions. As we alluded to earlier, there are scholars in Communication and other disciplines who focus their research entirely on developing and validating good measures that can be used by others. Most questionnaires in academic survey research are a combination of existing scales with newly written questions. However, whether compiling a questionnaire from existing scales or creating a completely new questionnaire, you have to make choices about the best way to structure and arrange your questions across the entire instrument. The three commonly used question formats are: tunnel, funnel, and inverted funnel formats.

> **Tunnel Format.** In the **tunnel format**, questions tend to be similar in terms of breadth and depth throughout the questionnaire. They are organized by similarity and vary little in terms of depth.
>
> **Funnel Format.** In a **funnel format**, the questions begin with broad, often open-ended questions followed by narrow, more closed-ended questions. Think of this as a format moving from general to specific.
>
> **Inverted Funnel Format.** Finally, the **inverted funnel format** is the polar opposite of the funnel format. It generally begins with more closed-ended, narrow questions moving throughout the questionnaire to the most open-ended, broad questions. Think of this format as moving from specific to general.

tunnel format
A type of question format in which questions tend to be similar in terms of breadth and depth throughout a questionnaire. Questions are organized by similarity and vary little in terms of depth.

funnel format
A type of question format in which questions begin with broad, open-ended questions followed by narrow, more closed-ended questions.

inverted funnel format
A type of question format that generally begins with more closed-ended, narrow questions moving throughout the questionnaire to the most open-ended and broad questions.

How to Choose the Right Format. As we have suggested throughout the book, the preferred questionnaire structure is the one best suited to your research question and/or hypotheses. Just as the questions determine the type of methodology that is best, the same components assist you in determining the most appropriate format for your question. For example, your author Ken Lachlan conducted a study of people's media dependencies and opinions of emergency information received following the collapse of a highway bridge in Minneapolis, Minnesota (Lachlan, Spence, & Nelson, 2010). When designing the instrument, he and his coauthors knew that they had to ask very specific questions about an incident that had happened about a week before the data collection. This included how they first heard of the bridge collapse, what sources they turned to for additional information, the types of information they received, and how satisfied they were with information that came from emergency managers, first responders, the mainstream media, and police. It also included questions concerning what the audience wanted to find out about most, and whether or not these needs were satisfied. Knowing that these were tough questions that required quite a bit of cognitive effect, they chose the inverted funnel format, putting these questions at the front of the survey. Easier questions, such as general media habits and demographics, went toward the end of the survey, since even a somewhat tired participant should be able to recall these things easily.

If you have ever answered a survey and thought, "I think I already answered that question," it may be that you have indeed answered a similar question—often one written that is the opposite of the first. For example, in McCroskey's (1982) Personal Report of Communication Apprehension Scale, one item states, "Ordinarily I am very tense and nervous in conversations," while another statement asks you to respond to the following, "Ordinarily I am very calm and relaxed in conversations." These items are written to minimize the tendency people have to start answering without much thought. This is called a *response set*. Reversing the polarity of some of the items on scales as you write is a good technique for avoiding a response set when participants complete your survey.

Survey Administration

When administering a questionnaire, researchers have choices to make about how best to deliver the material to the individual participating in the study or completing the questionnaire. This is known as questionnaire administration and we have three options: researcher-administered, self-administered, and interviews. In their content analysis of survey research in communication, Macias and colleagues (2008) found that the most common method of administration of surveys, by far, was mail (self-administered) surveys, used in 54 percent of research reviewed. Interviews over the telephone or in-person each were used in 11 percent of research reviewed. Web and fax surveys were rarely seen (only in 1% of studies reviewed).

Researcher-Administered. In **researcher-administered questionnaires**, the researcher is present when the participant completes the survey questionnaire, usually in a group setting. When a person fills out her own survey instrument, regardless of whether the researcher is present at the time, the instrument is called a *questionnaire*. Researcher-administered surveys allow the researcher the opportunity of answering any questions participants may have. Another primary benefit to researcher-administered questionnaires is that, when administering questionnaires to a large group of people at one time, data collection is quick and efficient. However, the disadvantage to administering a survey in such a setting is that participants sometimes feel less anonymous, as the researcher is present. Another disadvantage of administering a survey to a group of people is that groups can sometimes bias an individual's own responses. We may answer the survey differently if we feel that the information can be tied to us or if we feel that there is the chance someone in the group may find out about our responses.

researcher-administered questionnaires
A researcher is present when a participant completes a survey.

Self-Administered. In the past, most **self-administered questionnaires** were either handed out and sent home or mailed; however, the advent of technology allows us to collect data in a self-administered questionnaire via the Internet. Macias et al. (2008) found that, on average, self-administered surveys via mail yielded a 42 percent response rate, via e-mail yielded a 30 percent response rate, and via fax yielded a 66 percent response rate. Mailing and allowing participants to take paper surveys home tends to decrease the response rate. In other words, the number of individuals who complete and return the surveys is consistently lower than if we had used researcher-administered questionnaires, regardless of the specific means of self-administration. For example, imagine that you are studying how stress impacts college student communication with roommates and you are using a longitudinal design. In the past, you might have sent home a packet with a questionnaire for both a student and her roommate to complete and return to the communication department. What are the odds that the surveys will be returned? More than likely, they will be excavated at the end of the semester, when the student cleans out the backseat of her vehicle before returning home for break. That will affect the outcome of your survey and diminish your response rate. Some researchers provide incentives to increase response rate. What incentives motivate you to respond to a survey request? Scholars may use extra credit, money, and/or gift cards to entice you to participate in their study and thus to increase their response rate. Sometimes, incentives appeal to some groups more than others and therefore can call into question the representativeness of the sample.

self-administered questionnaires
Surveys that are completed individually, with no researchers or other people present.

In their study on intensive care unit communication between physicians and nurses, Manojlovich, Antonakos, and Ronis (2012) were interested in communication's impact on patient outcomes. One part of their research design distributed surveys to 866 registered nurses; they collected 462, a response rate of 53.3 percent. Pretty good based on our discussion above. However, it is important to recognize that we don't know why the other 46.7 percent chose not to participate. There may be something consistent about almost half of those approached to participate that then calls the generalizability of the findings into question.

A key advantage to self-administered questionnaires over researcher-administered questionnaires is that individuals completing the survey tend to be more honest in their answers as neither researchers nor others are present. This protects an individual's sense of privacy, ensuring that their data is anonymous. However, one of the trade-offs you make in self-administered questionnaires is that researchers are not present to answer any questions that may arise, so participants may guess at what you are asking them.

There are also pros and cons to conducting Web-based self-administered surveys. One large consideration for Web-based research is the representativeness of a sample that is able to access a questionnaire on the Web. There are still many people who don't have Internet access, or who are not comfortable with being on the Internet and thus might be less likely to complete a Web-based survey. Some research suggests that response rates for Web surveys are low, relative to other methods such as paper questionnaires (Couper & Miller, 2008). You can maximize representation of your sample by offering alternative modes of administration (Web and paper), but research suggests this also does not positively affect response rates (Couper & Miller, 2008). On the other hand, if your population is technologically savvy, a Web-based survey might be more attractive to them, and it is easier for you to work with since the data is already entered into a database ready for your analysis.

Interviews. When the researcher asks the study participant the survey questions and records the responses, this is called an **interview**, and the researcher is called an *interviewer*. Interviewing can take place in person or over the phone. The survey instrument used in an interview is often called an *interview guide*, *interview protocol*, or *survey*. Essentially, what we are talking about here is a *quantitative* survey methodology, which differs from qualitative interviewing (which we cover in Chapter 11), and as such, utilizes a different set of rules. Macias and colleagues (2008) found that interviews conducted in person yielded on average a 79 percent response rate, the highest of all the methods they studied, and telephone interviews yielded a 61 percent response rate on average.

The first concern in this type of survey is the validity of interview data. Here, the validity of the data depends highly on how participants view the interviewer, as well as how effectively the interviewer manages the interaction. It is important to be capable of recording participants' answers unobtrusively, as well as knowing how to expand a person's answer with additional questions—also known as probing and clarifying.

---

interview
A research practice with individual participants, or groups of participants, to obtain responses to survey questions by direct questioning.

The key to good quality interviews is the skill and training of the interviewers. There are, in fact, several validity threats related to interviewer issues. Interviewers can inadvertently create a personal attribute effect (when characteristics of the researcher—gender, for example—influences people's behavior) or unintentional expectancy effect (by influencing participants by letting them know the behaviors the interviewer desires, such as by smiling or frowning). When conducting an interview, it's important that you don't predispose a participant to answer in some set manner. When you write your questionnaire or survey protocol, disguise your questions so the respondent does not continually try to outguess you or anticipate the answer you want. Unskilled interviewers can damage the validity of a well-designed survey. They can bias participants' responses, they may record responses incorrectly, and they can misrepresent the goals and questions of the survey. All of these create problems with the validity of the research at hand. Often, these types of interviews are conducted by multiple interviewers; therefore, it is necessary that all interviewers are carefully trained to follow a written protocol, which details what questions will be asked in what order and how the entire interview will be conducted. Interviewers should be knowledgeable about the research, familiar with the interview questions, practice interviewing, and be skilled at building rapport with participants.

It is important that an interview gets off to the right start. Most people decide within the first few seconds whether they are willing to participate; therefore, the tone of the initial meeting and greeting with the researcher sets the tone for the rest of the interview process. A good interview should begin when the researchers introduce themselves to potential participants and identify the research entity they represent. They should identify the general research topic, explain any selection criteria for the study, and explain the time commitment participants must make. Finally, their role in the introduction of the interview is to convince the participant that his or her contribution is important to the research.

Interviews can be conducted either face-to-face or via telephone. We suspect future textbooks will have to consider survey-designed interviews that will be conducted via instant messaging, text messaging, and other similar electronic methods. The beauty of a face-to-face interview is that it provides nonverbal data and demographic information; however, we sacrifice time, expense, and a decrease in privacy and anonymity. As Opdenakker (2006, para. 3) points out, "Face-to-face interviews allow synchronous communication of time and place." As you have seen throughout this text, there is no perfect design; there is always some trade-off. That is true of telephone interviews, too! Using a telephone interview structure is less costly and time consuming and simultaneously increases privacy and anonymity; however, it sacrifices nonverbal data that cannot be collected. Yet, it has the added advantage of providing the opportunity to interview people over vast geographic distances. Telephone interviews can be difficult. A relatively new barrier to collecting data via the telephone is the "Do Not

Call" list. This is a national registry where individuals can request to have their number listed, so solicitors and telemarketers are prohibited from calling. This severely limits the proportion of the population who is available via telephone, which brings the representativeness of a random telephone sample into question. An additional barrier to collecting data via the phone is that it is easy for individuals to make an excuse, avoid the call (thanks to caller ID), or even hang up in the middle of an interview. In addition, since cell phone numbers are typically not available via traditional directories, researchers must make additional effort to obtain a good cross-section of all numbers. However, telephone interviews are advantageous in that they do allow for "synchronous communication of time and asynchronous communication of place" (Opdenakker, 2006, para. 3).

There are both advantages and disadvantages to using interviews (researcher asking the questions and recording the answers) in place of questionnaires (in which participants fill out the instrument themselves). Interviews usually have a higher response rate than questionnaires. This is particularly true of self-administered questionnaires when the researcher is not present while the questionnaire is being completed. Another benefit of interviews, when compared to traditional survey design, is that you can minimize the number of "don't know" responses. The facilitator or interviewer can use a probe, asking the question in a different way or allowing the respondent to provide additional detail concerning their answer. Interviews also allow us to guard against misunderstandings. The interviewer or facilitator can clarify what she is asking. This provides more flexibility to your design, allowing for a deeper understanding.

In addition to recording verbal data when interviewing, an important advantage is that the interviewer can observe, as well as ask questions. Things such as race, age, and nonverbal communication cues can all be noted by the interviewer.

One example of face-to-face interviewing is the use of the Oral History Interview (OHI; Buehlman & Gottman, 1996; Buehlman, Gottman, & Katz, 1992; Krokoff, 1984). The OHI provides a useful tool for investigating perceptions about marriage as evidenced by how the couple communicates about their marital experience. The OHI is a structured interview that asks couples a series of open-ended questions about their relationship story; that is, the couple's dating and marital history, their philosophy of marriage, and how their marriage has changed over time (Buehlman & Gottman, 1996).

As a graduate student, interviewing for an oral history relational study, Heather Powell Gallardo interviewed a college-age dating couple using the OHI. As she interviewed this particular couple, their answers didn't seem to add up. They answered the questions, but there was something strange about the way they acted. After talking with another research assistant at the lab, who had watched the interview from the control room, she called the director of the study and let him know the concerns. When asked later, the couple admitted that they had never been in a relationship and just participated for the incentive (extra credit), even though there were alternative ways to earn the same incentive. Had she just had them fill out a self-administered questionnaire, it is unlikely she would have discovered their cheating, negatively impacting the validity of the study.

Thus far, we have detailed the strengths of interviewing over questionnaire survey techniques; however, interviewing is not without disadvantages. One major drawback to interviewing is that it can be very expensive and time intensive. While time and expense can be overcome, a more substantial problem with interviews is that they may be subject to problems associated with social desirability. Remember social desirability is the idea that we may fudge our answers to present ourselves in a positive light. As such, participants are often inclined to provide answers they think we want to hear—regardless of whether they are true. Face-to-face interviews are most affected by social desirability compared to other methodological options available to use. Some argue that interviewers, through the use of rapport, try to increase honest answers, whereas others argue that social desirability is still a major concern. In any case, while surveys provide at least some sense of anonymity, having to actually disclose information to a live person—whether face to face or over the phone—may impact social desirability effects.

When interviewing, we need to be certain that the interviewing is conducted in a consistent manner each time, regardless of who is interviewing the participants. Remember survey-designed interviews follow a detailed protocol and, while it is necessary to probe respondents for more complete answers, interviewers must follow the protocol consistently. This differs from qualitative interviewing techniques.

So What?

Surveys will continue to be popular research tools; technology is contributing to their prevalence in assessing many different types of research questions and hypotheses, and there are many uses and advantages to this research method. We have examined survey design and many considerations a scholar must take into account when designing a questionnaire. You should know the difference between a cross-sectional and longitudinal design and when each is the appropriate study design. Survey-designed interviews have an important function in the assessment of many communication issues. Finally, we compared the uses, advantages, and disadvantages of using interviews and self-administered questionnaires. All methods and procedures have pros and cons and appropriate and inappropriate uses. The bottom line is—your research question or hypothesis drives what you do and how you do it. We will continue to revisit that notion in upcoming chapters.

Glossary

Cohort study
A study in which responses from specific subgroups of a population are identified and compared over time.

Cross-sectional survey
A survey design that describes the characteristics of a sample representing a population at one point in time.

Evaluation research
Research that is designed to assess the effectiveness of programs or products during development or after their completion.

Funnel format
A type of question format in which questions begin with broad, open-ended questions followed by narrow, more closed-ended questions.

Interview
A research practice with individual participants, or groups of participants, to obtain responses to survey questions by direct questioning.

Inverted funnel format
A type of question format that generally begins with more closed-ended, narrow questions moving throughout the questionnaire to the most open ended and broad questions.

Longitudinal survey design
A survey design that gathers data from respondents at several points in time.

Market research
Research that is designed to study consumer behavior.

Panel study
A study in which a sample is drawn from a population or universe and those same people or objects are measured at multiple points in time.

Political polls
One of the most common and readily available uses of surveys. They provide a detailed account of who is leading whom in the run for a particular office during an election.

Researcher-administered questionnaires
A researcher is present when a participant completes a survey.

Self-administered questionnaires
Surveys that are completed individually, with no researchers or other people present.

Survey design
A method of asking research participants questions that provides researchers with a method of information gathering from a large number of people over a relatively short period of time.

Trend study
Measurement occurs at two or more points in time, from different samples selected from the same population. This type of study is designed to identify changes or trends in people's beliefs about a variable of interest.

Tunnel format
A type of question format in which questions tend to be similar in terms of breadth and depth throughout a questionnaire. Questions are organized by similarity and vary little in terms of depth.

References

Atkin, C. K., & Freimuth, v. (2000). Formative evaluation research in campaign design. In R. E. Rice & C. K. Atkin (Eds.), *Public communication campaigns* (pp. 125–145). Thousand Oaks, CA: Sage.

Botta, R. A., & Dumlao, R. (2002). How do conflict and communication patterns between fathers and daughters contribute to or offset eating disorders? *Health Communication, 14*(2), 199–219.

Buehlman, K. T., & Gottman, J. M. (1996). *The oral history interview and the oral history coding system*. Mahwah, NJ: Erlbaum.

Buehlman, K. T., Gottman, J. M., & Katz, L. F. (1992). How a couple views their past predicts their future: Predicting divorce from an oral history interview. *Journal of Family Psychology, 5*, 295–318.

Carlsen, F. L. (Ed.). (2010). *Harris Michigan industrial directory*. Austin, TX: Harrisinfosource.

Center, A. H., & Broom, G. M. (1983). Evaluation research. *Public Relations Quarterly, 28*(3), 1–3.

Couper, M. P., & Miller, P. v. (2008). Web survey methods: Introduction. *Public Opinion Quarterly, 72*(5), 831–835.

Epps, C. S., Armstrong, M., Davis, C. S., Massey, T. O., McNeish, R., & Smith, R. B. (2007). *Development and testing of an instrument to measure mental health literacy*. Tampa, FL: Louis de la Parte Florida Mental Health Institute. University of South Florida.

Krokoff, L. (1984). The anatomy of blue-collar marriages (Doctoral dissertation, University of Illinois at Urbana-Champaign, 1984). *Dissertation Abstracts International*.

Lachlan, K.A., Spence, P.R., & Nelson, L. (2010). Gender differences in psychological responses to crisis news: The case of the I-35 collapse. *Communication Research Reports, 27* (1), 38–48.

Lim, V. K. G., & Teo, T. S. H. (2009). Mind your E-manners: Impact of cyber incivility on employees' work attitude and behavior. *Information & Management, 46*, 419–425.

Macias, W., Springston, J. K., Lariscy, R. A. W., & Neustifer, B. (2008). A 13-year content analysis of survey methodology in communication related journals. *Journal of Current Issues and Research in Advertising, 30*(1), 79–94.

Manojlovich, M., Antonakos, C. L., & Ronis, D. L. (2012). Intensive care units, communication between nurses and physicians, and patients' outcomes. *American Journal of Critical Care, 18*, 21–30.

Massey, O. T., Davis, C. S., Smith, R. B., Armstrong, M., & Vergon, K. S. (2008). *Refinement of an instrument to measure mental health literacy among caregivers and providers and a qualitative examination of interventions to enhance mental health literacy*. Tampa, FL: Louis de la Parte Florida Mental Health Institute. University of South Florida.

McCroskey, J. E. (1982). Oral communication apprehension: A reconceptualization. In M. Burgoon (Ed.), *Communication yearbook* (Volume 6, pp. 136–170). Beverly Hills: Sage.

Opdenakker, R. (2006). Advantages and disadvantages of four interview techniques in qualitative research. *Forum Qualitative Sozialforschung/Forum: Qualitative Social Research*, 7(4) <Electronic version>. Retrieved March 18, 2009, from http://www.qualitativeresearch.net/index.php/fqs/article/view/175/392

The Quotations Page. (n.d.). Retrieved June 15, 2009, from http://www.quotationspage.com/quote/706.html

The Quote Garden. (n.d.). Retrieved June 15, 2009, from http://www.quotegarden.com/tv-turnoff-week.html

Salmon, C. T., Park, H. S., & Wrigley, B. J. (2003). Optimistic bias and perceptions of bioterrorism in Michigan corporate spokespersons, Fall 2001. *Journal of Health Communication, 8*, 130–143.

Segrin, C., & Flora, J. (2000). Poor social skills are a vulnerability factor in the development of psychosocial problems. *Human Communication Research, 26*, 489–514.

EXPERIMENTS

Chapter Outline

1. What Is an Experiment?
   a. Independent and Dependent Variables
      i. What Are Independent Variables?
      ii. What Are Dependent Variables?
   b. Good Questions for Experiments
2. Understanding Experimental Notation and Language
   a. Observation
   b. Induction
   c. Random Assignment
   d. Terminology
3. Designs and Validity
4. Preexperimental Designs
   a. One Shot Case Study Design
   b. One Group Pretest Posttest Design
   c. Static Group Comparison Design
5. Quasi-Experimental Designs
   a. Time-Series Design
   b. Nonequivalent Control Group Design
   c. Multiple Time-Series Design
6. True Experimental Designs
   a. Pretest Posttest Control Group Design
   b. Posttest-Only Control Group Design
   c. Solomon Four-Group Design
7. Factorial Design
8. Field and Natural Experiments
9. So What?

Key Terms

Baseline
Between-subjects design
Control group
Dependent variables
Experimental group
Factorial design

Independent variable
Induction
Preexperimental designs
Posttest
Pretest
Quasi-experimental designs

Random assignment
Social experiment
True experimental designs
Within-subjects design

115

CHAPTER OBJECTIVES

1. To understand what experiments are
2. To understand the questions that can be addressed with experiments
3. To understand different types of experiments
4. To understand how different experiments address different validity threats

▼ What Is an Experiment?

Earlier in the book, we talked about some of the general conceptions and misconceptions people have about social research. In particular, we talked about how people can readily think of examples of research in medicine, engineering, computer science, and so on, while they may have a more difficult time coming up with examples of social research. Social researchers also frequently perform experimental research, although usually without a white coat or a Bunsen burner. Communication scientists have relied upon experimental procedures since the birth of the discipline to answer a variety of questions concerning the ways in which people use and respond to information. Experimental designs have been used for decades to address how people respond to interpersonal interactions, mediated information, workplace dynamics, and interactions with computers. Of course, this raises the question of exactly what an experiment is, by definition.

By definition, a **social experiment** is a procedure in which researchers take human subjects, do something to them, and observe the effects of what they did to them (Baxter & Babbie, 2004). This chapter will discuss some of the nuances associated with this seemingly simple procedure, including the use of subjects, random assignment, inductions, control groups, and multiple measures. More importantly, it will discuss how you can use these design elements to build confidence in your findings by ruling out particular validity threats.

social experiment
A procedure in which researchers take human subjects, do something to them, and observe the effects of what they did to them.

Independent and Dependent Variables

Experimental researchers deal with independent and dependent variables. We use these terms to describe causes and effects. A variable is anything that can be measured or observed by the researcher. The independent versus dependent distinction is related to the researcher's involvement in the observation.

First, let's explain some concepts about variables in experiments. Remember that—for all research—variables can be measured through self-report, measured through other report, or measured through observation. In an experiment, the independent variable can also be "manipulated" (we will get to inductions and manipulations shortly).

So, if—in your experiment—you are measuring a variable to determine beliefs, attitudes, or opinions, or to collect retrospective information about behavior or meaning, you would measure that variable using a *survey*. If, in your experiment, you are measuring a variable to analyze the content of media messages, you would measure that variable using a *content analysis*. Finally, if you are measuring a variable to analyze the content of an interpersonal message, you would measure that variable using an *interaction analysis*. So, to recap, surveys can be used as a stand-alone method, or as a way to measure a variable during an experiment. The same is true for interaction analysis.

What Are Independent Variables?

By definition, an **independent variable** is any observation that is controlled by the researcher. So, for example, you may want to test the effectiveness of an antismoking public service announcement (PSA). You develop two types of PSAs, one that uses a fear appeal to attempt to scare people into compliance and one that does not. You then show the fear ad to one group of people and the non-fear ad to another group.

In this instance, the independent variable is the type of ad that is being shown. While the researcher will make the observation that a particular group saw one ad or the other, it was the researcher who decided which group would see which and what those messages would look like. Any differences in the responses of the participants might be attributable to this decision. This leads us to our next way of thinking about independent variables: they are causes. Independent variables are the things that are manipulated by the researcher in order to produce a particular outcome.

independent variable
Any observation that is controlled by the researcher.

What Are Dependent Variables?

Dependent variables, on the other hand, are effects. They are observations made by the researcher that are not directly controlled by the researcher, but may be attributable to decisions surrounding the independent variable. In our example above, let's say the people who saw the fear appeal ad report that they are less willing to take up smoking. In this case, the dependent variable is willingness to take up smoking. It is the assumed result of a change in the independent variable.

Why do we call it a dependent variable? Because it is dependent on the independent variable. In short, independent variables are causes, while dependent variables are effects, or consequences.

dependent variables
Observations made by the researcher that are not directly controlled by them.

Good Questions for Experiments

If you remember earlier in the text, we talked about how social scientists use hypotheses to build theory, making educated guesses about the social world, and then testing those guesses through observation. In Chapter 5, we further discussed the formation of research questions and hypotheses, and how these may inform the selection of particular types of research design. As a classification of research design, experiments lend themselves best to particular types of questions. They are very useful for answering micro-level questions concerning responses to information. In particular, they lend themselves well to questions of *causation*. As we will see, this is because most experimental designs involve some kind of pretest; by examining someone before you expose her to a stimulus, then examining her again after the stimulus, you can argue to a certain extent that what you did to her may have caused any changes that you observe. So, if you are trying to answer a question such as: "Do video games *cause* people to respond more aggressively?" or "Does attractiveness *cause* people to disclose more information?" then an experimental design might be the way to go. Experiments are not particularly useful for descriptive purposes (since they are limited in the scope of phenomena they can address), nor are they particularly useful for drawing non-causal associations. They are, however, very useful for establishing causal relationships between independent and dependent variables.

Of course, it is not quite that simple. There are a myriad of internal validity threats that can undermine a simple "X causes Y" statement. Non-spuriousness (making sure the independent variable is the only cause for the observed effect on the dependent variable) also becomes an issue, as it may be difficult to rule out alternative explanations ("third variables") that account for what you observe. Different types of experimental designs may be more or less effective at dealing with these concerns. In this chapter, we'll discuss different designs, what they might look like, and how well they may address these concerns and problems.

Experiments are used in business and industry as well as in scientific and social science research. When author Christine Davis worked for a marketing research firm, they frequently used an experimental design to test alternative advertisements. Following a pretest posttest control group design, they were able to determine if the test ad led to an increase in potential product usage.

▼ Understanding Experimental Notation and Language

Before discussing different types of designs, it may be essential that we discuss the notation that is used when describing experimental procedures. We can identify three basic elements in an experimental design: observation, induction (or manipulation), and random assignment.

Observation

If you are reading the shorthand that scientists use to describe experimental designs, you will, at the very least, see a capital "O." This symbol is used to represent an *observation*. In communication research, this is typically some kind of written, spoken, or observed behavior or attitude. It is the basic building block of experimental design, which is after all a series of observations.

Induction

You may also see a capital "X." This symbol is used to convey some kind of **induction**—an induction is what you *do* to the participant. So, in our video game example from above, this may be the part of the design where you make someone play a certain type of game. In a persuasion experiment, it may be a certain kind of argument that is delivered to the participant. In a television violence study, it may be a short film clip that you show. In any case, this is what you do to the participant, the independent variable, the effect of which you are examining.

induction
What is done to a participant in an experiment.

Inductions are often incorrectly labeled as *manipulations*. Technically, an induction is only a manipulation if it actually works. The act of doing something to a participant, regardless of whether it affects them in any way, is more accurately referred to as an induction. In some fields, especially health communication, this is sometimes called an *intervention* or *treatment*.

Random Assignment

You may also encounter a capital "R" in experimental notation. This refers to the **random assignment** of participants to different groups within your design. In a true experimental design, you would want to assign people at random to different groups. Why? Well, if we were concerned about ruling out spuriousness, you would want all the groups in your study to be as similar or comparable as possible. Similar how? It depends on your study, but certainly if you're studying health literacy you might want the two groups to have an equivalent distribution of education, and perhaps health status and/or experience with health-care providers. If you're studying employee productivity, you might want to make sure both groups are equivalent in terms of work experience and training. If you're studying the politeness level of communication on e-mail versus voice mail (see Duthler, 2006), you might want to make sure participants in both groups have equivalent distributions in terms of their relationships with the communication recipients. If you randomly assign people to groups—if everyone has an equal chance of being in a particular group, then (theoretically) they should be roughly

random assignment
The assignment of people at random to different groups in an experimental design.

experimental group
The group of participants to whom you give the induction.

control group
A group that does not receive induction in an experiment.

between-subjects design
Designs comparing multiple groups.

within-subjects design
Designs looking at the same group multiple times.

baseline
An examination of someone before you expose him or her to a stimulus in order to argue, to a certain extent, that what was done to the subject may have caused any changes that are observed. Also called pretest.

pretest
An examination of someone before you expose him or her to a stimulus in order to argue, to a certain extent, that what was done to the subject may have caused any changes that are observed. Also called baseline measurement.

posttest
An examination or measurement conducted after administration of the induction.

the same. Of course, sometimes it is not logistically possible to have true random assignment. In these cases, you will sometimes see lines between conditions indicating that participants were not randomly assigned.

Terminology

There are also some key terms you should know in reading and understanding experiments. We just told you that you randomly assign participants to different groups. One of the groups is the group to whom you give the induction—this is called the **experimental group**. If you have more than one type of induction, you might have more than one experimental group. Ideally, you also have another group to whom you give no induction—this is called the **control group**. It's a group against which you can compare the experimental group. When you compare multiple experimental groups, this is known as a **between-subjects design**. When you only look at an experimental group, you call this a **within-subjects design**.

In many experiments, we measure the dependent variable both before and after exposure to the induction. The measurement before the induction is called a **pretest**, or **baseline** measurement. The measurement after the induction is called a **posttest**.

Designs and Validity

As we discussed earlier, there are a number of threats to validity that have to be taken into consideration when designing research. If you recall, there are a number of *internal validity* concerns that are relevant to the research process. These include history, or when something outside of the procedure takes place that skews your observations. Subjects may change over time, a process known as maturation. Testing describes the phenomenon in which participants respond differently as they become accustomed to your measures. Instrumentation refers to problems associated with using different measures to get at the same idea, and how well they measure the same things.

Fortunately, one of the advantages of the experiment is that in addition to allowing for causal statements, you can design studies in different ways to address each of these concerns. As we will see in the following descriptions, you can determine which of these issues concerns you the most, and design your study accordingly to rule it out as an internal validity threat. There is even one seldom-used design that rules out all of them. While no experimental design can ever rule out all plausible alternative explanations, thinking about internal validity concerns and designing a study appropriately can at least help you have more confidence in your findings.

Preexperimental Designs

One Shot Case Study Design

The simplest possible design in this research family is known as the One Shot Case Study (Campbell & Stanley, 1963). In this design, there is only one group. You give participants some sort of induction and observe the results:

$$X \quad O$$

For example, you could bring a group of participants into the lab and show them an ad for blue jeans. You could then pose a series of questions asking them about their likelihood to purchase the jeans. Since they seem to feel favorably toward the jeans, you conclude that the ad must have worked.

Do you see any problems here? There is no pretest, so you have no idea where the participants stood before seeing the ad. It is literally impossible to determine if your ad actually affected the results, since there is no measure of prior attitudes toward the product. The results could have come from anywhere: long-standing disposition toward the product, something that happened outside the laboratory, instrumentation that leads them in a certain direction, and so on. In this design, you really can't have any confidence in the results. As you can see, this experimental design doesn't account for anything in terms of validity concerns. In fact, it is almost never used. So why would we show you this design? Because it is a point of departure from which we can observe various means of ensuring against validity threats and providing results in which you can have more confidence.

Campbell and Stanley (1963) label these as **preexperimental designs**, since are either missing a pretest or a control group. Here are two more preexperimental designs.

preexperimental designs
Experimental designs that do not involve a true control group; no pretest, posttest, or control group.

One Group Pretest Posttest Design

Here is another example of a preexperimental design that lacks a control group:

$$O_1 \quad X \quad O_2$$

This is known as the One Group Pretest Posttest Design. It is a slight improvement over the One Shot Case Study. It still does not have a control group, so it is not possible to make comparisons between participants who did or did not receive the induction. But at least you can draw comparisons within this group of people in terms of where they stood before and after the induction. In our blue jeans example, you could ask people how they felt about the jeans, then show them the ad, then ask them again. You could then at least say that this group of people—whoever they are—did or did not feel more inclined to buy them.

Static Group Comparison Design

The final preexperimental design is the Static Group Comparison Design. This design looks just like the One Shot Case Study, except that you (kind of) add a control group:

$$X \quad O_1$$
$$O_2$$

Note that now, in addition to participants who get the induction, then take a posttest, you have added another group that takes the posttest without getting the induction. You can then compare those who get the induction to those who don't.

Returning to our example, you now have a second group: one that does not see the ad or take the pretest, but are simply asked about the jeans. Of course, there are still problems with this design. You can't really tell if people in the experimental group got used to your measures. If you run these groups at different time points, you can't tell if something outside the procedure affected the results. Most importantly, you don't know if these two groups felt differently about the jeans before the study.

Quasi-Experimental Designs

quasi-experimental designs
Experimental designs that use pretests and posttests in more complicated ways, but still lack random assignment.

This brings us to our next family of designs: the **quasi-experimental designs**. This term is used by Campbell and Stanley (1963) to describe designs that use pretests and posttests in more complicated ways, but that still lack random assignment. These designs are a marked improvement over the preexperimental, and while not perfect by any stretch, they are commonly used by communication researchers.

Time-Series Design

The first of these is the Time-Series Design:

$$O_1 \; O_2 \; O_3 \quad X \quad O_4 \; O_5 \; O_6$$

This design is geared primarily to rule out history and maturation as validity threats. As you can see, you have several pretests, an induction, and several posttests. In our example, we could ask a group of people how they feel about the jeans several times over the course of a few weeks. We could show them the ad, then measure their attitude several more times over the course of a few weeks. Looking at the results, we could tell if the participants' attitudes were already shifting before seeing the ad, or perhaps find evidence that something happened outside the lab that would influence the results. There isn't really a control group, but we can at least detect other threats.

Nonequivalent Control Group Design

Here is another quasi-experimental design, and one that is actually used quite commonly—the Nonequivalent Control Group Design:

$$O_1 \quad X \quad O_2$$
$$O_3 \quad \quad O_4$$

For logistical reasons related to random assignment, communication researchers often use this design. As you can see, we now have a true control group; these are people who get both the pretest and posttest, but not the induction. If we are to rule out a number of validity threats, it should be the case that people in the test group change from pretest to posttest, but those in the control group should remain exactly the same. This helps control against instrumentation, testing, and maturation as design threats. It does not do too much to address history, and there may be selection problems since there is no random assignment, but at least three major threats are controlled.

Multiple Time-Series Design

In order to improve this design to account for history, we can add multiple measures and produce the following, the Multiple Time-Series Design:

$$O_1 \; O_2 \; O_3 \quad X \quad O_4 \; O_5 \; O_6$$
$$O_7 \; O_8 \; O_9 \quad \quad O_{10} \; O_{11} \; O_{12}$$

As you can see, this design combines the advantages of the last two. We now have controls in place for testing, instrumentation, and maturation, and we have added a history safeguard by collecting pretest and posttest measures at different times. It is still not a perfect design, though. The lack of random assignment is still a concern.

true experimental designs
Experimental designs that randomly assign participants to both experimental and control groups.

....

True Experimental Designs

Fortunately, there is another class of design that, by definition, introduces random assignment: true experimental designs. Campbell and Stanley (1963) define **true experimental designs** as those that randomly assign participants to both experimental and control groups. Through random assignment, any subject-related concerns should be pretty much avoided. If everyone in your population has an equal chance of being in any group, then problems like evaluator apprehension, Hawthorne effect, and selection problems should not be a concern. Over a large enough group, if these problems are present then they are at least equally distributed.

Pretest Posttest Control Group Design

One classic example of this type of design is the Pretest Posttest Control Group Design:

$$R \quad O_1 \quad X \quad O_2$$
$$R \quad O_3 \quad \quad O_4$$

Note that this looks a lot like the Nonequivalent Control Group Design we discussed earlier, but that it simply adds random assignment. In doing so, it takes care of subject-related problems. Many classic experimentalists rely heavily on this design, as it rules out most validity threats, but is still fairly economical in design.

Heimendinger and colleagues (2005) used this design in a study to test four alternative messages designed to increase fruit and vegetable consumption among callers to the National Cancer Institute's (NCI) Cancer Information Service (CIS). They conducted a baseline interview when the callers initially called CIS. They then randomly assigned each study participant to one of three experimental conditions (different messages promoting fruit and vegetable consumption) or to a fourth group, a control group which received a different message (unrelated to fruit and vegetable consumption). Finally, they did posttest interviews with all participants both five months and twelve months later. Here's something else to note about this study—the researchers used a survey interview format to gather the information pre and post intervention. Their surveys included several scales, including some Likert scales to test reactions to the messages.

Posttest-Only Control Group Design

Similar to the Pretest Posttest Control Group Design is the Posttest-Only Control Group Design:

$$R \quad X \quad O_1$$

In 2001, Lee and Guerrero wanted to see how people interpreted different types of interpersonal touch. They set up an experiment in which they videotaped dyads in an interaction that ended with one of nine types of touch (handshake, clasping hands, soft touch on the forearm, arm around the shoulder, arm around the waist, soft touch on the cheek, tapping the shoulder in a condescending manner, push against the shoulder, and no touch). In their paper, they refer to this videotape as a *stimulus material*, another name for intervention or induction. One hundred ninety-three students were randomly assigned one of the touch videotapes. After watching the video, students were asked to rate their impressions of the interaction. From this experiment, Lee and Guerrero determined that different types of touch lead to different interpretations in terms of affection, romantic attraction, flirtation, and love, but not in terms of trust or happiness. They also found that face touch was interpreted to be the most intimate type of touch. Their design was limited by validity concerns about consistency across the videotaped dyads (since their videos used two women and two men with various ethnic combinations), reactions to touch initiated by women versus men, and reactions to the ethnic mix of the dyads. Since their experimental design did not account for these possible affects, they tested for them statistically. Again, note that the dependent variables were measured using Likert scale measurements in a survey interview format.

In their study on whether there is a difference between which type of communication is presented first—computer-mediated communication (CMC) or face-to-face (FTF) in diverse teams, Triana, Kirkman, and Wagstaff (2012) used an experimental design with twenty-five teams of four people each (three men and one woman) receiving the CMC first, then FTF. Another twenty-five teams communicated first utilizing FTF, then CMC.

As you can see, these designs also involve random assignment, although the absence of pretest measures may undermine your confidence in the results to a certain extent.

Solomon Four-Group Design

Finally, there is a true experimental design that controls for all of the commonly identified internal validity threats. Those that study experimental methodology hold this design as the gold standard in experimental methodology. It is known as the Solomon Four-Group Design:

$$R \quad O_1 \quad X \quad O_2$$
$$R \quad O_3 \quad \quad O_4$$
$$R \quad \quad X \quad O_5$$
$$R \quad \quad \quad O_6$$

Note that this design involves four different groups. There is a test group that receives both a pretest and posttest. There is a posttest-only experimental group, which should allow comparisons to evaluate testing and instrumentation as threats. There is a true control group, which can be used to rule out maturation and history as potential threats. The capacity to rule these out is further improved with the addition of a posttest-only control group. Random assignment should take care of any subject-related problems.

You may be reading the description of this design and wondering two things. First, you may be wondering why we have just walked though nine different designs to arrive at one that controls for everything. Next, you may be wondering why all experimental researchers don't just use the Solomon Four-Group. If this design is so effective at ruling out validity threats, then why wouldn't everyone use it?

Take a look at the design for a minute. You will notice that of the four groups, only one gets a pretest, an induction, and a posttest. This is the group that you would use to test your hypotheses. The other three groups simply exist as checks against validity threats. This makes the design a bit cumbersome and impractical at times.

Let's return to our blue jeans ad from a few pages ago. Suppose you wanted to use the Solomon Four-Group to test the effectiveness of the ad. You randomly sample 200 people from your population, then you randomly assign those 200 people to each of your four conditions. How many people do you actually get to test the ad on?

Fifty. Yes, that's correct. In this particular example, you would have to run (test) 200 research participants in order to obtain the results of fifty. While you could have strong confidence in your results, you would have to spend time, money, and resources collecting data from 150 people that you can't use to test your hypothesis. This lack of economy then increases multiplicatively. If you wanted to gauge the responses of 250 people, you would have to run 1,000 to get 250.

Communication researchers, like all social researchers, do not have unlimited resources. Given the parameters in which they operate—balancing budgets, lab time, student labor, and participant availability—they can seldom use this near perfect design. They are much more likely to think about their research problems, consider the validity threats they are most concerned about, and choose a less complex design, accordingly. In truth, the Nonequivalent Control Group design and the Pretest Posttest Control Group design are much more commonly used, and do an adequate job of ruling out validity threats for the purposes of the communication researcher.

▼ Factorial Design

There's another *wrinkle* to conducting experiments. We've discussed experiments in which the induction either is or isn't. People either see the ad, or they don't. You may have noticed from our real-world examples it's also possible for the induction to have different levels or types. Or, alternatively, you might want to test more than one induction or independent variable at a time. Remember our example earlier of the Lee and Guerrero (2001) study testing reactions to different types of dyadic touch. Their independent variable had nine different levels, or types. In an attempt to account for any changes that might be a product of the gender of the observer, they conducted what is known as a **factorial design**. As we've stated earlier, their type of touch had nine levels. Gender of the observer, obviously, had two levels (male/female). This gave them a 9 × 2 factorial design (read "nine by two") in which each possible combination of these two factors and levels would be shown to the different groups. You can multiply these numbers to tell you how many groups you would need to test all combinations of these factors (in this example, they needed 9 × 2, or 18, groups to test these factors). Here's how this 9 × 2 design would be notated:

factorial designs
Analyses that involve multiple independent variables.

$$R \quad X_{11} \quad O$$
$$R \quad X_{12} \quad O$$
$$R \quad X_{21} \quad O$$
$$R \quad X_{22} \quad O$$
$$R \quad X_{31} \quad O$$
$$R \quad X_{32} \quad O$$
$$R \quad X_{41} \quad O$$
$$R \quad X_{42} \quad O$$
$$R \quad X_{51} \quad O$$
$$R \quad X_{52} \quad O$$
$$R \quad X_{61} \quad O$$
$$R \quad X_{62} \quad O$$
$$R \quad X_{71} \quad O$$
$$R \quad X_{72} \quad O$$
$$R \quad X_{81} \quad O$$
$$R \quad X_{82} \quad O$$
$$R \quad X_{91} \quad O$$
$$R \quad X_{92} \quad O$$

This notation tells us that they had eighteen groups, randomly assigned, each of whom was exposed to a different experimental condition. Group one indicates that they viewed a videotape that includes level one of the touch (handshake) and the observer is categorized as level one on gender (male). Group two viewed a videotape that also uses the handshake but for whom the observer is female. Group three viewed a videotape that has the dyadic partners clasping hands, in which the observer is male. Group four viewed a videotape that has the dyadic partners clasping hands, in which the observer is female, and so on, through all eighteen groups. Of course, participants in each group would be administered the same interview after viewing the video. Using this design, we can easily determine which independent variable, and which combination of independent variables, affects the dependent variable. In case you are wondering, Lee and Guerrero (2001) found that male observers tended to find the touch gestures more flirtatious and indicative of love than did female observers, *regardless of the type of touch*. The authors could determine that these differences were accounted for by the gender of the observer and not by what type of touch they observed.

Communication-related studies frequently use a factorial design. Here's an example of one: Haumer and Donsbach (2009) conducted a study to see how a politician's nonverbal behavior influences his or her image. Using a mock television interview format, they tested viewers' reactions to politicians' communication. They had three independent variables, or factors: nonverbal behavior styles of the politician (active or passive), television host's reactions to the politician (negative, positive, or neutral), and television audience's reactions to the politician (negative, positive, or neutral). This gave them a 2 × 3 × 3 factorial design. Their dependent variables (the effects they expected the independent variables to influence) were the viewers' perceptions of the politician's problem-solving competence, leadership abilities, integrity, and personal qualities. They, again, measured the dependent variables using Likert scale questions in an interview format. They had eighteen groups (2 × 3 × 3) with twenty participants in each. Each group viewed a different video, representing all eighteen possible combinations of the three factors. Note that this is a post-only design, as they did not conduct a pretest prior to administration of the intervention.

▼ Field and Natural Experiments

As we've shown you throughout this chapter, when we talk about experimental designs, we almost immediately think of laboratory experiments. There are other kinds of experiments that can take place outside of the laboratory. A *field experiment* takes place in a naturalistic environment, but nonetheless involves the manipulation of independent variables and some of the design concerns we have already voiced. *Natural experiments* also generally take place in naturalistic environments, but they do not involve variable manipulation—they simply involve analysis of naturally occurring variables. While field and natural experiments may not be as precise as laboratory experiments in terms of control, they are nonetheless valuable in evaluating causal relationships. In fact, they both have one major advantage over laboratory experiments—they have much higher ecological validity. Thus, external validity versus control is a major consideration when deciding whether to do your experiment in the field or in a laboratory.

Here's an interesting example of a field experiment. Argo, Dahl, and Morales (2008) used a field experiment to see how attractiveness affects consumer consumption. Rather than set up a laboratory experiment (can you think of how they might have designed that?), they conducted an experiment in an actual retail shopping environment. They hypothesized that the attractiveness of a person touching a product affects the level of interest another consumer has in purchasing that product. Simply stated, the research was conducted in a university bookstore, and the researchers set up a *confederate* sales clerk (an actor who was in on the experiment) and a *confederate* shopper and had the shopper confederate only handle a T-shirt. They compared shopper attractiveness to interest in purchasing the T-shirt. Note the independent variable (shopper attractiveness) and dependent variable (purchase intent).

In a classic example of a natural experiment, the 1986 research of Holak and Reddy used the 1970 ban against cigarette advertising on television and radio as an independent variable (pre-ban, post-ban). Since the real world had already administered the induction, they were able to test the effect of the television and radio advertising ban on cigarette pricing, advertising spending, and product demand (dependent variables) and found that the ban affected all three of those variables.

Of course, a field experiment such as this one lacks the kind of control one could have in the laboratory. In fact, field experimentalists are often left to make sense of data where they have to decide what constitutes an independent or dependent variable. Complex designs, such as those we described above, are seldom utilized simply because the researchers don't have much control over the environment. They do, however, allow for consideration of causal relationships in more naturalistic settings.

So What?

So what have we uncovered? We have discussed how communication researchers use experimental designs to answer research questions, and in particular we have discussed how micro-level, causal research problems lend themselves well to these types of designs. We then went on to discuss different types of research designs, and how you can build confidence in your findings by strategically using design to address particular internal validity threats. We have discussed the differences between laboratory and field experiments. And finally, we have discussed the ways in which the data derived from an experimental design can be analyzed and interpreted.

Of course, there is a major validity concern related to experimental designs that cannot be overlooked: the problem of external validity. While experimental designs are very useful for demonstrating causal relationships between independent and dependent variables, the extent to which these procedures mirror real-life behaviors may be problematic. This is especially the case with laboratory research. When you go home after class today, you may turn on the television. It is highly unlikely that a stranger will ask you to fill out a survey first, then ask you to fill one out again when you are done. When you talk to a friend, no one subsequently asks you to report how disclosive you found him or her to be. While experiments are very effective at establishing relationships between independent and dependent variables, the extent to which these findings generalize into real-life situations is questionable. Future chapters will detail some research methods that deal more with the experience of communication, as opposed to linear relationships between causes and effects. Again, we will see that the proposition of different questions begs the use of different methods.

Glossary

Baseline
An examination of someone before you expose him or her to a stimulus in order to argue, to a certain extent, that what was done to the subject may have caused any changes that are observed. Also called pretest.

Between-subjects design
Designs comparing multiple groups.

Control group
A group that does not receive induction in an experiment.

Dependent variables
Observations made by the researcher that are not directly controlled by them.

Experimental group
The group of participants to whom you give the induction.

Factorial designs
Analyses that involve multiple independent variables.

Independent variable
Any observation that is controlled by the researcher.

Induction
What is *done* to a participant in an experiment.

Preexperimental designs
Experimental designs that do not involve a true control group; no pretest, posttest, or control group.

Pretest
An examination of someone before you expose him or her to a stimulus in order to argue, to a certain extent, that what was done to the subject may have caused any changes that are observed. Also called baseline measurement.

Posttest
An examination or measurement conducted after administration of the induction.

Quasi-experimental designs
Experimental designs that use pretests and posttests in more complicated ways, but still lack random assignment.

Random assignment
The assignment of people at random to different groups in an experimental design.

Social experiment
A procedure in which researchers take human subjects, do something to them, and observe the effects of what they did to them.

True experimental designs
Experimental designs that randomly assign participants to both experimental and control groups.

Within-subjects design
Designs looking at the same group multiple times.

References

Argo, J. J., Dahl, D. W., & Morales, A. C. (2008). Positive consumer contagion: Responses to attractive others in a retail context. *Journal of Marketing Research, 45,* 690–701.

Baxter, L. A., & Babbie, E. (2004). *The basics of communication research.* Belmont, CA: Wadsworth.

Campbell, D., & Stanley, J. (1963). *Experimental and quasi-experimental designs for research.* Chicago: Rand-McNally.

Duthler, K. W. (2006). The politeness of requests made via email and voicemail: Support for the hyperpersonal model. *Journal of Computer-Mediated Communication, 11*(2), article 6, http://jcmc.indiana.edu/vol11/issue2/duthler.html

Haumer, F., & Donsbach, W. (2009). The rivalry of nonverbal cues on the perception of politicians by television viewers. *Journal of Broadcasting & Electronic Media, 53*(2), 262–279.

Heimendinger, J., O'Neill, C., Marcus, A. C., Wolfe, P., Julesburg, K., Morra, M., Allen, A., Davis, S., Mowad, L., Perocchia, R., Ward, J. D., Strecher, V., Warnecke, R., Nowak, M., Graf, I., Fairclough, D., Bryant, L., & Lipkus, I. (2005). Multiple tailored messages are effective in increasing fruit and vegetable consumption among callers to the Cancer Information Service. *Journal of Health Communication, 10* (Supplement 1), 65–82.

Holak, S. L., & Reddy, S. K. (1986). Effects of a television and radio advertising ban: A study of the cigarette industry. *Journal of Marketing, 50*(4), 219–227.

Lee, J. W., & Guerrero, L. K. (2001). Types of touch in cross-sex relationships between coworkers: Perceptions of relational and emotional messages, inappropriateness, and sexual harassment. *Journal of Applied Communication Research, 29*(3), 197–220.

Triana, M. d. C., Kirkman, B. L., & Wagstaff, M. F. (2012). Does the order of face-to-face and computer-mediated communication matter in diverse project teams? An investigation of communication order effects on minority inclusion and participation. *Journal of Business and Psychology, 27,* 57–70.

QUALITATIVE RESEARCH AND CASE STUDIES

CHAPTER OUTLINE

1. Why Do Case Studies Matter?
2. When Should You Use a Case Study Approach?
3. What is a Case?
4. Limiting Your Case Study
5. Determining the Right Type of Case Study
6. Single or Multiple Case Study Design?
7. Types of Decisions with Case Design
8. Data Management
9. Analysis of Results
10. Compiling the Report
11. Ensuring Trustworthiness of Findings
12. So What?

KEY TERMS

Case
Case Study
Conceptual Framework
Constructivist Paradigm
Explanatory Case Study
Issues
Proposition

CHAPTER OBJECTIVES

1. To understand the importance and significance of a case study
2. To appreciate the differences between the various case study approaches and methodologies
3. To realize the significance of the various case study approaches and the appropriate applications
4. To understand how to conduct a case study and assemble the findings

case studies
A tool that provides researchers with the opportunity to contextually explore an observed phenomenon using a variety of data sources.

Writing a case study is never easy. To students new to case study methodology, there is usually a misunderstanding about what a case study is and how it works. If done properly, a well-developed case study can inform, and ultimately influence, professional practice or evidence-based decision-making.

Contrary to the common belief that case studies can only be used to study individuals or specific historical events, a well-developed qualitative **case study** provides researchers with the opportunity to contextually explore a phenomenon using a variety of data sources. It also empowers researchers to observe individuals or organizations through complex interventions, relationships, communities, or programs (Yin, 2003) and supports the dissection and reconstruction of various phenomena.

Why is this important? Simply put, it ensures that the issue is not explored through one lens but rather a variety of lenses, which allows for multiple facets of the phenomenon to be discovered and understood. There are two key approaches that guide case study methodology; one proposed by Robert Stake (1995) and the other by Robert Yin (2003). Both aim to ensure the research topic of interest is well explored, and the essence of the phenomenon is revealed, but the methods they each use are vastly different.

constructivitst paradigm
A belief based on the principal that truth is relative and dependent upon an individual's perspective.

Both Stake (1995) and Yin (2003) base their approach to case studies on a **constructivist paradigm**. Constructivists claim that truth is relative and dependent on one's perspective. This paradigm "recognizes the importance of the subjective human creation of meaning, but doesn't reject outright some notion of objectivity. Pluralism, not relativism, is stressed with focus on the circular dynamic tension of subject and object" (Crabtree & Miller, 1999, p. 10). Constructivism is built on the belief of a social construction of reality (Searle, 1995). One of the advantages of this approach is the close collaboration between the researcher and the participant, while enabling participants to tell their stories (Crabtree & Miller, 1999, p. 14). Through these stories, participants can describe their views of reality, and this enables the researcher to better understand the participants' actions (Lather, 1992).

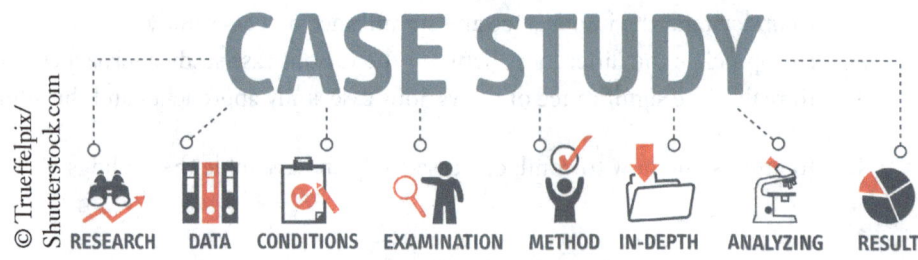

When Should You Use a Case Study Approach?

Before we jump into talking about the nuances of case studies and their use in qualitative research, it is important to point out that a case study approach should not be used for everything. According to Yin (2003), a case study design should be considered when: (a) the focus of the study is to answer "how" and "why" questions; (b) you cannot manipulate the behavior of the participants in the study; (c) you want to cover contextual conditions because you believe they are relevant to the phenomenon under study; or (d) the boundaries are not clear between the phenomenon and context. For example, a study of the decision-making of nursing students conducted by Baxter (Baxter and Rideout, 2006) sought to determine the types of decisions made by nursing students and the factors that influenced them. A case study approach was chosen because the case was the decision-making of nursing students, but the case could not be considered without the context, the school of nursing, and, more specifically, the clinical and classroom settings. It was in these settings that the decision-making skills were developed and utilized.

It would have been impossible for this author to have a true appreciation of the nursing students' decision-making without thinking about the context within which it occurred. Determining the case/unit of Analysis while considering what your research question will be is also something that must be accounted for. This may sound simple, but determining what the unit of analysis (case) is can be a challenge for both novices and seasoned researchers alike.

What Is a Case?

The **case** is defined by Miles and Huberman (1994) as "a phenomenon of some sort occurring in a bounded context. The case is, "in effect, your unit of analysis" (p. 25). Asking yourself the following questions can help determine what your case is; do I want to "analyze" the individual? Do I want to "analyze" a program? Do I want to "analyze" the difference between organizations? For example, with reference to the Baxter study, your question could be "How do women in their 30s who have had breast cancer decide whether or not to have breast reconstruction?" In this example, the case could be the decision-making process of women between the ages of 30 and 40 years who have experienced breast cancer. However, it may be that you are less interested in the activity of decision-making

case
An occurrence that a researcher wishes to analyze.

and more interested in focusing on the experiences of 30- to 40-year-old women. In the first example, the case would focus on the decision-making of the group of women, while the second would analyze the individual experiences of 30- to 40-year-old women.

What is examined has shifted in these examples—one is focused on a group process, whereas the other looks at individual experiences.

▼ Limiting Your Case Study

Once you have determined what your case will be, you must consider what your case will *not* be. One of the common problems associated with case study methodology is that there is a tendency for researchers to attempt to answer a question that is too broad. Or they choose a topic that has too many objectives for one study. In order to avoid this problem, several authors, including Yin (2003) and Stake (1995), have suggested that placing boundaries on a case can prevent this explosion from happening. Researchers have offered many suggestions on how to set parameters for a case, including: (a) By time and place (Creswell, 2003); (b) By time and activity (Stake, 1995); and (c) By definition and context (Miles & Huberman, 1994). By setting limits on the study, you help to ensure your study remains reasonable in scope.

In the example of the study involving women who must decide whether or not to have reconstructive surgery, established boundaries would need to include a precise definition of breast cancer and reconstructive surgery. It would have to indicate where the women received care or where they made decisions and the period of time researchers were interested in learning about, for example, within nine months of a radical mastectomy.

It would be unreasonable to look at all women in their 30s across a country who had experienced breast cancer and their decisions regarding reconstructive surgery. It would be simply too large a population to study. Another approach would be to look at single women in their 30s who have received care in a tertiary care center as opposed to a large, research hospital. As is evident by the scope, the boundaries indicate what will and will not be studied in the research project. By setting boundaries in a qualitative case study, you are establishing parameters similar to the development of inclusion and exclusion criteria for sample selection in a quantitative study. The difference is these boundaries also indicate the breadth and depth of the study and not simply the sample to be included.

Determining the Type of Case Study

Once you have determined that the research question is best answered through a qualitative case study approach, it is important to consider what type of case study will be conducted. The selection of a specific type of case study design will be guided by the overall study purpose. Are you looking to describe a case, explore a case, or compare between cases? Yin (2003) and Stake (1995) use different terms to describe a variety of case studies. Yin categorizes case studies as explanatory, exploratory, or descriptive. He also differentiates between single, holistic case studies and multiple case studies, whereas Stake labels them as intrinsic, instrumental, or collective.

Yin's Case Study Ideas

Below is a brief description of each of Yin's suggested case approaches:

- **Explanatory:** This approach is suggested if you are looking to answer a question that is attempting to explain the presumed causal links in real-life interventions that are too complex for the survey or experimental strategies. In evaluation language, the explanations would link program implementation with program effects (Yin, 2003).
- **Exploratory:** This type of case study is used to explore situations in which the intervention being evaluated has no clear, single set of outcomes (Yin, 2003).

- **Descriptive:** This type of case study is used to describe an intervention or phenomenon and the real-life context in which it occurred (Yin, 2003).
- **Multiple Case Studies:** A multiple case study approach enables the researcher to explore differences within and between cases. The goal is to replicate findings across cases. Because comparisons are drawn, it is important that the cases are chosen carefully. This empowers the researcher to predict similar results across cases or forecast contrasting results based on a theory (Yin, 2003).

Stake's Case Study Ideas

The following list provides an overview and brief explanation of each Stake's case study approaches:

- **Intrinsic:** This approach should be taken when researchers, who have a genuine interest in the case, want to gain a better appreciation of the situation. This methodology is typically used in unusual cases. It is not undertaken because the case represents other cases or because it illustrates a particular trait or problem. It is usually used because in all its particularity and ordinariness, the case itself is of interest. The purpose is *not* to understand some abstract construct or generic phenomenon (Stake, 1995).

- **Instrumental:** This approach is used to accomplish something other than understanding a specific situation. It provides better insight into an issue or helps to refine a theory. With this approach, the case is of secondary interest because it truly facilitates our understanding of something else. The case is looked at in depth, its contexts scrutinized, and its ordinary activities detailed (Stake, 1995).
- **Collective:** Collective case studies are similar in nature and description to multiple case studies. Once again, it is important that the cases being examined are of similar scope so the researcher can draw logical conclusions based on the data being examined (Stake, 1995).

Single or Multiple Case Study Designs

In addition to identifying the "case" and the specific "type" of case study to be conducted, researchers must consider if they should conduct a single case study. Or, if a better understanding of the phenomenon would be gained through by conducting multiple case studies. For example, if we re-consider the topic of breast reconstruction surgery, we can begin to discuss how to determine the "type" of case study and the necessary number of cases to study.

A Single Case Study

A single holistic case might be the decision-making of one woman or a single group of 30-year-old women facing breast reconstruction. But it is also important to take the context into consideration: Are you going to look at these women in one environment because it is a unique or extreme situation? If so, you can consider a holistic single case study (Yin, 2003).

If you were interested in looking at the same issue, but were fascinated by the different decisions made by women attending different clinics within one hospital, then a holistic case study with embedded units would enable the researcher to explore the case while considering the influence of the various clinics and associated attributes on the women's decision-making. The opportunity to look at subunits that are situated within a larger case is powerful when you consider that data can be analyzed within the subunits separately (within case analysis), between the different subunits (between case analysis), or across all of the subunits (cross-case analysis). The challenge researchers often encounter is they analyze at the individual subunit level and fail to return to the macro issue they initially set out to address (Yin, 2003).

Multiple Case Studies

If a study contains more than a single case, then a multiple case study approach is required. This is often associated with multiple experiments. You might find yourself asking, "What is the difference between a holistic case study with embedded units and a multiple case study design?" Simply put, the context is different for each of the cases. A multiple or collective case study methodology allows the researcher to analyze within each setting and across settings. A holistic case study, by contrast, with embedded units allows the researcher to understand only one unique/extreme/critical case. By using a mutiple case study design, researchers can examine several cases to understand the similarities and differences between the cases. Yin (2003) describes how multiple case studies can be used to either "(a) predict similar results (a literal replication) or (b) predict contrasting results but for predictable reasons (a theoretical replication)" (p. 47). This type of design has its pros and cons. Overall, the evidence created from this type of study is considered robust, but it can also be extremely time consuming and expensive to conduct. Using the same example, if you wanted to study women in various health-care institutions across a country, then a multiple or collective case study would be employed. The case would still be the decision-making of women in their 30s, but you could also analyze the different decision-making processes engaged in by women in the different centers.

Stake (1995) uses three terms to describe case studies: intrinsic, instrumental, and collective. From Stake's perspective, if you are interested in studying a unique situation, you should use an intrinsic approach. This simply means you have an inherent interest in the subject and are aware that the results have limited transferability. If the intent is to gain insight and understanding of a particular situation or phenomenon, then Stake recommends using an instrumental case study to gain understanding. He uses the term collective case study when more than one case is being examined. The same example used to describe multiple case studies can be applied here.

Once the case approach has been identified and the boundaries determined, it is important to consider the additional components required for designing and implementing a rigorous case study. These include: (a) propositions (which may or may not be present) (Yin, 2003; Miles & Huberman, 1994); (b) the application of a conceptual framework (Miles & Huberman, 1994); (c) development of the research questions (generally "how" and/or "why" questions); (d) the logic linking data to propositions; and (e) the criteria for interpreting findings (Yin, 2003).

Propositions
A guideline a researcher uses in the execution of the research study.

Propositions

Propositions are helpful in any case study, but they are not always present. When a case study proposal includes specific propositions, it increases the possibility that the researcher will be able to place limits on the scope of the study and increases the feasibility of completing the project. The more a study contains specific propositions, the more it will stay within feasible limits. So where do the propositions come from? Propositions may come from the literature, personal or professional experience, theories, and/or generalizations based on empirical data.

For example, one proposition included in a study on the development of nursing student decision-making in a clinical setting stated that "various factors influence nurse decision making including the decision maker's knowledge, and experience, feelings of fear, and degree of confidence" (Baxter and Rideout, 2006). This proposition was based on the literature found on the topic of nurse decision-making. The researcher can employ multiple propositions to guide the study, but each must have a distinct focus and purpose. These propositions later influence the data collection and discussion. Each proposition serves to focus the data collection, determine direction and scope of the study, and together the propositions form the foundation for a conceptual structure or framework (Miles & Huberman, 1994; Stake, 1995).

It is important to realize that propositions may not be present in exploratory holistic or intrinsic case studies because the researcher does not have enough experience, knowledge, or information on which to base propositions. For those familiar with quantitative approaches to experimental studies, propositions can be equated to hypotheses in that they both make an educated guess to the possible outcomes of the experiment/research study. A common challenge for case study researchers is to include too many propositions and then find they are overwhelmed by the number of propositions that must be returned to when analyzing the data and reporting the findings.

Propositions versus Issues

To contribute to the confusion that exists surrounding the implementation of different types of qualitative case study approaches, where Yin (2003) uses "propositions" to guide the research process, Stake (1995) applies what he terms "issues." Stake states, "**Issues** are not simple and clean, but intricately wired to political, social, historical, and especially personal contexts. All these meanings are important in studying cases" (p. 17). Both Yin and Stake suggest the propositions and issues are necessary elements in case study research because they lead to the development of a conceptual framework that guides the research.

Both Stake (1995) and Yin (2003) refer to conceptual frameworks, but they don't fully describe them or provide a model of a conceptual framework for reference. An excellent source for examples of conceptual frameworks is Miles and Huberman (1994). These authors explain that a **conceptual framework** serves several purposes: (a) identifying who will and will not

Issues
A complexity relating to the research study.

conceptual framework
The foundation for a research study that is designed by the researcher.

be included in the study; (b) describing what relationships may be present based on logic, theory, and/or experience; and (c) providing the researcher with the opportunity to gather general constructs into intellectual "bins" (Miles & Huberman, 1994, p. 18). The conceptual framework serves as the foundation for the study and is referred to at the stage of data interpretation.

For example, an initial framework was developed by Baxter (2003) in her exploration of nursing student decision-making. The framework was based on the literature and her personal experiences. The major constructs were proposed in the following manner: (Adapted from Baxter, 2003, p. 28). The reader will note that the framework does not display relationships between the constructs. The framework should continue to evolve and be completed as the study progresses, and the relationships between the proposed constructs will emerge as data are analyzed. A final conceptual framework will include all the themes that emerged from data analysis.

Yin (2003) suggests that returning to the propositions that initially formed the conceptual framework ensures the analysis is reasonable and that it provides structure for the final report. One of the drawbacks of a conceptual framework is that it could limit the inductive approach when exploring a phenomenon. To protect the study from being deductive, researchers are encouraged to record their thoughts and decisions and discuss them with other researchers to determine whether their thinking has become too influenced by the framework.

▼ Types of Decisions

A key trait of case study research is the use of multiple data sources, a strategy that also enhances data credibility (Patton, 1990; Yin, 2003). Potential data sources include documentation, archival records, interviews, focus groups, direct observations, and participant-observation. Unique in comparison to other qualitative approaches, within case study research, investigators can collect and integrate quantitative survey data, which allows reaching a holistic understanding of the phenomenon being studied.

In case studies, data from these multiple sources are then combined in the analysis process rather than handled individually. Each data source is one piece of the "puzzle," with each part contributing to the researcher's understanding of the larger picture. This convergence adds strength to the findings as the various pieces of data are brought together to promote a greater understanding of the case. Although the opportunity to gather data from multiple sources is attractive because of the rigor associated with this approach, there are potential challenges.

One possible pitfall is the collection of overwhelming amounts of data that require management and analysis. Often, researchers find themselves overwhelmed by the data. In order to bring organization to the data collection, a computerized database is often used to organize and manage the voluminous amount of material.

Data Management

Both Yin (2003) and Stake (1995) recognize the importance of effectively organizing data. The advantage of using a database is that raw data is available for independent inspection. Using a database also improves the reliability of the case study as it helps the researcher track and organize data sources including notes, key documents, narratives, photographs, and audio files.

Analysis

As in any other qualitative study, the data collection and analysis occur concurrently. The type of analysis employed depends on the type of case study. Yin (2003) briefly describes five techniques for analysis: pattern matching, explanation building, time-series analysis, and logic models. In contrast, Stake (1995) describes categorical aggregation and direct interpretation as types of analysis. It is important to review various types of analysis and to determine which approach you are most comfortable with for your study and work.

Below is a list and brief explanation of each of Yin's data analysis techniques:

- **Pattern matching:** Pattern matching is the comparison of two patterns to determine whether they match (i.e., that they are the same) or not (i.e., that they differ). Pattern matching is the core procedure of theory-testing with cases (Mills, Durepos, & Wiebe, 2010).
- **Explanation building:** An explanation—a good, successful, satisfactory, adequate, or acceptable explanation—is intended to act as an answer to a specific research question. What counts as an explanation depends on the interest of the researcher (Mills, Durepos, & Wiebe, 2010).
- **Time-series analysis:** Time series analysis is a statistical technique that deals with time series data, or trend analysis.

Time series data means that data is in a series of particular time periods or intervals (Yin, 2003).
- **Logic models:** A logic model is a visual diagram that illustrates how your program will work to fill a researcher's identified needs for their research project (Yin, 2003).

Below is a listing and explanation of Stake's two approaches for data analytics:
- **Categorical aggregation:** Entails compiling a collection of themes from the data, hoping that significant meaning about lessons to be learned about the case will result (Stake, 1995).
- **Direct interpretation:** Literal interpretation of a situation as or after it occurs (Stake, 1995).

From Yin's perspective, an important practice during the analysis phase of any case study is the return to the propositions. This is important for several reasons, according to Yin. First, it leads to a focused analysis when the temptation is to analyze data outside the scope of the research questions. Second, exploring rival propositions is an attempt to provide another explanation of a phenomenon. Third, by partaking in this process the confidence in the findings is increased as the number of propositions and rival propositions are addressed and accepted or rejected.

One pitfall associated with the analysis phase is that each data source is treated independently and the findings reported separately. This is not the purpose of a case study. Rather, the researcher must ensure the data are synthesized in an attempt to understand the overall case, not the parts of it or the contributing factors that influence it. One strategy that helps ensure a researcher remains focused on the original case is to involve other research members in the analysis phase. It is also important to ask for feedback on the data sources, as well as the integration of the findings. Such perspectives can provide a researcher with insights and out-of-the-box ideas of possible applications of their findings.

Reporting a Case Study

Reporting a case study can be a hard task for any researcher because of the complex nature of this approach. It is tough to report the findings in a concise manner, and yet it is the researcher's responsibility to convert a complex phenomenon into a format that is readily understood. The goal of the report is to describe the study in such a comprehensive manner as to ensure the reader feels as if he or she had been an active participant in the research. It is important that the researcher describe the context within which the phenomenon is occurring, as well as the phenomenon itself. There is no one correct way to report a case study. However, some suggested ways are by telling the reader a story, by providing a chronological report, or by addressing each proposition.

Addressing the propositions ensures the report remains focused and deals with the research question. One of the biggest hurdles in report writing is not being distracted by the mounds of interesting data that are superfluous to the research question. Returning to the propositions or issues ensures the researcher avoids this pitfall. Yin (2003) suggests six methods for reporting a case study. These include linear, comparative, chronological, theory building, suspense, and unsequenced. (Refer to Yin for full descriptions.)

Strategies for Achieving Trustworthiness in Case Study Research

Many frameworks have been developed to evaluate the rigor or assess the trustworthiness of qualitative data (e.g., Guba, 1981; Lincoln & Guba, 1985), and strategies for establishing credibility, transferability, dependability, and confirmability have been extensively written about across fields (e.g., Krefting, 1991; Sandelowski, 1986, 1993). In addition, guidelines for critically appraising qualitative research have also been published (e.g., Forchuk & Roberts, 1993; Mays & Pope, 2000).

For beginning researchers, designing and implementing a case study project, there are several basic key elements to the design of the study that can be included to enhance the overall quality of the study. For example, researchers using this method will want to ensure sufficient detail is provided so readers can assess the validity or credibility of the work. It is important that researchers ensure that: (a) the case study research question is clearly written, propositions are provided, and the question is substantiated; (b) case study design is appropriate for the research question; (c) purposeful sampling strategies appropriate for case study have been applied; (d) data are collected and managed; and (e) the data are analyzed correctly (Russell, Gregory, Ploeg, DiCenso, & Guyatt, 2005).

Case study research design principles lend themselves to including numerous strategies that promote data credibility or "truth value." Triangulation of data sources and data types is a primary strategy that can be used and would support the principle in case study research that the phenomena be viewed and explored from multiple perspectives. The collection and comparison of this data enhance data quality based on the principles of idea convergence and the confirmation of findings (Knafl & Breitmayer, 1989). It is also important to look for opportunities to have extended exposure to the phenomenon being examined within its context so that relationship with participants can be established. It also helps to ensure a number of perspectives can be collected and understood and to reduce the potential for social desirability responses in interviews (Krefting, 1991).

As data are collected and analyzed, researchers may want to integrate a process of member checking, where the researchers' interpretations of the data are shared with the participants and the participants have the opportunity to discuss and clarify the interpretation and contribute new or additional perspectives. Additional strategies employed in qualitative studies include the use of reflection or the maintenance of field notes and peer examination of the data. At the analysis stage, the consistency of the findings can be promoted by having multiple researchers independently code a set of data and then meet to come to a consensus on the emerging codes and categories (Krefting, 1991).

Case study research is more than simply conducting research on a single individual or situation. This approach has the potential to deal with everything from the simplest to the most complex situations. It enables the researcher to answer "how"- and "why"-type questions, while taking into consideration how a phenomenon is influenced by the context within which it is situated.

So What?

In summary, there is no right or wrong way to carry out a case study. So much of the case study approach, relies on the objectives of the research an the goals of the researcher. It is important to consider the differences between the perspectives and methodologies before deciding the best path.

Glossary

Case
An occurrence that a researcher wishes to analyze.

Case studies
A tool that provides researchers with the opportunity to contextually explore an observed phenomenon using a variety of data sources.

Conceptual framework
The foundation for a research study that is designed by the researcher.

Constructivitst paradigm
A belief based on the principal that truth is relative and dependent upon an individual's perspective.

Issues
A complexity relating to the research study.

Propositions
A guideline a researcher uses in the execution of the research study

References

Baxter, P. 2003. "An Exploration of Student Decision Making as Experienced by Second Year Baccalaureate Nursing Students in a Surgical Clinical Setting." Unpublished master's thesis, McMaster University, Hamilton, ON.

Baxter, P., and Jack, S. (2008). Qualitative Case Study Methodology: Study Design and Implementation for Novice Researchers . *The Qualitative Report, 13*(4), 544–559. Retrieved from https://nsuworks.nova.edu/tqr/vol13/iss4/2

Baxter, P., and L. Rideout. 2006. "The Development of Nurse Decision Making: A Case Study of a Four Year Baccalaureate Nursing Programme." Unpublished doctoral thesis, McMaster University, Hamilton, ON.

Campbell, R., and C. E. Ahrens. 1998. "Decision Making of 2nd year Baccalaureate Nursing Students." *Journal of Nursing Education, 45*(4), 121–128.

Crabtree, Benjamin F. and William L. Miller. 1999. *Doing Qualitative Research.* 2nd ed. Sage Publications.

Creswell, J. 1998. "Innovative Community Services for Rape Victims: An Application of Multiple Case Study Methodology." *American Journal of Community Psychology, 26,* 537–571.

Creswell, J. 2003. *"Research Design: Qualitative, Quantitative and Mixed Methods Approaches "* 2nd ed. Sage Publications.

Forchuk, C., and J. Roberts. 1993. *Research Design: Qualitative, Quantitative, and Mixed Methods Approaches.* 2nd ed. Thousand Oaks, CA: Sage.

Guba, E. 1981. "How to Critique Qualitative Research Articles." *Canadian Journal of Nursing Research, 25,* 47–55.

Hancock, D. R., & B. Algozzine. 2006. "Criteria for Assessing the Trustworthiness of Naturalistic Inquiries." *Educational Resources Information Center Annual Review Paper, 29,* 75–91.

Handel, N., M. Silverstein, E. Waisman, J. Waisman, and E. Gierson. 1990. *Doing Case Study Research: A Practical Guide for Beginning Researchers.* New York: Teachers College Press.

Hellström, I., M. Nolan, and U. Lundh. 2005. "Reasons Why Mastectomy Patients do not have Breast Reconstruction." *Plastic Reconstruction Surgery, 86*(6), 1118–1122.

John R. Searle. 1995. *The Construction of Social Reality.* Simon & Schuster. New York.

Joia, L. A. (2002). "We Do Things Together." A Case Study of "Couplehood" in Dementia. *Dementia, 4*(1), 7–22.

Knafl, K., & B. J. Breitmayer. (1989). "Analyzing a Web-Based E-Commerce Learning Community: A Case Study in Brazil." *Internet Research,* 12, 305–317.

Krefting, L. March 1991. "Rigor in Qualitative Research: The Assessment of Trustworthiness" *American Journal of Occupational Therapy,* 45, 214–222.

Lather, P. (1992). "Rigor in Qualitative Research: The Assessment of Trustworthiness." *American Journal of Occupational Therapy,* 45, 214–222.

Lincoln, Y. S., & E. A. Guba. 1985. "Critical Frames in Educational Research: Feminist and Post-Structural Perspectives." *Theory into Practice, 31*(2), 87–99.

Lotzkar, M., & J. Bottorff. 2001. *Naturalistic Inquiry.* Beverly Hills, CA: Sage.

Luck, L., D. Jackson, and K. Usher. 2007. "An Observational Study of the Development of a Nurse/Patient Relationship." *Clinical Nursing Research,* 10, 275–294.

Mays, N., & C. Pope. 2000. "STAMP: Components of Observable Behavior that Indicate Potential for Patient Violence in Emergency Departments." *Journal of Advanced Nursing,* 59, 11–19.

Miles, M. B., & A. M. Huberman. 1994. "Qualitative Research in Health Care: Assessing Quality in Qualitative Research." BMJ, 320, 50–52.

Mills, A. J., Durepos, G., & Wiebe, .E. 2010. *Encyclopedia of Case Study Research*. Sage, 2010.

Patton, M. (1990). *Qualitative evaluation and research methods* (pp. 169–186). Beverly Hills, CA: Sage.

Russell, C., Gregory, D., Ploeg, J., DiCenso, A., & Guyatt, G. (2005). Qualitative research. In A. DiCenso, G. Guyatt, & D. Ciliska (Eds.), *Evidence-based nursing: A guide to clinical practice* (pp. 120–135). St. Louis, MO: Elsevier Mosby.

Stake, R. 1995. *The Art of Case Study Research*. Thousand Oaks, CA: Sage Publications.

Yin, R.K. 2003. *Case Study Research: Design and Methods*. London: Sage.

PUTTING IT ALL TOGETHER

CHAPTER OUTLINE

1. Developing the Basics of Your Communication Research Toolkit
2. Research Theory and Logic
3. Research Objectives and the Research Question
4. Research Hypothesis
5. Determining Your Variables
6. Relationships Between Variables
7. Research Techniques: Sampling
   a. Establishing a Sampling Framework
8. Research Techniques: Surveys
   a. Benefits of Survey Research
   b. Designing Your Survey
   c. Specific of Longitudinal Design
   d. Building a Survey Questionnaire
   e. Arranging the Survey Questions
   f. Administering a Research Survey
9. Research Techniques: Experiments
   a. Building Blocks of an Experiment
   b. Important Terms in Experiment Design
   c. Designing Your Experiment
10. Research Techniques: Field Work
11. Research Techniques: Focus Groups
12. Candidate Selection
13. Budgets
14. Timelines
15. Research Study Checklist
16. So What?

KEY TERMS

confounding variables
dependent variables
experiments
extraneous variables
fact pattern
field work

focus groups
hypothesis
independent variables
mediating variables
moderating variables
relationships

research objectives
research questions
sampling
surveys
variables

149

Chapter Objectives

1. To realize the various techniques and opportunities available to researchers in the design of a communication research study
2. To identify the advantages and limitations of each of the various techniques
3. To understand how to design and implement a strategic and comprehensive communication research study

When it comes to the real world, and more importantly the real world of communication research, the challenge is figuring out which techniques to implement at which point in the research process. In addition to understanding the pros and cons of each technique, as well as the advantages and disadvantages of each, there are many additional factors that come into play when recommending and ultimately deciding which tools to use.

In this chapter, we will explore the communication research toolkit and review the appropriate tools for use at specific points in the process. In addition, we will review the external factors that come into play including budget, timelines, access to candidates, and other environmental factors that can influence the outputs of the communication research process.

▼ Developing the Basics of Your Communication Research Toolkit

Imagine you are working at one of the big advertising, public relations, or marketing firms and your client comes to you with an idea for a new product. They have asked you to evaluate the product's potential with insights on possible target markets, product appeals, and overall marketability. Sounds great but where do you start?

In this complicated world of old school and new school research techniques, it is important to start by simply examining all of your options and determining what will work best for your client. Let's start with some of the ideas we explored in Chapter 2 "Research, Questions, Objectives and Hypotheses," where we discussed the concepts of theory, research objectives, research questions, and the research hypothesis. As explained, these concepts are critical in setting the agenda and framework for the research process. Not only do these concepts help interpret the realities of a situation, but they also allow researchers to see the short-term ramifications as well as, predict the long-term effects of changing the elements of situation.

Research Theory and Logic

The first step in setting the research agenda is determining **which type of research is going to be conducted and the type of theory and related logic that will be applied.** There are two primary paths to consider—*the positivist paradigm* that is based on deductive rationale or *the interpretive paradigm* that is based on inductive rationale. Each varies greatly as far as their perspective and subsequent approach are concerned. With the positivist paradigm, the research questions and hypotheses are built on existing theory and look to extend, test, or further enhance its foundational understanding. In general, researchers that use this approach believe reality is predictable, manageable, and objective.

By contrast, with the interpretive paradigm, the focus is on the exploration and development of new theory or ideas. As a result, researchers with this approach seek responses to open-ended questions, often resulting in new insights on an existing theory or possible basis for an entirely new one. The majority of researchers following the interpretive paradigm believe reality is subjective, unpredictable, and difficult to control.

Regardless of whether you elect to use a deductive or inductive approach, all theories begin with the adoption of a **fact pattern or question**. Simply put, the fact pattern is the factual relationship occurring frequently throughout a research project, while the question is the quest for the answer as to why something happens.

fact pattern
The factual relationship that occurs frequently throughout a research project.

Research Objectives and the Research Question

After deciding the approach and basis for your theory, you **have to set your research objectives.** As explained earlier in the text, research objectives are the rationale for a research project. In many ways, they set the stage for the creation of your research questions and the formulation of your hypothesis. When asked to initiate a research study, the first thing you will do is decide your area of inquiry and then determine your specific focus. It is important the focus be specific enough to develop a research agenda around it.

Simply put, your research objectives communicate the overarching purpose of the research study and what you hope to learn from it. It can be as simple as filling in the blanks in the following statement: "I am studying _____, because I want to find out [who/what/when/where/whether/how] _____ is, in order to understand _____". All research studies should relate to a larger issue in some way. Think of it as filling in the last piece

research objectives
The rationale for the research project.

Research questions
Primary questions that guide the focus of the research study. Simply put, they are the areas or issues that you are exploring.

of a giant puzzle—your research can be the piece that solves a problem or provides a critical insight. Often research objectives are the platform for the formulation of research questions or the research hypotheses.

Research questions play a critical role in any research study as they are the basis for the exploration. In communication research, most of these questions are about the nature of communication or the relationship between two or more factors. Most of them focus on the who, what, when, where, and how of communication. There are two primary types of research questions: *questions of definition* and *questions of fact*.

Research Hypothesis

research question
The overarching question you are trying to answer as a result of your research study.

hypothesis
A statement about the relationship of at least two variables of a research study.

After you have formed you primary **research question,** the next step is determining your **hypothesis.** As a reminder, a hypothesis is a statement about the relationship between at least two of the variables of the research. In most cases, it is the researcher's guess as to how these concepts are thought to be related. Researchers typically form a hypothesis based upon prior knowledge of or experience with the subject matter. Within the hypothesis, there are two key types of relationships that are specified: relationship of association and relationship of causation. A relationship of association suggests that where one variable is found, the other will also be found. In contrast, a causal relationship implies that one variable causes a change in the direction of the other.

Now that we have revisited the concepts of research theory, research objectives, research questions, and a research hypothesis, let's focus on setting up your research toolkit. Just like the hammer, screw driver, wrench, and tape measure are essential to any hardware toolkit, there are a few critical elements for the communication research toolkit, namely, variables, sampling, surveys, and experiments. The first area we will explore is variables.

Determining Your Variables

As described in Chapter 4, "Understanding Variables," variables can be any concept with the ability to take on more than one value. There are two primary considerations to take into account when deciding your variables. The first is the conceptual definition—the way you describe the variable you intend to study. The second is the operational definition—the observable characteristics of a concept. Without a clear understanding of the conceptual and operational definitions, it is incredibly challenging to determine variables that sufficiently answer the research questions and hypothesis.

The hardest part of defining a variable is in the conceptual fit between what is measured and what you intended to measure. In other words, it is how closely your operational definition matches your conceptual definition. To gauge your conceptual fit, some of the questions you can ask is:

- Is the operational definition adequate or complete?
- Does it include all of the essential aspects of a variable? Is it accurate?
- Do you agree with how the research measured the variable? Does it make sense?

It is important to realize that while researchers try to be as thorough and complete in their operational definition, most are not all encompassing. In addition, it is almost impossible to capture the true meaning of some constructs with a single variable. The bottom line: Nothing is perfect. As the researcher, you need to decide based upon the conceptual and operational definitions if you have an acceptable conceptual fit to support the focus of the research. If not, it is important to recalibrate both factors so that you do.

In terms of establishing your variables for a communication research project, it is important to remember that there are two basic types: independent and dependent. An **independent variable** is the variable that is thought to predict or strongly influence the value of another variable. The **dependent variable** is the variable that relies on or is determined by another variable. In pragmatic terms, the independent variable is the one the researcher changes or what the research changes, while the dependent variable is what the researcher gauges.

Occasionally, a third type of variable, called an **extraneous variable,** will make discovering the true relationship between the independent and the dependent variables tough. Why? It is because the additional variable is another possible cause of the effect on the dependent variable. Usually, the extraneous variable is considered to be unpredictable and uncontrollable by the researcher or one that wasn't part of the original research design. A specific type of extraneous variable called a **confounding variable** periodically makes it way into a research study. In a sense, these variables confuse a research study as they muddle the relationship between the independent and dependent variable. When designing a research study and identifying your variables, it is important to try to identify possible confounding variables and eliminate them in the design of the study.

As a reminder, there are two additional variables that can also effect the dependent variable: **mediating variables and moderating variables.** These are vastly different from extraneous variables as they are usually predicted and controlled by the researcher.

independent variable
A variable that is thought to predict or strongly influence the value of another variable.

dependent variable
A variable that relies on or is determined by another variable.

extraneous variable
A variable that was unpredicted or unforeseen by the researcher. It can have a significant impact or pose a significant threat to the success of the research study.

confounding variable
A variable that causes a conflict between the dependent and independent variables.

mediating variables
A variable that explains the relationship between the dependent variable and the independent variable.

moderating variables
A variable that changes the strength or direction of an effect between two variables X and Y.

Relationships Between Variables

After deciding the variables for your research study, you must consider the potential **relationships** between them. There are several types of relationships that exist:

- *Reversible vs. Irreversible:* Reversible relationships can go either way, while irreversible ones can only go one way.

relationships
The interplay between variables in a research study. There are several possible types.

- *Deterministic vs. Stochastic:* Deterministic relationships occur when the dependent variable must result from the independent, while stochastic relationships are ones that are likely to occur.
- *Sequential vs. Coextensive:* Sequential relationships are those where the ordering of the variables is imperative and must occur sequentially, either chronologically or in order. In coextensive relationships, the variables in the relationship co-occur or happen simultaneously.
- *Sufficient vs. Contingent:* In sufficient relationships, the presence or change in one variable can cause a change in a second variable, while in contingent relationships one variable is enough to warrant a third variable, if necessary.
- *Necessary vs. Substitutable Relationships:* With necessary relationships, one variable must be present for the second one to be present, whereas substitutable relationships are those where other forces might bring about the same effect as a necessary relationship.

A final thing to consider when determining your research variables are the dimensions or the complexity of them. Some variables are considered unidimensional as they are not complicated and require only one question or a short series of questions to answer. However, there are other variables that are substantially more complicated, often requiring more than one component or dimension. These are called multidimensional.

Research Techniques: Sampling

Now that we have talked about determining the variables for your study, we will move into reviewing the techniques you could use to conduct your study. The first technique we will review and explore is **sampling**. Sampling is a critical component of most research studies. It is considered crucial for ensuring the quality, validity, and credibility of any research study. Without exposing the idea or the product to actual users from the proposed target market, the plausibility of the idea can be easily questioned. Proper sampling ensures you are adequately representing the group you claim to be representing.

As discussed in Chapter 5, "Understanding Sampling," there are several key components of any sample study:

- *Sample:* Representatives of the population you are studying
- *Population:* Group of people you are claiming to generalize based on the sample
- *Sampling Frame:* A realistic version of your population you can easily identify and access. In most cases, it is a list representative of your potential sampling population.

sampling
A research technique where a researcher tests out a potential product or idea with a probable target market.

- *Sampling Units:* What your unit of analysis will be in the sampling such as individuals, sites, activities, events, times, or artifacts.

Establishing a Sampling Framework

After you determine the population you are going to sample, identify the sampling frame, and define the unit of analysis, the next step is to establish which sampling method you will use. As discussed in earlier in the book, there are many sampling methods to choose from so we will do a quick review of them for both the quantitative and qualitative forms of research. Let's start with the choices for conducting quantitative research:

- *Simple Random Sampling:* A group of subjects are chosen from a larger group for participation in a sampling study. In this case, everyone in the original population has an equal chance of being selected.
- *Systematic Random Sampling:* A list of the sampling population is created, a seed number is selected, and participants are chosen based upon multiples of the seed number. For example, every tenth or twelfth individual or unit would be an example of this method.
- *Stratified Sampling:* A technique where different subcategories of the sample are determined and then randomly selected.
- *Proportional Stratified Sampling:* A method of sampling where different subcategories of the sample are identified and then chosen relative to their representation in the population.
- *Cluster Sampling:* A form of sampling where groups are identified based upon their overall representation of the population. These groups are then sampled randomly, resulting in each group representing the population.
- *Nonrandom Sampling:* A sample that is not a random sample.
- *Convenience Sampling:* It is the sampling of a group of people that are easy and simple to access.
- *Volunteer Sampling:* The sampling of a group of people who volunteer to be tested.
- *Snowball Sampling:* The creation of a sampling study based on referrals. After completion of the first sample group, the respondents are asked to refer additional participants.
- *Network Sampling:* The creation of a sampling group based on the selection of participations from specific business or social networks.

Now let's examine the choices for conducting qualitative research:

- *Purposive Sampling:* Samples chosen for a specific purpose.
- *Quota Sampling:* A type of non-probability technique that establishes quotas for each of the primary categories to identify

the number of members of the sample that should be put into each of the categories.
- *Maximum Variation Sampling:* A method that chooses participants for a study who represent a broad range of traits that are present in the population and relevant to the research study.
- *Theoretical Construct Sampling:* An approach that selects participants with characteristics representing theories on which a study is based.
- *Typical Instance Sampling:* The testing of units with traits primarily found within a population.
- *Extreme Instance Sampling:* The sampling of subjects with tendencies vastly different from the rest of the population.

▼ Research Techniques: Surveys

A second important technique in conducting communication research is surveys. When most of us think of research and conducting a research study, we think of taking a survey. Ever since the concept of research came into being, surveys have been everyone's go-to methodology for gauging opinion. **Surveys** come in all shapes and sizes and are used across a variety of industries. Think of all of the surveys you have taken in your life, they probably range from teacher and restaurant evaluations to design reviews or movie ratings. Regardless of where you live or what college or university you attend, you have inevitably taken a lot of surveys and will take even more in the future.

Why are surveys so popular? It is for four primary reasons:

- *Ease-of-Use:* It is an easy way of gathering a lot of information from a large number of people in a short period of time.
- *Simple and Inexpensive:* They are relatively simple and cost-effective to administer.
- *Easily Understood:* It is a straightforward research strategy and a reliable measurement technique.
- *Design Flexibility:* Researchers can design them to include both quantitative and qualitative questions.

Benefits of Survey Research

Given the immense number of benefits that come with this research technique, it is used to measure a variety of perspectives:

- *Attitudes:* Anytime you are creating a campaign to promote a product, service, or behavior, you will more than likely want to analyze your potential target market to gauge how they feel

Surveys
A research technique where a researcher collects feedback from a potential user through a formal question asking process. Surveys can be administered in-person, on-line, in small groups or randomly carried out.

about your topic. Designing and implementing a survey is one of the most effective ways to do it.
- *Past Behavior:* Sometimes you may want to measure how a target group felt about something in the past as compared to how they currently feel about it. Creating a detailed survey about the event or product can provide significant help to researchers in judging a change in attitude or perspective.
- *Politics:* Political surveys are incredibly popular, especially leading up to an election. Their success and validity varies according to the research techniques and strategies used, the quality of the sampling, the sample size, the response rate, and the questions asked.
- *Evaluations:* Often when trying to launch a product, especially one that is new to the market, developers conduct a survey to judge the effectiveness of their design. This is called *formative research*. However, sometimes developers will wait until the first version of a product is complete—often called the Beta product—to garner feedback. If that is done, it is called *summative research*. In addition, researchers might conduct a *needs analysis*, which is a way of identifying problems experienced by a group of people by comparing what already exists with what participants desire.
- *Market Research:* Considered one of the most classic and coming forms of research, this is research designed to study consumer behavior. A survey can be a huge asset in assessing consumer behavior. In theory, it can help researchers determine what people consume, how often, why, and how much they might need in the future of a given product or service.

Designing Your Survey

Given all of the advantages and simplicity of surveys as a research tool, it is highly likely you would elect to use one when conducting research for client. What are the must-haves for an effective survey? We'll run you through them here:

1. Sample Frame: A sample frame is a list of all the members of a population that your survey is designed to study.
2. Cross-Sectional vs. Longitudinal Design: After developing your sample frame, you need to determine whether you will use a cross-sectional or longitudinal design:
    - *Cross-Sectional:* A survey focused on the attitudes or feelings of a population at a specific point in time. It is important to keep in mind this type of survey design assumes the

variables and factors being studied have reached stability. The challenge is often that is not the case as most things are constantly in flux. If you are looking to achieve a simple point-in-time measurement or opinion, then a cross-sectional survey will work for you. If you are looking for more than that, it is best to consider other options.
- *Longitudinal Design:* In contrast to the cross-sectional design, a longitudinal survey design enables researchers to collect data from respondents at several points in time. With the design, you have an incredible ability to gather large amounts of data from your targeted population. It is ideal for gauging the impact of unusual environmental events on a population or assessing whether a population's beliefs or attitudes have shifted over time. It also enables you to judge causal relationships. If you elect a longitudinal design for your research, there are three ways of conducting it: trend study, cohort study, and panel study.

Specifics of Longitudinal Design

Given the fact there are three options for designing a longitudinal study, it is important to examine the advantages and disadvantages of each before selecting one:

- *Trend Study:* With this format, measurement occurs at two or more points in time from different samples selected from a population. This format is great for identifying trends and changes in people's beliefs about the variables of interest or in the correlations between them at different points in time. This format offers data on the varying opinions within subsets of a population but does not account for changes within a subset.
- *Cohort Study:* With this format, a specific subgroup of a population is selected and their responses to a set of variables are tracked over time. This works well if you are interested in studying a select group within a population that share a common characteristic due to a life experience such as the year they graduated from high school. The group being studied (the cohort) is usually defined relative to time or history. In contrast to a trend study, it only offers the perspective of one group within a targeted population.
- *Panel Study:* With this type of study, a sample is selected from a population and those same people are measured or tested at multiple points in time. This method affords true tests of causality, as it enables the researcher to look at correlations over time and dismiss confounding variables. Due to their duration

and the level of commitment required, the biggest problem with panel studies is that many participants drop out of the study.

Building a Survey Questionnaire

Once you've determined the type of study you would like to complete, the next step is to design the questionnaire. Below are some guidelines to keep in mind for the design of survey questions:

- Written clearly and easy to understand
- Focus on one issue
- Avoid biased or leading words and making assumptions
- Refrain from offending participants

There are two basic types of questions that can be included in a survey questionnaire:

- *Closed-ended:* With this type of question, you give the respondent certain possible answers that their responses must fit into, such as "yes/no" or a scaled response. This format is best for eliminating interviewer interpretation, eliminating coding and editing interpretations, making recording of the data easier as the interview is being conducted, and ensuring consistency in interviewing.
- *Open-ended:* With this style of question, there is no suggested response but rather the answer is subject to the respondent's opinion. This format is preferred when you need to measure a participant's level of knowledge, recall of something, or detailed explanation of an opinion. Examples include: "What do think of _____?" or "Why did you day that?" The challenge with the style of question is that they often require a significant amount of probing on the part of the interviewer. Sometimes, the interviewer fails to do it, which results in incomplete findings.

Arranging the Survey Questions

Once you have formulated and written the questions, you need to put them together in the survey. Sadly, it isn't as simple as just laying them out in numerical order, but rather a significant amount of thought must go into how they are ordered in the survey.

There are three common ways of laying out questions in a survey:

- *Tunnel Format:* With this layout, questions are usually similar in terms of breadth and depth throughout the questionnaire. They are organized by similarity and vary little in terms of depth.
- *Funnel Format:* With this style, the questions begin with broad, open-ended questions followed by narrow, more closed-ended questions.

- *Inverted Funnel Format:* With this format, you begin with the more closed-ended questions, narrow questions, and then conclude with the most open-ended and bad ones.

Unfortunately, there is no cut and dry rule for deciding which format to use for the survey. It simply depends upon the one that is best suited to your research question and/or hypotheses. A final point to consider with respect to surveys is the way it will be administered.

Administering a Research Survey

What's the most effective way to administer a survey? It depends who you talk to.

Generally you pick one of three ways to administer your survey:

- *Researcher-Administered:* With this format, a researcher is present when a participant completes a survey questionnaire, usually in a group setting. This method allows the researcher to answer any questions participants may have, as well as receive fast results since they are present when the surveys are completed. Some challenges with this format are respondents feel less anonymous since the researcher is present and the group structure can sometimes influence the responses of the individuals.
- *Self-Administered:* These surveys are completed independently by the respondent, without other researchers or participants present. The biggest challenge with this format is that it is incredibly difficult to predict the response rate. Typically, the response rate with this format is significantly less than of one administered by a researcher. That being said, because there is no one present while the survey is administered, respondents tend to be more honest in their responses.
- *Interviews:* With this methodology, individuals or groups of participants are asked survey questions directly by an interviewer. It can be done in-person or over the phone. There are many challenges with this type of survey administration including quality of data, interviewer bias, interpersonal challenges between interviewer and interviewee and the interviewer directly effecting a respondent's answers. However, one huge advantage with in-person interviews is that the interviewers can record and interpret the respondent's nonverbal communication. It can also eliminate the presence of "N/A" or "Don't know" responses from participants as the interviewer can pose follow-up questions to draw an answer from the respondent.

Research Technique: Experiments

Another tool to consider for use in your research study is the **experiment**. A *social experiment* is a procedure in which researchers take individuals, do something to them, and observe the effects of what they did to them. All experiments include two major factors: *independent* and *dependent variables*. A variable is anything that can be observed or measured by the researcher. To break it down further, an independent variable is any observation that is controlled by the researcher, while the dependent variables are effects.

experiment
A research technique where the researcher exposes a potential user to one or a series of scenarios to gauge their interest in a potential product or service.

Building Blocks of an Experiment

Now that we've reviewed the two most fundamental concepts of an experiment, let's discuss some of the procedural specifics: observation, induction, and random assignment:

- *Observation:* Typically recorded as capital "O" in the notation of an experiment, this is some type of written, spoken, or observed behavior or attitude. It is the basic building block of experiment design.
- *Induction:* Usually symbolized as capital "X" in the notation of an experiment, this is what you do to a participant.
- *Random Assignment:* Typically recorded as capital "R" in the notation of an experiment, this refers to the assignment of people at random to different groups in an experimental design.

Important Terms in Experiment Design

The concepts of observation, induction, and random assignment are the essential building blocks of any experiment. In addition, there are few other terms that are important to understand:

- *Experimental Group:* The group of individuals to whom you give the induction.
- *Control Group:* A group that doesn't receive any induction in an experiment. It is a group you can compare the experimental group to before and after the experiment.
- *Between-subjects Design:* An experiment designed to compare the results of multiple groups.
- *Within-subjects Design:* An experiment designed to look at the same group multiple times.
- *Pretest or Baseline Measurement:* The practice of measuring the dependent variable before exposure to the induction in an experiment.
- *Posttest:* The practice of measuring the dependent variable after exposure to the induction in an experiment.

Designing Your Experiment

If you are going to use an experiment in your research study, you need to keep in mind that you also have to give some thought to its design. Similar to the considerations of surveys, the design of an experiment is critical to its success. To recap from earlier in the text, there are five primary types of design to consider before constructing your experiment:

- *Pre-experimental Design:* Experiments that do not involve either a true control group or a pre-/posttest.
- *Quasi-Experimental Design:* Experiments that incorporate pretests and posttests but lack random assignment. This design is very common in communication research.
- *True Experimental Design:* Experiments where the participants are randomly assigned to both experimental and control groups.
- *Factorial Design:* Experiments where the analysis involves multiple independent variables.
- *Field Experiments:* Experiments that take place in a naturalistic environment—in the field or where participants live, work, or play— that incorporate the manipulation of independent variables.
- *Natural Experiments:* Experiments that occur in a naturalistic environment but *do not* include the manipulation of variables. They focus on the analysis of naturally occurring variables.

So far we have reviewed the research techniques found most commonly in quantitative research studies. Now, we will do a quick review and summary of the most popular qualitative techniques that can be integrated into quantitative research.

Research Techniques: Field Work

field work
A research technique where the researcher exposes the potential target market to concepts or ideas about a product/idea in an unstructured setting.

Sometimes, as part of your research study, you have to go into the inner workings of an industry, social group, or country to truly understand the potential or appeal of your product or service. Called **field work** by researchers, this is the practice of immersing yourself in a culture or setting and gaining research data during the experience. Traditional forms of field work include: observation, participation in local activities, casual conversations, and formal interviews. People that provide a significant amount of information or intelligence to researchers are called informants.

Since field work involves some form of immersion, there are typically other research techniques that are integrated into it. Some of the most popular ones include sampling and interviewing.

Research Techniques: Focus Groups

Used primarily with qualitative research, focus groups offer researchers a quick and relatively simple way of gaining immediate feedback from a target market or sample group. From a definitional stand point, **focus groups** are in-depth group discussions on a specific situation or topic of interest, usually consisting of five to twelve individuals and a moderator.

Traditionally, focus groups were held in a small face-to-face group setting. Today, an increasing number of them are being conducted over the phone, via Skype, and by other digital means. Focus group participants are either strangers selected randomly based upon their demographic or socioeconomic profile or a group of people who all know each other. Regardless of the format or the type of participant, it is always led by a moderator. Usually, the focus group meets just once or regularly over a defined period of time.

Focus groups offer researchers many advantages including the ability to see the group's reaction to the product, service, or idea in real time. In many ways, it can be said that focus groups are more natural than other research techniques as they tap into a person's everyday thoughts and feelings. Especially when done in a traditional face-to-face setting, respondents tend to give their immediate, unfiltered thought. This can prove to be incredibly insightful for researchers, especially when trying to gauge reactions to a product or service. That being said, it is important to remember that with focus groups there is the possibility of bias or influence on the respondents due to the format and live setting. Some participants may be influenced by what they hear others say or the tone in which the questions are asked.

Now that we have reviewed the basics of research design and the techniques available to complete the work, it is important to explore the challenges of candidate selection, budgets, and timelines.

focus group
A research technique where the researcher exposes a pre-qualified group of individuals to a potential product or service to gain qualitative feedback.

Candidate Selection

Choosing participants for a research study can be expensive and time consuming. Before selecting the type of research tools you are going to incorporate into your study, it is important to think about the amount of money and time you have to complete it.

For candidate selection, there are typically two options: do it yourself or hire someone to do it for you. If you elect to outsource candidate selection, then the participants for the study will be selected primarily by the firm you are using. You will be presented with a list of candidates before the research begins and ultimately you will have the right to reject anyone you don't deem qualified. But, if you don't have the money to hire a candidate recruiting agency, then you will have to do it yourself.

One way to find candidates is to build a research panel. This involves creating a list of potential research participants for your study. Initially time is required upfront to research and compile the potential list of participants, but in the end it gives you a great repository of people to choose from for the various facets of the study.

Another way to discover candidates is to turn to your client's customer support team. Take a look at the calls and complaints received in the call center or through the website. This is a simple and easy way of identifying qualified participants for your study. Along the same lines, another technique could be to engage with customers while they are on the company's website. By sending website visitors an instant message, commonly known as an IM, or launching a pop-up asking them if they have any questions could be an additional way to solicit participants for your study.

In addition to actually using it as a way to conduct research, social media can be another great way to recruit candidates for your study. Through a company's LinkedIn, Facebook, Twitter, or Instagram platforms, you could advertise the launch of the study and enroll qualified candidates. Another easy way to get participants is to simply ask a few of the qualified candidates for referrals. Offer them a referral bonus if they recommend someone to the study who is truly qualified.

▼ Budgets

In addition to the complexities of candidate selection, another huge challenge with research studies is the budget. Many clients want huge market research studies to be conducted but they simply don't have the money to pay for it. Sometimes, they have the money but they don't have an appreciation for the cost. Many times, this can actually be more challenging than the actual budget.

There is no right or wrong way to get around budget constraints. The client wants the stars but you can only offer them the moon. So, what do you do? There are a couple of approaches to consider:

- *Phased Approach:* If money is a problem, then suggest to your client that you take a phased approach. This simply means that you start off with the easiest and least expensive appropriate research technique and then expand as budget allows. This way your client can get a taste of the results and—if they are insightful—ask you to continue.

- *Now and Later:* Another way to approach fiscal challenges is to put together a timeline that affords small, inexpensive research techniques across a specific time period. This will provide the client with results leveraging a variety of techniques over an extended time period.
- *Local and Limited:* A third option is to conduct the research study using easily accessible candidates in a very focused and specific manner. This is almost a friends and family approach to research. Under this scenario, you would use referrals and/or members of the local population to serve as research subjects. You would also employ the research techniques that were most easily accessible to you.

Timelines

For any research project, it is essential the client and the researcher agree on a realistic timeframe as a basis for the study to be conducted. It is important to factor in any potential delays that could occur with candidate selection or research technique that's adopted. You should always strive to conduct your research study on time and within budget.

Research Study Checklist

Now that we have reviewed the nuances of completing a research study, let's summarize the steps you must take in putting one together:

1. Determine what type of research will be conducted
2. Decide the theory and type of logic you will apply
3. Choose your fact pattern
4. Set your research objectives and question
5. Establish your hypothesis
6. Determine your variables
7. Understand the relationships between your variables
8. Select your research techniques
9. Pick your candidates
10. Conduct your study using your techniques
11. Collect your data
12. Analyze and summarize your results
13. Write your report

14. Present your findings
15. Make your determination

It is highly probable that you will need to rework some of these steps as the unexpected will inevitably occur. But, with a focused and systematic approach, the chances are likely you will provide your client with the insightful and strategic knowledge data they need to make a decision about their product, service, or idea.

So What?

 Conceiving, creating and conducting a research study is complicated. It involves making many decisions that will accurately support the focus of the research study. In designing your research framework, it is incredibly important to keep your research objectives in mind and realize the potential variables that could come into play. Following a systematic process in the design of your research study, will allow you to safeguard against potential pitfalls and ensure the greatest probability of achieving credible results.

Glossary

Confounding Variable
A variable that causes a conflict between the dependent and independent variables.

Dependent Variable
A variable that relies on or is determined by another variable.

Experiment
A research technique where the researcher exposes a potential user to one or a series of scenarios to gauge their interest in a potential product or service.

Extraneous Variable
A variable that was unpredicted or unforeseen by the researcher. It can have a significant impact or pose a significant threat to the success of the research study.

Fact Pattern
The factual relationship that occurs frequently throughout a research project.

Field Work
A research technique where the researcher exposes the potential target market to concepts or ideas about a product/idea in an unstructured setting.

Focus Group
A research technique where the researcher exposes a pre-qualified group of individuals to a potential product or service to gain qualitative feedback.

Hypothesis
A statement about the relationship of at least two variables of a research study.

Independent Variable
A variable that is thought to predict or strongly influence the value of another variable.

Mediating Variables
A variable that explains the relationship between the dependent variable and the independent variable.

Moderating Variables
A variable that changes the strength or direction of an effect between two variables X and Y.

Relationships
The interplay between variables in a research study. There are several possible types.

Research Objectives
The rationale for the research project.

Research Questions
Primary questions that guide the focus of the research study. Simply put, they are the areas or issues that you are exploring.

Research Question
The overarching question you are trying to answer as a result of your research study.

Sampling
A research technique where a researcher tests out a potential product or idea with a probable target market.

Surveys
A research technique where a researcher collects feedback from a potential user through a formal question asking process. Surveys can be administered in-person, on-line, in small groups or randomly carried out.

APPLYING YOUR SURVEY RESEARCH

10

Imagine that after months and months of work, you have completed your communication research study. You've interviewed dozens of participants, tabulated results from hundreds of surveys, and compiled observations from experiments. Now what? Where do you go from here?

For many researchers, that's the next big challenge—determining what to do with the data. Much of this decision comes from the overall objective of the study. The natural thing to want to do is to share the research with the external world. Before you write up your findings and release them to the public, there are many things to consider.

Chapter Outline

1. Importance of Communicating Your Research Findings
2. Application of Research Findings
3. Determining the Target Audience
4. Types of Research Users
5. Understanding Your Audience's Wants and Needs
6. Learning More About Your Target Research Audience
7. Clarifying Your Research Findings
8. Identifying the Implications of Your Study
9. Imagining the "What If" of Your Research
10. Out-of-the-Box Applications of Your Work
11. Writing Your Key Messages
12. Broadcasting Your Content
13. Choosing Your Communication Medium
14. So What?

Key Terms

Baby Boomer
Conceptual Application
Epistemological

Generation X
Generation Y
Generation Z

Instrumental Application
Millennial
Strategic Application

Chapter Objectives

1. Realize the importance of knowing your research audience and understanding their concerns, interests, and needs.
2. Appreciate the importance of communicating key messages about research findings.
3. Understand how to craft specific messages for your target research audience and the importance of disseminating them in a timely manner.

▼ Importance of Communicating Your Research Findings

epistemological perspective
The idea that a researcher's findings contribute to the greater good of society.

epistemology
The study of knowing nature.

Whether you like it or not, it is one of the underwritten rules that most research findings, unless they are proprietary or labeled confidential, will get released into the public domain. "The responsibilities of the researcher extend beyond the immediate design, conduct, and supervision of the research. Those additional responsibilities have both **epistemological** and ethical implications for what it means to do work that goes by the name of research, and those implications have to do with how the research is circulated and shared" (Willinsky, 2006, p. 439).

What is **epistemology**? It is the study of knowing nature. From an epistemological perspective, it is important that a researcher shares their findings because it is a way for it to get global exposure and contribute to society. Most researchers believe that in order for a study's conclusions to be validated, they must be subject to public scrutiny. As a result, it is critical that the results of a study get published. (Willinsky, 2006).

Another major reason that most researchers publish their work is for the overall benefit of the research community. In order for researchers to secure additional funding, they must show traction in the marketplace. The more a researcher communicates the success of a study, the greater the likelihood he or she receives additional funding to conduct another study. This concept applies to all types of research projects—government, private, nonprofit, etc. An example of this is shown in a request for proposal (RFP) from the Nuffield Foundation:

Your application must include a broad dissemination plan, including proposed outputs, and identification of your target audience(s). You should outline the key mechanisms you will use, such as conferences, seminars, meetings with senior policy makers, or the production of publications aimed at wider audiences. [...] While we welcome the production of academic journal articles these are not usually the primary outputs of the projects we fund. (Nuffield Foundation, 2015, p. 14)

In this case, it is obvious that while the research study itself is important, the communication of the findings is equally as significant. A third reason the communication of research is so significant is the connection between research and the value it provides to society. As noted by OECD (2011, p. 1), "Public research organizations are increasingly aware that they must demonstrate performance, impact and quality to their parent funding bodies, to their private clients and to the international research community. A big part of this demonstration of performance, impact and quality is effective communication of research outputs and outcomes to appropriate audiences." This same pressure is felt in the university sector. As Willinsky (2014, p. 575) points out, "Educational researchers would seem to face an increased responsibility for the reach and 'impact' of their work."

An additional reason the communication of research is so incredibly important is the effect on society. Rickinson (2005) summarized the factors affecting the use of research under four broad headings:

1. Nature of the research
2. Nature of the practitioners
3. Nature of the professional context
4. Nature of the wider context of support.

After reviewing studies that were done in the United Kingdom and United States and published between 1999 and 2005 on the ways in which higher education practitioners access and use research, Rickinson observed how "two issues that recur in studies of practitioners' perceptions of research are complaints about the inaccessibility of the language and the challenge of locating work that is relevant" (Rickinson, 2005, p. 24).

The two examples cited were a study of science teachers and one of local education authorities. In the study of the science teachers, it was found that "the inaccessibility of many research reports in both location and style [was] seen as a barrier to the impact of research" (Rickinson, 2005). In the one of education authorities, it was felt that, in general, it is difficult to access research findings and that there is lack of relevant and practical content in the research that is published (Rickinson et al., 2003, pp. 11-12).

In recent research studies, similar problems have been noted (Nutley et al, 2007). Such observations only reinforce the need for researchers "to reflect critically on the ways in which research findings and research-based resources are developed, designed, and distributed within current education systems" (Rickson, 2016, p. 5).

A final reason it is important to think about how and why you are going to communicate your research findings is the quickly changing world of the social media and the Internet. Online and open source publishing, the growth of social media, and the popularity of mobile devices have led to the proliferation of more varied, rapid paced avenues of communication. What this means for researchers is that the way to most effectively publish research is constantly changing. (Willinsky, 2014, p. 581).

Although these and other developments offer new avenues for the publication of research, it does not make it any easier. The reality is that everyone is competing to have their research published. Before you submit your research for consideration for publication to a journal, magazine, or website, it is important to seriously consider the avenue and audience to which it is most appropriately suited.

▼ Application of Research Findings

By this point, I am sure you understand and appreciate the reason that you should publish your research findings. Now, let's review the different applications of research data before we move right into crafting messages and determining your target audiences.

When trying to get your research data published, it is important to think about the type of research that you have generated. It is important that research data is understood in connection with the way it will be utilized. A simple framework for understanding the utilization of research data is in terms of its instrumental, conceptual, and strategic research use:

Instrumental
An instrumental application is a concrete application of research.

Conceptual
A conceptual application is research knowledge that influences how practitioners define or view problems.

Strategic
A strategic application is one where the research data and findings can be used to defend a position.

- **Instrumental:** A concrete application of research, "where the research has often been translated into a material or usable form . . . is used to direct specific decisions and/or interventions." This research provides specific and immediately applicable solutions.
- **Conceptual:** This is when "research may change one's thinking but not necessarily one's particular action . . . In this kind of research utilization, research informs and enlightens the decision-maker." This research offers concepts that play a part in how practitioners define problems, and it is one among several sources of knowledge upon which practitioners use.
- **Strategic:** This "involves the use of research as a persuasive or political tool to legitimate a position or practice." This form of research generates data that can be used to justify or defend a position.

Source: Estabrooks (2001, pp. 283-284)

When developing strategies for disseminating research findings, it is important to think about the possibility of distributing different types of research. Maybe some of your data is instrumental, while other aspects of it are conceptual? The flaw most researchers make is that they tend to focus on instrumental use by individual professionals (Nutley et al., 2007). In reality, "evidence use is best characterized as a continual and iterative process, one that draws on diverse kinds of knowledge through many different channels" (Davies et al., 2008, p. 190).

In this section, we've looked at how researchers think about the communication of their work. To be successful in getting it published, researchers must think about: (i) the communication of the research in relation to actual research conducted; (ii) the relationships between research, policy, and practice; (iii) the idea of research communication as a process; and (iv) the use of research in the modern world (Rickinson, 2016).

What Effective Research Communication Involves

When thinking about successful research communication, it is important to recall the phrase "Getting the right information to the right people in the right format at the right time" (Nutley et al., 2007, p. 14). Although simple in concept, it can be quite tricky in execution. Some of the many questions that arise are the following: How do you decide the target audience for your research findings? What should you say about it? How should you communicate it to the market?

Deciding the who, what, and where of your research communication comes down to four basic things: questions of audience (target market), questions of content (the messaging and appeals), questions of outputs (the communication channels), and questions of other influences (timing). Now, let's look at the communication of research from these four vantage points:

- Understanding your audience
- Formulating key messages
- Crafting outputs
- Identifying potential influences

Understanding Your Audience

Before you can even begin to think about communicating the results of your research, you need to have a keen sense of your audience. As explained by Brewer, "The process of impact can be simplified by reducing it to three questions which all social scientist can ask themselves about their research [...]: Who are the users of our research? How do I engage with them? What has been/could be the effects of this engagement?" (Brewer, 2013, pp. 118-119).

To simplify Brewer's point even further, it all comes down to *who is going to be interested in your research? Essentially, who is your target market?* Sadly, all things do not appeal to all people, so it is vital that you give significant thought to who is the best audience for your findings. Periodically, the results of the study may differ significantly from your hypothesis. If that's the case and your target market has changed, give a lot of thought to the nuances of this new group.

How do you figure out the best audience for your research? This is something you should think about not after you have conducted the study but beforehand. The clearer you can be at the beginning about whom your research is targeted toward, the greater the likelihood you will generate findings and theories that will appeal to that audience. It is important from the very beginning of a research study to take the time to

- carefully define the target audience
- consider the potential and opportunities for work across traditional boundaries
- appreciate the wants and needs of the intended audiences

Defining the Target Audience

When you ask yourself the question "whom is the research for?" the answer is probably more complicated than you think. Most of us have a general response: educators, adults, academics, or other researchers. Such responses can help provide direction for the general potential audience, but they offer no specifics. As Foster and Hammersley (1998) argue,: "It is important to remember that there is not one single, well-defined, and internally homogenous professional audience, but rather multiple, overlapping publics whose boundaries and characteristics are ill-defined" (p. 613).

As Foster and Hammersley (1998) suggest, it is the responsibility of the researcher to attempt to understand the nuances and complexities of their potential target audience. Learning more about the market requires study and interaction with them. It can be said, "This process is about trying to work from the general to the specific, from the broad brush to the fine grained, from the undifferentiated to the nuanced. It means remembering that users are in one sense everyone and thus in another sense no one, they need specification to be meaningful (Brewer, 2013, p. 90)."

As a result, it is helpful to think about target audiences in terms of not only the specifics of their profession but also how they might use the results of the research. Another way to think about it is to segment out those you would like to use your research (primary market); those you would like to promote your research (secondary market); and those who you would like to know about your research (tertiary market) (Rickinson, 2016).

Consider the Breadth of Your Target Research Audience

In addition to thinking about the specifics of your target audience, it is also important to think about it in terms of breadth, that is, across traditional categorizations (Rickinson, 2016). This is important in situations where researchers (either individually or collectively) have developed a tendency to work on issues relating to particular groups of research users (Rickinson, 2016).

Brewer has observed that "Most social scientists have preferred working either with organic publics, local, community-based and non-market groups, without much access to formal power, or with people in these very systems of formal power, such as governments and policy-makers" (Brewer, 2013, p. 161).

Types of Research Users

- When trying to determine whom a piece of research is best suited for, it is helpful not only think to about the potential audiences, but also to think broadly about the different categories of end users (Rickinson, 2016).
- When thinking across different categories of research users, it is important to consider the wide range of intermediary organizations operating within and across the categories, e.g., media, specialist media, professions, corporations, entrepreneurs, consultants, think tanks, policy communities, and NGOs (Rickinson, 2016).

Types of Research Users	
Business/Corporate Sector—Corporations, small and medium-sized enterprises, start-ups. **Government and Public Policy Sector**—Local and regional government, national government. Groups and Unions: Trade unions, interest groups, lobbyists, think tanks, and NGOs. **Media:** National/international/local print and broadcast media, Web-based media, social media, bloggers. Source: Bastow et al. (2014)	**Culture**—Educators, cultural consumers, librarians, schools, media, public bodies, private organizations, charities, individuals, families, etc. **State**—Governments (local, national, and regional), political parties, politicians, policy makers, and civil servants. **Market**—Business, industry, trade unions, consumers, workers, etc. Source: Brewer (2013)

Understanding Your Research Audience's Wants and Needs

In addition to determining the audience's specific research needs and thinking across boundaries, it is also important to try to understand the mind of your target audience. This involves more than just thinking about how they will interpret your research or the impact it might have on their daily lives. It means trying to figure out how your target audience thinks—what are their values? What are their concerns? What keeps them up at night? By asking "Who are the main audiences for this research?" you are only scratching the surface. A concerted effort must be made to delve into their concerns, interests, and needs. Why does this detail matter? Simply put, it will help you to communicate more effectively the salient details of your study to the intended audience. A researchers' decision about what and how to communicate must be supported by an understanding of their intended audiences in terms of how the research relates to the:

- *interests*
- *activities*
- *concerns*
- *communication preferences*
- *time-scales and schedules*

With a clearer understanding of such issues, you will be able to craft key messages and develop outputs that are better suited to your target audiences (Bastow et al. (2014).

Learning More About Your Target Research Audience

The process of understanding your audience's needs and interests requires specific skills, patience, and time. This isn't something that will happen overnight or over the course of a few days. It takes time, and it starts at the beginning of the research process. As you interact with research subjects and observe how they respond to the various tools, you will gain an understanding of what matters to them. Over time, this will translate into clues about their value systems and how they think.

Developing Your Research Messages

Crafting your key messages is an integral part of the communications research process. Without specifically written messages, users will not realize the true merit of your research study. People want to know the significance of a study, ramifications of the findings, and potential impact. That being said, the primary function of any research summary is to communicate the main findings and implications of a research study to a specific audience or group of audiences. Sounds easy right? Believe it or not, the key messages often get lost within a large research summary. You can avoid this mistake by clearly identifying your findings and potential implications of the study.

Clarifying Your Research Findings

What are some ways to clearly communicate your findings? Consider using a number of tools to highlight your results:

- *lists and bullets* to showcase main findings and implications
- *quotes and scenarios* to reinforce qualitative findings
- *charts, tables, and numbers* to highlight quantitative findings
- *photos, diagrams, and videos* to bring ideas to life
- *short sections, catchy titles, and boxes* to make it easier to follow

To clarify your findings, you need to go beyond employing simple stylistic techniques. It involves balancing the potential clash between clarity of the communication and sophistication of the argument (Rickinson, 2016). It is about trying to preserve the subtlety of a study's findings while simultaneously searching for easy ways to make those findings accessible and comprehensible to intended audiences. The challenge is in figuring out a way to preserve the authority of the data while making it relatable to the intended audience. Clarity and brevity should not be about superficiality and simplification. As noted in an Australian study of education professionals, "Communicating research to practitioners/policy-makers is not actually a question of simplifying the material but of complicating it in just the ways that address the various needs of various audiences" (Figgis et al., 2000, p. 352).

Another challenge is the need for key messages to be placed in the proper context and described in a way that brings them to life for the target audience. The idea of clarity is not just about breaking down the key findings but also considering how they can best be illustrated and contextualized to different audiences. In addition, it is also important to consider how research findings can be presented in ways that encourage additional thought and discussion. Part of the goal of publishing your research should be to trigger a public discussion of it or debate about it. It is important to think about which communication vehicles will best support this goal. Not all channels and publications are the right place for your research.

As noted by Figgis et al. (2000, p. 357): "Research publications might profit from explaining not only the duration and usefulness of what had been found but indicating the questions and uncertainties that remain. The point of this is to invite [research users] to think about what fits or is at odds with their current thinking and whether in implementing the ideas there are unexpected consequences; and so on. In other words, design the publications to trigger the sorts of dialogues which [are] critical for mutual and beneficial exchanges to occur."

▼ Identifying the Implications of Your Study

In addition to making sure you have clear, well-crafted messages, it is also important to identify the potential implications of the research to users. The challenge is that research data does not simply translate into potential implications. As a result, it is important to think creatively about not only the research study and the findings, but also the potential implications of these research findings on the marketplace. Ultimately, this requires the researcher to go beyond thinking just about the research. He or she must be willing to contemplate the relationship between the research and its potential market applications (Sharples, 2013, p. 22).

▼ Imagining the "What If" of Your Research

Thinking about how your research findings could potentially be used in the marketplace could be a daunting task. You've spent weeks, maybe months, running experiments, conducting focus groups, and tabulating surveys, and the last thing you want to do is go beyond your analysis. So how can it be done? Here are a few suggestions:

Work on the development of research implications as a team: This will enable you to leverage each other's creativity and expertise and develop a variety of data "What If" scenarios. This could be done in many ways including:

- Relay interim findings back to research participants through various channels (face-to-face or online, individual or group, etc.) during the research process. This could help create an ongoing dialogue about the findings and their possible market implications.
- Discuss emerging findings and their potential implications at regular periods during the research process with a project advisory group that includes representatives of your potential target audience.
- Hold a workshop with specifically targeted stakeholders and relevant opinion-leaders midway through or at the end of the research process. Preview draft research findings and work together to brainstorm possible market implications (Rickinson, 2016).

If you elect to employ any of these techniques, it is absolutely paramount that the emphasis from the researchers is on listening more than talking. Otherwise, you risk losing the opportunity to learn from your fellow researchers and study participants.

Out-of-the-Box Applications of Your Work

In addition to receiving information from colleagues and participants about the applications of your research, it is important to gain the perspective of others that are not as familiar with it. The challenge is that sometimes we are so close to the work that we fail to realize some of the most obvious uses for it. What's the best way to gain some outside perspectives? Just ask. Preview your findings with colleagues, potential target audience members, interested media, and anyone else you think your work may appeal to. Be sure to give them time to review your work, and then ask questions such as:

- What parts of the research did you find the most interesting?
- What questions do you have about it?
- What concerns do you have?
- What issues does it bring to mind?
- What else would you like to know?
- Whom else do you think would find this interesting?
- In what communities or in what organizations do you think it could make the greatest impact?
- What groups do you think could leverage the data the most effectively and why?
- Are there any professional groups you think could benefit from it?

Answers to these and many other questions will help you realize new opportunities and avenues for the publication of your work. Very often, we fail to realize the most obvious opportunities.

Another way to discover the potential for your data is to consider the development of different case studies for targeted end-user groups. Similar to the development of key messages about your work, the more finite you can be about the implications of your work, the easier it will be to identify end users and generate additional opportunities for it.

Instead of viewing the data from the research community's perspective, try to view it from that of the end user. Consider how it could help one of the targeted end-user groups fulfill their daily needs, conquer a workplace challenge, or solve a societal problem. If your data related to the field of education, for example, you could consider the way your findings could specifically help school leaders, classroom teachers, or special education coordinators. By bifurcating the implications of the data from the perspective of the end user, you will realize implications and uncover applications that hadn't originally occurred to you or the research team (Rickinson, 2016).

Writing Your Key Messages

Now that you've clarified your findings and considered the implications of your work, it is time to write your key messages. Sounds easy? Sadly, it isn't, but here are a few suggestions for ways to simplify the process:

- Use crisp, action-oriented words to convey the key points of your study.
- Write in a way that is familiar to your targeted user-group. Don't use acronyms or complex words unless you know your audience understands them.
- Avoid the past tense and write in the active voice.
- Be purposeful and pick points that will resonate with the target audience.
- If you have multiple end-user groups, craft messages specific to each of them.
- Keep it simple—think of the messages as the selling points of your research.
- Organize your points in the most impactful way possible based on the interests of the target audience.

Broadcasting Your Content

Once the target audience is understood, the application and impact of the data realized, the key messages written, it is time to communicate your findings to the world. Traditionally, the most popular and traditional medium for the dissemination of research has been a journal article, book, or research report. These opportunities were limited, highly competitive, and involved an incredibly arduous submission process. Today, however, with the popularity of the Internet and social media, there is a vast array of opportunities available to researchers. Not only do these new mediums offer researchers more chances to publish their work, but they also expose them to new audiences around the globe. Studies measuring the impact on research studies have shown that different audiences require different kinds of communication vehicles (e.g. Nutley et al., 2007; Sharples, 2013).

Instead, researchers need to leverage the constantly expanding world of opportunities for presenting and sharing their findings. What this means for researchers is that not only is crafting targeted messages important but communicating them via the right medium matters as well. That being said, here are some things you need to keep in mind when deciding where to disseminate your work:

- **Create an identity:** Use the Internet to create an identity for your study. Leverage resources such as Twitter, Linked In,

Facebook, blogs, and relevant e-zines to announce the launch of the study and provide regular updates.
- **Mix it up:** Use a combination of digital (e.g., e-newsletter, webinar, website, blog post, podcast, videos, infographics, social media, etc.) and **print** (e.g., research report, magazine article, journal article, press release, policy brief, fact sheet, etc.) formats.
- **Bring it to life:** Hold events (e.g., workshops, meetings, conferences, boot camps) and participate in live media opportunities such as television or radio interviews as well as debates and public speaking engagements.
- **Make it accessible:** Create resources (e.g., teaching resource, website, workbook, checklist, and guidelines) for understanding and applying your research findings.
- **Keep it current:** Post online and publish regular updates about the study's progress and also the final conclusions and implications of the work, as well as final outputs.

▼ Which Medium? Think About the Consumption Habits of Your Target Market

Clearly, there are a myriad of mediums through which you can publish your research. In fact, there are so many it can be overwhelming. How do you decide where to start? Think about which medium will resonate most with your target end user. The majority of the population fits into one of seven categories:

Generation Name:	Births Start/End		Min. Age	Max Age
The Silent Generation	1925	1945	74	94
Baby Boomer Generation	1946	1964	55	73
Generation X (Baby Bust)	1965	1980	40	54
Millennials Generation Y, Gen Next	1980	1994	25	39
iGen/Gen Z	1995	2012	7	24
Gen Alpha	2013	2025	1	6
Source: *Robinson, 2017*				

Here's some background information on each of the four most popular categories—iGen/Gen Z, Millennials, Generation X, and Baby Boomers:

iGen/Generation Z: The iGen or Gen Z refers to anyone born between 1995 and 2012. This emerging group of consumers is still figuring out its position relative to other generations. But what researchers have observed so far is fascinating. In general, Gen Zers are much more open in the way they think, as well as more accepting of different cultures, sexual orientations and races than prior generations. In addition, they are:

- Risk adverse and cautious
- Independent thinkers
- Critical of authority figures in both religion and government
- Less interested in alcohol and narcotics than Millennials
- Spending less time in shopping malls and at the movie theater
- Prefer Instagram and Snapchat over Facebook

(Source: *Tweng, 2017*)

Some potential challenges for Gen Z are:

- Grew up more supervised and protected than other generations
- Have had less experience talking to people "face-to-face" due to the prevalence of smartphones
- Less likely to read books, newspapers, and magazines
- Lack experience with teen jobs and earning money in high school
- Possibly more depressed than prior generations
- Feel more lonely and not needed

Generation Z
Anyone born from 1995–2012.

Millennials/Gen Y: Millennials are individuals born between 1980 and 1994. They are the largest generation in U.S. history, with approximately 83 million living in this country. They grew up in a technology-rich

Millennials/ Generation Y
Anyone born between 1980–1994.

period when almost every home in the United States had a computer and Internet connection. They were alive during the 9/11 terrorist attacks on the World Trade Center and the Pentagon. They have been the generation at the forefront of technological growth, with companies such as Google, Facebook, SalesForce.com, LinkedIn, EBay, and PayPal being part of their everyday vocabulary (Robinson, October 2017).

Some other interesting facts about Millennials are:

- Most have less than $1,000 in their savings accounts; many have no savings at all.
- Many have less credit card debt and car purchases than previous generations.
- More than 65% don't have a credit card.
- Corporate social responsibility (CSR) and environmental friendliness have a significant impact on their buying decisions.
- When making a purchase, they either follow their own instincts or rely on recommendations from peers but ultimately consider price to be the most important factor.
- Follow brands online for discount opportunities—66% of Millennials would switch brands if offered at least a 30% discount.
- About 60% say they will be brand loyal if they are treated well by the company; otherwise they will try something else.
- In addition to valuing CSR and environmental friendliness, they believe in authenticity, giving back to community/society and ethical production.
- Facebook, YouTube, and Instagram are their favorite social media sites.

Source: Costin, 2019.

generation X
Anyone born between 1965–1980.

Generation X: Gen X is anyone born between 1965 and 1980. Before we start talking in depth about this generation, let's explain the name. The original name of Gen X was actually "Gen Bust" because their birth rate was much lower than that of the Baby Boomers. They were around to see the collapse of the Berlin Wall and the downfall of the Soviet Union. They watched music videos on channels such as MTV and VH-1. They were also old enough to fight in the first Gulf War (Robinson, 2017). Here are some other interesting facts about them:

- Heaviest users of Facebook with over 20 million active users per month in 2018. This number is expected to decline to 43.8 million by 2022.
- Instagram is their second favorite social media platform, with approximately 23.5 million users in 2018. That number has increased slightly in 2019 but isn't expected to increase that much more (e-marketer, 2018).

Baby Boomers: A Baby Boomer is anyone born between 1946 and 1964. They grew up in a time of economic prosperity devoid of any war or extreme violence. Baby Boomers are viewed as the ultimate consumer, having a reputation for spending every dollar they made. Although they didn't grow up during the Internet boom, they were the first generation to have two cars in every garage and a television in most living rooms. Despite all of this prosperity, Baby Boomers also witnessed several assassinations, the Cold War and the Vietnam War (Robinson, 2017).

As for their social media preferences, here's how it looks:

- Favorite social media site is Facebook, with over 20 million active users per month in 2018, which is expected to stay constant over the next couple of years.
- Second favorite social network is Pinterest, with 12.9 million users in 2018.
- Snapchat is their third favorite site, with 3.8 million users in 2018 (e-marketer, 2018).

Greater detail on the generations and their social media preferences is included in the following chart:

> **Baby Boomers**
> *Individuals born between 1946 and 1964. They are the parents of Gen X.*

US Social Network Users, by Platform, 2017-2022
millions, % change and % of social network users

	2017	2018	2019	2020	2021	2022
Facebook	167.9	169.5	171.1	172.9	174.6	176.3
—% change	1.0%	0.9%	0.9%	1.1%	1.0%	1.0%
—% of social network users	86.5%	85.0%	83.8%	82.8%	81.9%	81.0%
Instagram	92.6	104.7	113.3	120.3	125.7	130.7
—% change	28.9%	13.1%	8.2%	6.2%	4.5%	4.0%
—% of social network users	47.7%	52.5%	55.5%	57.6%	59.0%	60.1%
Snapchat	79.2	84.8	90.4	95.6	100.2	103.6
—% change	25.8%	7.1%	6.6%	5.8%	4.7%	3.4%
—% of social network users	40.8%	42.5%	44.3%	45.8%	47.0%	47.6%
Pinterest	72.3	77.4	80.9	83.6	85.5	87.2
—% change	13.8%	7.0%	4.6%	3.4%	2.2%	2.0%
—% of social network users	37.2%	38.8%	39.6%	40.0%	40.1%	40.1%
Twitter	54.7	55.2	55.7	56.1	56.5	56.9
—% change	2.1%	0.9%	0.9%	0.8%	0.7%	0.6%
—% of social network users	28.2%	27.7%	27.3%	26.9%	26.5%	26.1%

Note: internet users who use social networks via any device at least once per month
Source: eMarketer, Aug 2018

Source: © Kendall Hunt Publishing Company. Adapted from www.eMarketer.com.

So What?

 In this chapter, we've talked about the rationale, challenges, and techniques of communicating the results of your research study. Clearly, you have many potential avenues for publication. The challenge comes in picking the right one for your targeted end user. Remember that you need to give your data the chance to appeal to more than just one group and that the trick to success comes in the clarity and precision of your communication.

Glossary

Baby Boomers
Individuals born between 1946 and 1964. They are the parents of Gen X.

Conceptual
A conceptual application is research knowledge that influences how practitioners define or view problems.

Epistemological perspective
The idea that a researcher's findings contribute to the greater good of society.

Epistemology
The study of knowing nature.

Generation X
Anyone born between 1965–1980.

Generation Z
Anyone born from 1995–2012.

Instrumental
An instrumental application is a concrete application of research.

Millennials/Generation Y
Anyone born between 1980–1994.

Strategic
A strategic application is one where the research data and findings can be used to defend a position.

References

Bastow, S., P. Dunleavy, and J. Tinkler. 2014. *The Impact of the Social Sciences*. London: Sage.

Brewer, J. *The Public Value of the Social Sciences*. London: Bloomsbury. 2013

CareerPlanner.com. 2017.

Costin, Gui. May 1, 2019. "Millennial Spending Habits and Why They Buy." Forbes.

Davies, H., S. Nutley, and I. Walter. 2008. 'Why "Knowledge Transfer" is Misconceived for Applied Social Research', *Journal of Health Services Research Policy 13*(3): 188-190.

E-Marketer. August 28, 2018. "Facebook is Tops with Everyone but Teens: Snapchat Expands Lead Among 12-17 Year Olds.".

Estabrooks, C.A. 2001. "Research Utilization and Qualitative Research." In: Morse, J.M., J.M. Swanson, and A.J. Kuzel. (Eds.) *The Nature of Qualitative Evidence*. London: Sage.

Figgis, J., A. Zubrick, A. Butorac, and A. Alderson. 2000. "Backtracking Practice and Policies to Research." In: DETYA *The Impact of Educational Research*. Canberra: DETYA.

Foster, P. and M. Hammersley. 1998. "A Review of Reviews: Structure and Function in Reviews of Educational Research", *British Educational Research Journal*, 24, 5, 609-628.

Nuffield Foundation. 2015. *Grants for Research and Innovation Guide for Applicants*. London: Nuffield Foundation.

Nutley, S., I. Walter, and H.T.O. Davies. 2007. *Using Evidence: How Research Can Inform Public Services.* Bristol: Policy Press.

OECD. 2011. *OECD Issue Brief: Research Organization Evaluation.* Paris: OECD.

Rickinson, M. 2005. *Practitioners' Use of Research.* London: National Educational Research Forum.

Rickinson, M. 2016. "Communicating Research Findings", In: D. Wyse, E. Smith, L. E. Suter, and N. Selwyn. (Eds.) *The BERA/Sage Handbook of Educational Research.* London: Sage.

Robinson, Michael T. 2017. The Generations: *Which Generation Are You?*

Robinson, Michael T. October 7, 2017. Millennials. The Mystery Generation How the Boomers Screwed an Entire Generation. CareerPlanner.com

Sharples, J. 2013. *Evidence for the Frontline.* London: Alliance for Useful Evidence.

Tweng, Jean M. August 2017. iGen: Why Today's Super-Connected Kids Are Growing Up Less Rebellious, More Tolerant, Less Happy and Completely Unprepared for Adulthood—and What that Means for the Rest of Us. Simon & Schuster.

Willinsky, J. 2006. "When the Research's Over, Don't Turn Out the Lights", In: K. Tobin and J. L. Kincheloe. (Eds.) *Doing Educational Research: A Handbook.* Rotterdam: Sense.

Willinsky, J. 2014. "The New Openness in Educational Research", In: A. D. Reid, E. P. Hart, and M. A. Peters. (Eds.) *A Companion to Research in Education.* New York: Springer.

Wilson, R., J. Hemsley-Brown, C. J., Easton, and C. Sharp. 2003. *Using Research for School Improvement: the LEA's Role* (LGA Research Report 42). Slough: NFER.

CASE STUDIES IN COMMUNICATION RESEARCH

CHAPTER OUTLINE

1. University of Minnesota: "The Other Hangover"
2. Domino's Social Media Crisis Communication
3. A Whale of a Problem: A Strategic Communication Analysis of SeaWorld Entertainment's Multiyear *Blackfish* Crisis
4. Connecticut Light & Power's (CL&P) Crisis Communication Response
5. The Jersey Shore and Superstorm Sandy
6. Deflated: The Strategic Impact of the "Deflategate" Scandal on the NFL and Its Golden Boy

CHAPTER OBJECTIVES

1. To appreciate how communication research techniques are used in the real world
2. To realize the potential impact of a well-designed and executed communication research study
3. To understand the limitations and potential pitfalls of the various research techniques in real-world applications

•••

After a thorough review of the approaches, techniques, and tools that form the basis for the world of communication research, it is important to explore the implementation of these ideas in the field. We will do this by reviewing a series of recent real-world campaigns from a variety of industries:

- Education: University of Minnesota
- Consumer:
  - Domino's
  - Sea World
  - Connecticut Light & Power
  - State of New Jersey
- Sports: The New England Patriots

University of Minnesota: "The Other Hangover"

The first case study we will review was done in 2010 at The University of Minnesota—the focus was binge drinking on campus. To no one's surprise, binge drinking is a massive problem across most colleges and universities including at the University of Minnesota. In an attempt to mitigate the problem, a student-designed and -initiated campaign was launched on campus. Rather than create a campaign centered on the health effects of binge drinking, the students used an untraditional approach: focus on the social consequences of overconsumption, such as damage to one's reputation and the loss of friendship.

Heavily designed and executed by undergraduate students, the campaign, titled "The Other Hangover," took a unique approach to a health issue that had largely been seen as extraordinarily difficult to build due to students not caring about the potential health risks (Gilkerson, Gross, & Ahneman, 2013). Prior to designing and executing the campaign, the research team conducted an extensive study on the University of Minnesota campus about student attitude toward drinking. Why? It was important to gauge students' current perception of the issue in order to design a campaign that would resonate most effectively with them. This was done through a combination of surveys, focus groups, interviews, and research techniques. Through this comprehensive research study of their peers, the students discovered that 75% of students believed their behavior when binge drinking had negative social consequences (Gilkerson et al., 2013). As a result of the data, they decided to construct a campaign centered on the behavioral effects of excessive drinking, realizing it would potentially reap greater rewards than a traditional antibinge drinking campaign.

Comprised of eight undergraduate and two graduate students, the team was given a $75,000 grant from the Century Council to implement the campaign on the University of Minnesota campus during the Fall 2010 semester (Gilkerson et al., 2013). The team chose three platforms as the primary vehicles upon which to execute the campaign: social media (Facebook), the University's website, and traditional advertisements.

The advertisements featured across the University of Minnesota's campus consisted of posters, billboard, and digital ads in the football stadium and on the JumboTron. There were also campaign posters and coasters handed out to students at local bars and restaurants (Gilkerson et al., 2013). These posters depicted different stereotypes of poor binge drinking behavior with titles like "The Creep," "Fighter," "Make-out," "Crier," and "Flasher." The stereotypes, just by name, are obviously relatable to any college student who has ever spent any amount of time at a bar or a party where binge drinking occurs and were essential to the success of the campaign.

Simply put, the strategy largely worked. In an evaluation of the campaign's effectiveness, surveys found there was an effective 58.2% unprompted recall rate, while 86% of participants recognized the campaign's logo (Gilkerson et al., 2013). Those numbers are impressive for a campaign for binge drinking, especially one implemented over such a short period of time.

Why was it such a success? The messages and messaging channels the team chose clearly resonated and grabbed students' attention. Using language and imagery that was relatable and familiar to the students, the campaign grabbed the audience's attention significantly more than similar ones in the past. By focusing on behavior that results from drinking, students were able to see themselves in these potentially socially damaging situations, or at least recognize the fact that they had witnessed that kind of behavior before. The visual imagery and themes of the posters and advertisements were one of the most influential elements of the campaign. Specifically, the posters with "The Creep" had the highest recognition rate (Gilkerson et al., 2013) by students.

As far as the effectiveness of campaign's themes and messages, 81.1% of students agreed the messages from the campaign were more relevant to them than those from other binge drinking campaigns. And 82.3% said the ads were more believable than prior campaigns. More than three-quarters of students—78%—said they liked the campaign itself (Gilkerson et al., 2013). Even the name of the campaign was a huge success as many students started to use "The Other Hangover" as a term to remind their friends not to drink too much.

While the postcampaign data and surveys did not show any actual change in attitudes or practices about binge drinking, the campaign was able to spark discussion and grab attention about a topic previously thought almost impossible to convey to college students. The chances are likely that if the campaign was implemented over a longer period of time, the results would be even more positive.

The project at the University of Minnesota was impressive as it effectively tackled a problem that many perceive as overdone. Clearly, the key to its success was identifying what current students thought of the issue and then designing a campaign around it. Now, we will look at how Domino's tackled a used communication research to combat a problem triggered by some of their employees.

Domino's Social Media Crisis Communication

In the social media era, companies and organizations need to be prepared to adapt to any and all crisis scenarios. As we all know, information can spread rapidly and without restraint. In 2009, Domino's Pizza faced a crisis when two store employees posted a video onto YouTube depicting them defaming certain items of food (Young & Flowers, 2012). Having only a small window of time with which a crisis communications response could be implemented, Domino's had to figure out how to deal with an issue that was, in effect, purely online.

With the vast nature of the Internet, as well as countless potential stakeholders as customers, bloggers, etc., all potentially becoming potential coproducers of messages about an organization (Young & Flowers, 2012), communication and public relations specialists need to be adaptable to any situation. The video posted by the Domino's employees reached one million views in the 2 days it was up on YouTube. Imagine in 2018, with the popularity of Twitter, Snap, and Instagram how many more individuals would have viewed the video.

Domino's has been in business since June 10, 1960, when it opened its first location in Ypsilanti, MI. Needless to say, the company has a significant amount of experience interacting and communicating with its customers. Given the time sensitivity of the situation, the communication team did not have the opportunity to do a full research study to determine the most effective response. Instead, they decided to implement the techniques they thought would most quickly remedy the situation with their customer base.

The first step was to pull down the video—this was done on Sunday, 2 days after it had been put up. The second was to respond to customers who had reacted to the YouTube video. The Domino's communication team used Twitter to connect with customers who had questions or concerns about the situation (Young & Flowers, 2012). Their third step was a video apology on their corporate website, but this technique proved ineffective as it wasn't viewed by many customers. The decision was made to place the video on YouTube—which was where the crisis originated—and it proved to be the right decision. Once on YouTube, the video apology was viewed by tens of thousands (Young & Flowers, 2012).

Integrating social media into the response was a critical move as it dramatically helped successfully spread Domino's apology. Why? It enabled the company to apologize and tell the truth in a timely manner to their target audience on the same medium on which they had been attacked. It helped that after their failed attempt on their corporate website, they had the insight to switch strategies and not continue to push information on an outdated platform.

Domino's successfully put out the fire due to a combination of speed, strategy, and sincerity. It helped that the problem wasn't necessarily the corporation's fault, as well as the fact it was more of an instance of a few bad actors in the company who were able to be identified, blamed, and fired. There's not much Domino's could have done better. They successfully walked the fine line between issuing a timely, thoughtful response and one that was done too quickly and incomplete. Part of their success came from the fact they did not overreact and panic; if Domino's had ramped up its response to an unnecessarily high level, more people would have been made aware of it than would have in the first place and the results could have been much more devastating.

With a crisis such as this, there is often not the time to do comprehensive research to determine the best course of action. Most companies have to rely on the knowledge they have of their existing customers to determine the most effective response. Sometimes companies know their customers well and are successful, and other times they are not.

The Arthur W. Page Society lists seven principles to public relations, which are especially helpful in times of crisis:

i. Tell the Truth
ii. Prove It With Action
iii. Listen to the Customer
iv. Manage for Tomorrow
v. Conduct Public Relations as if the Whole Company Depends on It
vi. Realize a Company's True Character Is Expressed by Its People
vii. Remain Calm, Patient, and Good-Humored

The Domino's team followed these principles in developing its response to this crisis. Research shows that when companies adhere to the Page Society's principles, they tend to have a more effective and successful public relations effort and less successful when they do not.

Now that we have looked at a proactive marketing campaign successfully created and launched at the University of Minnesota and a reactive crisis campaign issued by Domino's, we will explore another case study that is a blend of proactive and reactive. Specifically, we will look at problems experienced at Sea World.

A Whale of a Problem: A Strategic Communication Analysis of SeaWorld Entertainment's Multiyear *Blackfish* Crisis

Over the past 10 years, the executives at SeaWorld have had a rough time. The company and its theme parks used to be as American as apple pie. Sea World's aquariums were visited by millions per year and provided families with unforgettable happy memories. Unfortunately for Sea World, the tides have shifted and many are now upset by the company and its practices. Gone are the days when Shamu and the many other attractions were standing room only, today it is rare to find the stands filled.

As stakeholders have become more socially conscious as a group and traditional business models fight to stay relevant in the age of disruption, SeaWorld has found itself in a significant bind. *Blackfish*, a CNN documentary that first aired in 2013, has thrown SeaWorld a right hook it's still recovering from. Detailing the mistreatment of SeaWorld's popular Orca or "Killer" whales, the documentary exposed SeaWorld's practices that allegedly led to the death of Orca trainer Dawn Brancheau in 2010. Needless to say, this caused a significant amount of backlash against the company in the months following the airing of the documentary.

Initially, *Blackfish* was shown at The Sundance Film Festival in January 2013. It was then aired on CNN to the general public in October 2013. This gave SeaWorld executives nearly 1 year to prepare for how they would defend themselves once the documentary hit the public. Simultaneously, SeaWorld was also in an important period of transition for its business after being purchased by Blackstone in 2009 and was taken public on the NYSE (Duhon, Ellison, & Ragas, 2016). Clearly, SeaWorld and its executives were in a tough spot. It was critical their response to the film effectively tackle the issues and allegations outlined in it, as well as position it as a stable and efficiently run business.

Sadly, what happened after *Blackfish* aired was predictable. Artists cancelled shows at venues (Duhon et al., 2016, p. 10) and there was significant cultural backlash, much of which occurred on social media. Companies like Taco Bell, Hyundai, and Southwest Airlines ended partnerships with SeaWorld (Duhon et al., 2016, p. 10) and the company entered a relative free-fall after being such a reliable profit generator for so many years.

The initial response strategy deployed by SeaWorld was focused on advocacy with a defensive posture (Duhon et al., 2016). The company sent out a critique of the documentary to film critics, as well as posted it on their own website (Duhon et al., 2016). In December 2013, the company published an open letter in newspapers around the country, with a particular focus on the three cities where it had locations. In this letter, the company tried to defend itself and its care of the Orcas (Duhon et al., 2016). These traditional modes of communication weren't working for SeaWorld as most of the conversation around the film was taking place on social media.

Over 7.3 million people saw tweets about *Blackfish* on the night it aired alone, partially due to a trending #Blackfish promoted by CNN (Duhon et al., 2016). That's a significant social media impact in just one night, let alone the second life *Blackfish* found when it was released for streaming on Netflix. If stakeholders take to social media to complain about something,

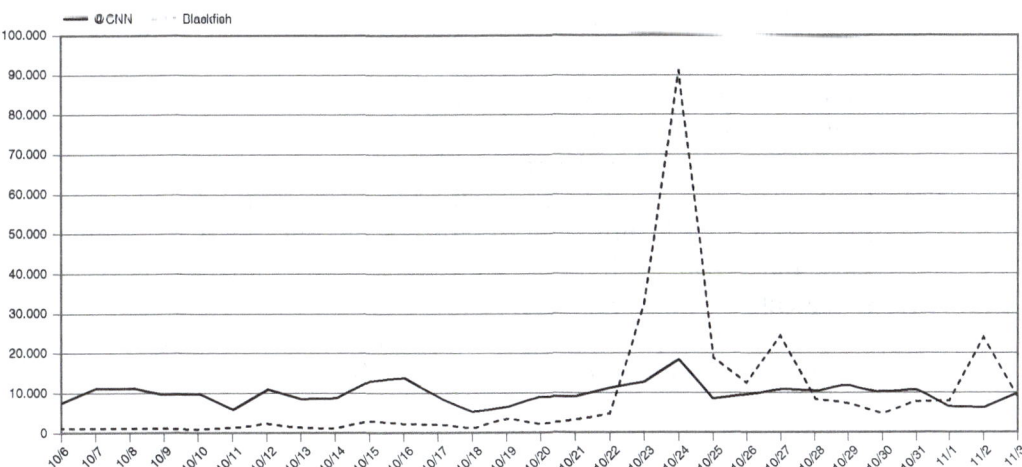

in most cases, the best way to engage and connect with the audience is on social media as well.

It took time but eventually the executives at SeaWorld began to shift their response to address questions and concerns of stakeholders (Duhon et al., 2016, p. 19), as well as rebuild its overall image. Initially, SeaWorld began a campaign largely built on advocacy in an attempt to win back the general public who had turned on them so quickly. In addition to making substantial changes to how they treated the Orca whales, the company pledged money to marine research. By 2015, SeaWorld had spend $10 million in efforts related to restoring its public image in the wake of *Blackfish* (Duhon et al., 2016).

Primarily due to the initial use of outdated and slow response techniques, SeaWorld was not able to effectively quell stakeholder outrage following the airing of *Blackfish* in a manner that was efficient, speedy, or significant. Instead, the company took a major hit at a volatile time, leaving the future of one of their main attractions up in the air. SeaWorld could have been more proactive, less accusatory, and more understanding about the stakeholders' anger. Instead, they allowed a narrative to take over and do significant harm to their reputation and their bottom line. Now, SeaWorld has to play a long game of catch-up as a result of this devastatingly poor perception of the company.

What could SeaWorld have done differently? Sea World should have used the 10 months between when the documentary first aired at Sundance and when it globally appeared on CNN to put together a comprehensive response strategy. This strategy should have been based upon research of its customers and stakeholders to gauge their concerns about the company. This research could have been done through focus groups, impromptu interviews with Park visitors, and online surveys. This could have been coupled with research with the initial viewers of the film. To conduct this research, a feedback survey could have been administered in-person to viewers immediately following the airing of the film. In addition, researchers could have conducted random, in-person, one-on-one interviews with viewers as they exited the viewing.

After completing both of these efforts, researchers could have compared the findings to see similarities in the responses. This would have helped them to further identify any sensitivities or concerns that customers or stakeholders had. With this data, they could have crafted the messages and statements for their responses.

Now that we have looked at the crisis at SeaWorld, let's examine an unexpected communication crisis caused by a national disaster in Connecticut in 2011.

Connecticut Light & Power's (CL&P) Crisis Communication Response

In late October of 2011, the state of Connecticut was slammed with a Nor'easter. It was one of the worst storms in the state's history, leaving a record number of residents without power. This happened just a few months after Hurricane Irene hit the state in August, and the citizens of Connecticut were once again without power for a prolonged period of time. CL&P, the state's main provider of power, was responsible not only for restoring homes and businesses with power, but also for keeping the public updated with information regarding the restoration.

Due to the severity of the storm, which was greater than initially predicted, CL&P was overwhelmed. Rather than proactively offering residents timely updates, information was limited to daily media briefings held at the designated emergency operation center. The company elected to use radio broadcasts and newspaper articles as its primary communication platforms. Since most customers did not have power, they couldn't access the radio broadcasts and many were also not receiving newspaper deliveries. Even for those with Internet access, updates from CL&P were impossible to receive as the company's website lacked current information and it neglected to use its social media channels as a primary information source.

Following a crisis, it is imperative to keep the stakeholders, who are in this case the Connecticut residents, updated with relevant, timely, and helpful information. Due to CL&P's response, the stakeholders' opinion of the company went from trusted to skeptical in a matter of days and resulted in the resignation of President and CEO Jeffrey Butler (Grantham, 2015, p. 1).

Looking at this response from the perspective of Situational Crisis Communication Theory (Coombs, 2007), it is clear that CL&P's reputation was at stake during the aftermath of the storm. In general, the three factors that shape stakeholders' feelings about a company following a crisis are: initial crisis responsibility, crisis history, and prior relational reputation.

CL&P had an enormous amount of responsibility, being the company working to restore power across the area. Having tackled a similar situation with Hurricane Irene earlier in the year, they were overly familiar with the enormous task ahead of them. Although their prior reputation was strong, the company found itself in a dubious position and needed to enact a clear communications campaign in order to satisfy the stakeholders.

What happened? The breakdown in communication occurred largely due to factors stemming from the crisis itself; lack of television service, lack of Internet access, etc. The messages were mostly conveyed over the radio and while they reached a large number of people, the medium itself made it difficult to properly explain when power was going to be restored and what strategies were being used to do it (Grantham, 2015). President and CEO Jeffrey Butler was also inadequately prepared to deal with the onslaught of press appearances and crisis communication that was needed to properly satisfy the needs and wants of the stakeholders.

Subsequent reports have found that CL&P's response time and recovery were actually adequate for the amount of damage that was done by the storm (Grantham, 2015, p. 18). That being said, public perception was that the company wasn't doing all it could to restore power in a timely manner. How did this come about? Customers recognize that CL&P was not responsible for the weather. The lack of information about the damage assessment process and the amount of time it would take to restore power, coupled with the fact there were ongoing injuries and deaths from people improperly trying to heat their homes, negatively influenced the public's perception of how CL&P was handling the restoration.

Event	Peak Outages	Date	Days to Substantially Complete Restoration
October Snowstorm	803,000	10/29/11	11
Storm irene	671,000	08/28/11	9
Hurricane Gloria	506,150	09/27/85	10
Superstorm Sandy	497,000	10/29/12	6
Hurricane Bob	275,000	08/19/91	4
Snowstorm	209,658	11/19/86	3
Thunderstorm	209,045	06/08/11	4
Thunderstorm	201,651	07/23/91	3
Windstorm	168,544	03/13/10	7

Source: "Historic Storm Response" (2012).

What went wrong? A big problem was that Connecticut's residents had no prior experience with this type of storm. There was no framework against which stakeholders could assess CL&P's activities. Although everyone had been prewarned about the potential severity of the storm and the possibility of being without power for some time, the vagueness of the restoration timeline was disconcerting. The perception that the flow of information from CL&P was delayed and inaccurate increased. The governor and the media quickly targeted CL&P as inefficient and ineffective.

What should CL&P have done? There are a few steps CL&P could have taken to remedy the situation faster and more successfully than they did:

1. CL&P's president should have been overseeing the damage assessment and restoration efforts rather than acting as the company's primary spokesperson. The spokesperson responsibility should have been assigned to another executive with experience in communicating information to the various stakeholders.
2. CL&P's CEO should have designed and communicated a reasonable time frame for damage assessment to the stakeholders' groups before specific plans could be made to restore power. Stakeholders did not understand the process involved, which is what ultimately led to their dissatisfaction.
3. Emergency services such as the National Guard and the Red Cross should have been summoned to assist with recovery efforts such as debris removal, temporary lodging, etc.
4. CL&P should have communicated the process they were using to restore power to residents. The company failed to explain it was strategically restoring power to the largest communities of residents first. Those living in the towns with the worst damage would likely have their power restored as those recovery efforts were more complicated and required substantial effort. The goal was to restore power to as many residents as quickly as possible.
5. CL&P should have enlisted the help of a crisis communication expert with technical expertise and media training to lead the company's external communication process.
6. CL&P should have educated the public, as well as local governments, on its damage assessment procedures. Many local and state officials did realize the two-step process CL&P uses to evaluate storm damage, which led to a significant amount of misinformation.

The reality is that CL&P was not prepared to implement the necessary communication outreach to properly handle a crisis of this size. The community liaisons had trouble conveying useful information to town mayors and selectmen (Grantham, 2015) and there weren't enough direct-to-consumer information channels such as text messages or social media alerts. Preparation is critical, and establishing a two-way dialogue with stakeholders prior to the crisis occurring is paramount in establishing postcrisis communication protocol (Grantham, 2015, p. 18). Poor communication led to a poor public image, mistrust from the stakeholders, and the eventual resignation of the president and CEO, despite the company quickly and adequately repairing all of the damage that was done.

CL&P ultimately dug themselves into a hole that they didn't need to be in. If they had utilized faster and more updated communication channels, such as social media, e-mail, or text message updates to communicate with customers, the situation would have gone much more smoothly. In addition, prior to the storm hitting, CL&P could have reached out to customers with a preview of the response plan it would be taking along with an associated timeline. This would have given customers a sense of the time and complexity associated with the storm repairs. To ensure timely and smooth communication with customers, CL&P could have surveyed customers prior to the storm to determine their preferred method of communication. All of these actions would have helped CL&P avoid the negative publicity that ultimately led to the departure of a CEO and the need for rehabilitation of public trust.

One year after the terrible Nor'easter hit Connecticut, another incredibly powerful, 100-year storm ravished the New Jersey coastline—none other than Superstorm Sandy. Unlike the failed communication campaign implemented by CL&P, the New Jersey State government and its various municipalities devised a proactive communication campaign that helped bring the area and its vital economy back to life.

The Jersey Shore and Superstorm Sandy

Superstorm Sandy devastated a significant portion of the Northeastern Seaboard, hitting New York and New Jersey the hardest. The Jersey Shore is one of New Jersey's most profitable economic systems, bringing in an estimated $40 billion a year (Harasta, 2014). The damage the storm did, as well as the rhetoric surrounding it in the aftermath, threatened to do serious harm to the Shore's bottom line the next summer, 2013, as well as for years to come. Putting the state back together, while simultaneously implementing multiple marketing, public relations, and communications campaigns, was a difficult task for the states' legislators to tackle.

Obviously, Sandy was destructive. It caused approximately $30 billion in damages to the state of New Jersey. (Harasta, 2014). Recovering from the devastation in time for the summer was going to be a tall task, but fighting the media war was going to be just as important. In the aftermath, news spread on both social and traditional media depicting total and complete destruction of certain areas like the Atlantic City Boardwalk, which was far from the truth (Harasta, 2014). Networks such as CNN shared false images and video, which were eventually taken down and apologies asked (Harasta, 2014), but the damage had already been done. Once an image has been shared on social media, it's difficult to police them and there's no control as to where it has gone to. And, much to the dismay of many NJ shore businesses, the beaches appeared to have suffered incredibly devastating, long-term damage. It was so bad that many wondered if the NJ shore would ever recover.

Beyond the potential long-term destruction to the New Jersey coastline, New Jersey's government faced an incredible near-term recovery effort—helping residents navigate through short-term devastation and the long-term destruction. The government needed to assemble a two-prong communication plan to support the immediate needs of New Jersey residents who faced housing shortages, food and water distribution deficiencies, electricity and fuel reductions, etc., as well as combat the potential devastation of its most significant industry.

To do this, The New Jersey Department of Tourism initiated a multiphase approach leveraging a combination of social media and traditional media to keep citizens up-to-date with information on the storm, as well as the state's efforts to help them, both in the short and long term. As time was of the essence, New Jersey's leaders leveraged the speed, pervasiveness, and efficiency of social media to reach out to millions of people whose smartphones were their only sources of information and only means of communication. It was the first time so many people in need of information, and ultimately relief, relied so heavily on this form of communication.

The social media app Twitter was heavily used by the governor, the state, and its many agencies to communicate with residents before, during, and after the storm. Governor Christie used Twitter to help keep residents, many of whom had lost power, updated on the storm. FEMA also urged its 163,400 Twitter followers to use social media and text messaging for updates and to communicate with relatives affected by the storm (Harasta, 2014).

In addition to the recovery efforts, the state needed to launch a persuasive information campaign to dispel the misperceptions Americans had about the long-term effects to New Jersey and the state's efforts to overcome Sandy's destruction. To combat the negative perception, the New Jersey government and its various municipalities devised a proactive, nation-wide communication campaign that depicted the coastline as open and ready for business. It was done in such a widespread and ubiquitous manner that the fake and real images of destruction were forgotten and replaced by ones of summer fun.

In March 2013, The New Jersey Department of Tourism launched a $25 million campaign focused on New Jersey residents and their summertime shore spending habits. It was accompanied by campaigns like "Stronger

Than The Storm," "Show Your Love For The Shore," and "Restore The Shore" (Harasta, 2014). Specifically, the "Show Your Love for the Shore" campaign was targeted toward internal planning among state leaders to promote the Jersey Shore from within the state. This included such groups as:

- State Business Administration's (SBA) NJ District Office;
- FEMA External Affairs at the NJ Joint Field Office—Private Sector;
- NJ Division of State, Division of Travel and Tourism;
- NJ Business Action Center;
- NJ Restaurant Association;
- NJ State Chamber of Commerce;

The biggest and most heavily funded campaign was "Stronger than the Storm," which featured a dedicated theme song and an appearance by Governor Christie. This $4 million, nationwide campaign was designed to reverse misconceptions about the Jersey Shore's condition and its readiness for tourists. The commercial concluded with the governor saying, "We're stronger than the storm and open for everyone." This campaign also had a large Internet and social media presence, as well as an online store that helped engage the audience across multiple mediums (Harasta, 2014).

Hurricane Sandy was one of the first major natural disasters to happen in the social media era, and it's footprints were seen before, during, and after the storm. Harnessing the immediate power of social media was imperative for the state immediately following the initial crisis. But, it ended up being just as important in the following months.

When the 2013 Summer season began, some numbers were unsurprisingly down from the year prior. The northern part of the shore experienced a larger decline than the south, partially due to visitors from New York, Northern New Jersey, and Connecticut still dealing with their own damage from Sandy as South Jersey relies less on visitors from those areas (Harasta, 2014). The "Stronger Than The Storm" campaign ran throughout the summer of 2013, and efforts to restore attendance didn't let up. By the end of the summer, attendance was skyrocketing, and when the official numbers came out in 2014 it was clear that the summer after Sandy was a record-breaking year in terms of total revenue, reaching $40.3 billion (Harasta, 2014).

In conjunction with each other, the campaigns were enormously successful, especially following such a destructive storm and media cycle. These campaigns are an example of a smart, well-implemented, and timely response to a potentially damaging occurrence that utilized social and traditional media to spread the word and redirect the public image of the Jersey Shore. One of the only complaints levied against the campaign was that it ignored people who were still suffering due to loss of homes or property (Harasta, 2014), which could have been addressed in a separate, but similar campaign. Nonresidential homes—homes on the shore that get rented out to vacationers—were not covered under the $16 billion recovery fund from the government. Ultimately, however, their owners did benefit from the number of people that took trips to the shore due to the marketing and public relations campaigns. Putting resources, time, and energy into the campaigns, which were built around a cohesive theme and messaging, ultimately made the Jersey Shore restoration a successful one.

Why was the New Jersey Shore campaign successful? Simple, they got it right from the start. By leveraging a mix of new world and old world techniques, the New Jersey State government was able to address both short-term communication challenges and long-term perception problems. In the end, it worked out better than anyone could have imagined.

A final case study we will examine is that of the New England Patriots and Deflategate. Clearly, this is much less serious than any of the other cases but it is an excellent example of how a small problem quickly turned into a big one.

Deflated: The Strategic Impact of the "Deflategate" Scandal on the NFL and Its Golden Boy

In 2015, the NFL faced yet another public image crisis. Following the incident regarding Ray Rice's domestic violence in 2014 (Strawser, Shane, Thompson, Vulich, & Simons, 2017, p. 62) the league once again found itself in something of a media tornado surrounding one of its flagship franchises.

The New England Patriots, led by poster boy quarterback Tom Brady and owned by outspoken owner Robert Kraft, has been accused by the Indianapolis Colts of purposefully deflating the footballs used in a playoff game in order to give Brady an advantage. The Patriots won the game, and the NFL began to look into the possibility of tampering with the footballs. What followed was a multiyear media cycle that ultimately ended up with both parties recovering from bruised reputations.

The NFL appointed its General Counsel Jeff Pash and Attorney Ted Wells to investigate the incident (Strawser et al., 2017). Pash and Wells took their time, but eventually came up with findings in May 2015 that the NFL thought useful and potentially damning. The investigators concluded that the Patriots did deflate the balls, but that it was unlikely that Tom Brady was unaware of the situation (Strawser et al., 2017). This led to the suspension of Brady for the first four games of the following season, as well as the loss of the team's first round draft pick in the upcoming draft, their fourth round draft pick in the following draft, and a one million dollar fine from the league (Strawser et al., 2017). The media jumped all over the story.

The Patriots, obviously, refuted the claims made by the NFL and had an appeal filed by the NFL Players Association (Strawser et al., 2017).

The arbitration for the case took place in August and September 2015, where the Judge nullified Brady's suspension. The NFL then appealed, continuing the legal saga, and March of 2016, The U.S. Second Circuit Court of Appeals sided with the NFL and Brady did not appeal, thus ending the legal portion of the ordeal.

One of the truly inciting incidents was when the NFL provided two prominent football journalists with incorrect information regarding what they found when investigating the case. The NFL told journalists they found 11 of the 12 footballs to be about 2 pounds per square inch underweight, and ESPN ran the story that caught serious traction (Strawser et al., 2017). It turned out this information was false. Despite the inaccurate information, ESPN never retracted the story or apologized publicly in any way for relaying completely false information. This could be partly attributed to ESPN's close partnership with the NFL and commissioner Roger Goodell. The NFL feeding bad info to journalists is an example of Agenda Setting, trying to shape the narrative in a certain way in order to serve some sort of agenda. In this case, the NFL wanted to stoke public mistrust of the Patriots franchise and Tom Brady as an individual, in order to win the reputation of the competition in the aftermath of the scandal.

The Patriots themselves embarked on a mission to rebuild their own image, which included denial, evasion of responsibility, reducing offensiveness, and mortification (Strawser et al., 2017). Brady, Kraft, and the Patriots denied all wrongdoing, painting themselves as victims of the NFL. Brady also evaded responsibility, as well as reduced offensiveness, by constantly downplaying the incident, such as comparing the situation to ISIS in order to illustrate how little it actually matters (Strawser et al., 2017).

What went wrong? The Patriots improperly handled the scandal from the beginning. Instead of truthfully handling the situation from the start, the team and its owners denied everything from the start. In a situation such as this, it would have been better to admit fault and then proactively reach out to Patriot fans with an apology. The team could have used a mix of traditional—newspaper ads, commercials, and radio ads—and modern techniques such as social media, websites, and blogs to communicate to the fans. Had they apologized immediately after the scandal broke, the chances are likely the situation would have quickly disappeared. But instead, it was drug out for a long period of time.

After reviewing these six cases, you can appreciate how various companies from different industries have used research techniques to tackle different communication challenges. Some have done it effectively such as the State of New Jersey, while others have gravely failed such as Domino's and the New England Patriots. Clearly, this is just a sampling of what some companies have experienced. There are thousands of others that could be reviewed, studied, and used as models for evaluation and study.

References

Duhon, S., Ellison, K., & Ragas, M. W. (2016). A whale of a problem: A strategic communication analysis of SeaWorld Entertainment's multi-year Blackfish crisis. *Case Studies in Strategic Communication, 5*, 3–37. Retrieved from http://cssc.uscannenberg.org/wp-content/uploads/2016/08/v5art2.pdf

Gilkerson, N., Gross, M., & Ahneman, A. M. (2013). "The Other Hangover," Implementing and evaluating an original, student-designed campaign to curb binge drinking. *Case Studies in Strategic Communication, 2*, 93–131. Retrieved from http://cssc.uscannenberg.org/wp-content/uploads/2014/01/v2art5.pdf

Grantham, S. (2015). Power to the people: CL&P's crisis communication response following the 2011 October nor'easter. *Case Studies in Strategic Communication, 4*, 3–28. Retrieved from http://cssc.uscannenberg.org/wp-content/uploads/2015/07/v4art2.pdf

Harasta, J. (2014). Jersey Srong, right? A communications analysis of New Jersey's post-Hurricane Sandy tourism recovery. *Case Studies in Strategic Communication, 3*, article 4. Retrieved from http://cssc.uscannenberg.org/cases/v3/v3art4

Strawser, M. G., Shain, S., Thompson, A., Vulich, K., & Simons, C. (2017). Deflated: The strategic impact of the "Deflategate" scandal on the NFL and its golden boy. *Case Studies in Strategic Communication, 6*, 62–88. Retrieved from http://cssc.uscannenberg.org/wp-content/uploads/2018/01/v6art3.pdf

Young, C. L., & Flowers, A. (2012). Fight viral with viral: A case study of Domino's Pizza's crisis communication strategies. *Case Studies in Strategic Communication, 1*, 93–106. Retrieved from http://cssc.uscannenberg.org/wp-content/uploads/2013/10/v1art6.pdf

OUTLINE

The Case for Envirocare: Prioritizing Stakeholders for Public Relations by Kenneth D. Plowman, Brigham Young University and Brad L. Rawlins, Arkansas State University from *Case Studies in Strategic Communication,* Vol. 7, 2017. www.csscjournal.org

"#BringDickieVtoMurray": *A Case Study Analysis of a Fan-Enacted Twitter Campaign* by John S. W. Spinda Clemson University from *Case Studies in Strategic Communication,* Vol. 7, 2017. www.csscjournal.org

"Maintaining Hope and Inspiration": Using Social Media to Encourage Internal Stakeholders by Emily S. Kinsky and Kimberly Bruce of West Texas A&M University and Kirk Scarbrough and W. Aaron French of Teach for America from *Case Studies in Strategic Communication,* Vol. 5, 2016. www.csscjournal.org

A Corporate Coming Out: Crisis Communication and Engagement with LGBT Publics by Erica Ciszek of The University of Houston from *Case Studies in Strategic Communication,* **Vol. 5, 2016.** www.csscjournal.org

The Brand Behind the Activism: Patagonia's DamNation Campaign and the Evolution of Corporate Social Responsibility by Derek Moscato of Western Washington University from *Case Studies in Strategic Communication,* **Vol. 5, 2016.** www.csscjournal.org

Exclusive and Aspirational: Teen Retailer Brandy Melville Uses the Country Club Approach to Brand Promotion by Sarah VanSlette of Southern Illinois University Edwardsville and Damion Waymer of University of Cincinnati from *Case Studies in Strategic Communication,* Vol. 5, 2016. www.csscjournal.org

A Cavalier Approach to Public Relations: The Unconventional Image Restoration of LeBron James by Kathleen Stansberry of Cleveland State University and Jessalynn Strauss of Elon University from *Case Studies in Strategic Communication,* Vol. 5, 2016. www.csscjournal.org

Book Battles: A Strategic Communication Analysis of Amazon.com's Dispute with Hachette Book Group and Authors United by Kelsey Dimar of Liquor Stores N.A., Rachel Ann Kuchar of *Weber Shandwick* and Matthew W. Ragas of DePaul University from *Case Studies in Strategic Communication*, Vol. 5, 2016. www.csscjournal.org

Protecting the Herd: An Analysis of Public Relations Responses to the 2015 Measles Outbreak Originating at Disneyland and Disney California Adventure Park by Shelley Aylesworth-Spink of University of West London from *Case Studies in Strategic Communication*, Vol. 5, 2016. www.csscjournal.org

Public Relations as Personal Relationships: How Top Bordeaux Wines are Promoted in China by Kara Alaimo of Hofstra University from *Case Studies in Strategic Communication*, Vol. 4. 2015. www.csscjournal.org.

The Hazelwood Coal Mine Fire: Lessons from Crisis Miscommunication and Misunderstanding by Jim Macnamara of the University of Technology Sydney from *Case Studies in Strategic Communication*, Vol. 4. 2015. www.csscjournal.org.

"Team Sarah": How a Small Group of Public Relations Volunteers Helped a 10-Year-Old Get New Lungs and Changed U.S. Transplant Policy by Marjorie Kruvand of Loyola University Chicago from *Case Studies in Strategic Communication*, Vol. 3. 2014. www.csscjournal.org.

Making a Case for Virtual Healthcare Communications: Mayo Clinic's Integration of Virtual World Communities in its Social Media Mix by Donna Z. Davis University of Oregon from *Case Studies in Strategic Communication*, Vol. 3. 2014. www.csscjournal.org.

Please note: The contents for these cases must be accessed through the book's website. Please follow the instructions located on the inside front cover of the book